Manifesting Divinity

CHINMAYA VISION ON EDUCATION

Published by

Chinmaya Mission West
P.O. Box 129, Piercy, CA 95587 U.S.A.
Tel: (707) 247-3488
Email: publications@chinmayamission.org
Website: www.chinmayamission.org

First Edition: December 2012, 8,000 copies

Gratitude and prostrations to Pūjya Guruji for his love and guidance.

Grateful acknowledgment to Ācaryās, Chinmaya Vidyalaya and Chinmaya College Management, Principals, teachers and students for their contribution towards the book. Many thanks to CM Delhi, Anjali Singh, Nanki Singh, Nancy Patchen, Brni. Prarthana Chaitanya, Brni. Vibhooti Chaitanya, Chinmaya Archives, *Tapovan Prasad*, Chinmaya Jeevan Darshan CCMT Publications, Chinmaya Kalpanam, and devotees of Chinmaya Mission. We thank Brni. Nivedita Chaitanya for her endearing Siddha illustrations and Devendra Sharma for his illustrations of Gurudev. Special thanks to Ramani Thyagarajan of the CCMT Education Cell for her invaluable support.

Authors

Swamini Vimalananda and Vishva Sodhi

Project Co-ordinator

Shibani Khorana

Content, Edit, and Design Support

Kumkum Bhatia and Sharda Chawla

Support by the Mananam team

Swami Shantananda, Margaret Dukes, David Dukes, Neena Dev,
Rudite Emir, Br. Eric, Rashmi Mehrotra, Arun Mehrotra,
Padmashree Rao, and Aarthi Ramalingam

Illustrations, Design, and Layout by

Nidhi Wadhwa and the Bluefish Designs team

Printed by

Silverpoint Press Pvt. Ltd., India

Library of Congress Control Number: 2012953222

ISBN: 978-1-60827-010-1

THE mananam SERIES
CHINMAYA BIRTH CENTENARY CELEBRATION SERIES

Manifesting Divinity

CHINMAYA VISION ON EDUCATION

CHINMAYA PUBLICATIONS
CHINMAYA MISSION WEST PUBLICATIONS DIVISION

TRAINING THE MIND IS THE ESSENCE OF EDUCATION. BY QUIETENING AND DISCIPLINING THE MIND'S WANDERINGS, WE CAN BRING OUT THE DIVINITY ALREADY INHERENT IN US.

| SWAMI CHINMAYANANDA |

ॐ

Foreword

Birds are gifted with the ability to fly just as fish spontaneously swim. Man is gifted with an intellect to question, think, reason, discriminate, observe, innovate, and create. We begin to question right from our childhood and when told not to, we ask, 'why not?'

Possessing a violin does not make me a violinist. In the same way, possessing an intellect does not necessarily make me intelligent. Rigorous training and practice is required to become a master violinist. In the same way, education trains the intellect to excel. The vast majority utilize the intellect merely for survival, to earn a livelihood and live in comfort. Others use it for gaining mastery in a field or for gaining more name, fame, power, prosperity, or comforts for themselves. Indeed, the intellect is a powerful instrument, and, if misused, can destroy those around us as well as ourselves. Thus the primary function of education is to cultivate an intellect so that it blesses us and benefits others.

It is the duty of parents to ensure a good education for their children. This includes secular and spiritual knowledge, as well as value education. To receive a good education is the right of every child and it is the responsibility of the government to provide it. The scriptures say that if citizens commit wrong acts as a result of an education devoid of values, the government is to be held responsible. All over the world, governments spend billions each year producing and procuring arms and ammunition while paying much less attention to education. We see that costly and high-precision guided missiles are in the hands of misguided minds. In schools, students disrespect teachers. We also hear of students carrying weapons and indiscriminately killing other students in schools. In such extreme cases, police are required to maintain law and order on school and college campuses. When value education was an inherent component of education, such things were heard of less often.

Education begins with literacy — learning the three R's — reading, writing, and arithmetic. This opens up the treasure trove of all knowledge. A literate person can learn and master any field of knowledge he so wishes. Thus, literacy leads to knowledge and mastery over a subject.

A machine stopped working in a factory, and an expert was called to fix it. He studied the machine for an hour, banged it in a couple of places, and set it right. A young graduate who was watching the expert asked, "How can you charge two thousand and two dollars for a couple of taps?" The expert said, "I charged two dollars for the taps and two thousand for knowing where to tap." Indeed, once a subject has been mastered, the student should use the knowledge to bless himself and benefit others — that is wisdom.

Should education be job-oriented? Is the purpose of education only to earn a living? Of course, education must make us capable of earning. A degree is useless if with it we cannot even get a job. Yet today, many with a degree are still unemployable or unemployed. Therefore education must empower us with the knowledge and skills to stand on our own feet. The government must provide opportunities for employment or encourage self-employment. Each individual must be educated, able to work, besides being enterprising enough to create employment for others, and capable of creating wealth and prosperity. But knowledge is not only meant for creating wealth and buying comfort. It should give us a vision, make us independent, and transform our thinking and lives.

Education is important, but dedicating our knowledge, skills, talent and profession to a noble cause or a higher altar is even more important. We see many authors dedicating their books to their family and friends who support them and some to their ideals who inspire them. When our knowledge or talent is employed for a higher cause, the returns are greater. A sportsman winning for a club gets name, fame, and money, but when he wins for his country, he gets greater name, fame, money, and inner satisfaction. Pelé is well-known even now, not for winning club matches, but for scoring in the World Cup which brought victory to Brazil.

Scientists who work for the cause of science, artists who dedicate their life to art, social workers who work for the betterment of society, and saints who dedicate their lives to God are honored, awarded, and revered. So education must also bring dedication in our lives.

Ancient India had a very well-developed education system. There were thousands of gurukulas spread throughout the country, which offered basic and advanced education in various secular and spiritual subjects. Students were given professional expertise according to their inclination, but a spiritual and cultural education was common to all. The Guru set a high standard of values and conduct which the students were expected to follow, even when they returned home. The students lived a simple and disciplined life, dedicated to knowledge and service of the Guru. The students graduated with mastery in their vocation and a strong character, which helped them to face life's challenges and build a successful life of their own. The Gurus were neither concerned with making money nor the country's politics even though all the great and important persons of the city or country, including the rulers of the land were their students. They led an inspired and an inspiring life, which was dedicated to education.

Lal Bahadur Shastri, the former Prime Minister of India was a teacher before he joined politics. It is said that he got a monthly pay of ₹15 with which his wife met the household expenses. Once his wife inquired why he looked so worried. He said that one of his friends was in dire need of money. To his surprise his wife gave him ₹50 from her kitty for the friend. She said that she had managed to save ₹2 per month from his pay and had thus collected ₹50 over the years. The next day after giving his friend ₹50 he went to the school management and said, "Please reduce my pay by ₹2 as my wife manages all our needs in ₹13." Such high values and conduct in a teacher is indeed difficult to find.

Parents, teachers, family, and society together help beautify and refine the behavior and mind of the child. The scriptures give us life-skills to manage our personal and professional life. This is called Saṁskṛti. Holistic education also refines the person and makes him cultured. Customs, traditions, festivals, ceremonies, spiritual practices, rituals, and art forms are all practical means of inculcating culture and values. All these, along with fine arts and performing arts in India were taught, mastered, and perfected to the highest degree. All of them were dedicated to God and became a means to worship God.

The Indian education system, management skills, and culture can be practiced even today, as they are at once ancient and time-tested, yet very relevant and modern. Pūjya Gurudev visualized a holistic education program (now called the Chinmaya Vision Programme) by which the best of the ancient and modern systems of education could be integrated. This, he ascertained, was the right means to manifest the inherent divinity in man. For, it is knowledge that empowers, knowledge that elevates and knowledge alone that liberates man.

Swami Tejomayananda
Head, Chinmaya Mission Worldwide

Contents

An offering of love, at the sacred feet of
Pūjya Gurudev, Swami Chinmayananda

ॐ

Preface

> The Truth which is the Self is called the 'fourth.' (caturthaṁ manyante sa ātmā)
> — Māṇḍūkya Upaniṣad 7

Education refines, beautifies, and transforms the soul of man. It has the power to manifest his inherent divinity. *Manifesting Divinity — Chinmaya Vision on Education* is the 'fourth' book in the Mananam Series published to commemorate Gurudev's Birth Centenary. It explores Gurudev's own secular and spiritual education in the chapter — 'Making of a Master,' his vision for an ideal education in 'An Experiment in Education — Chinmaya Vision Programme,' its manifestation as 'The Edifice of Education — The Chinmaya Education Institutions' and its 'Unifying Link — CCMT Education Cell.' The book also delves into Gurudev's thoughts and influence on management principles and its practitioners in the chapter — 'Age of Management,' and his lofty vision for the arts is captured in the 'The Heart of Art.' What is in the beginning and the end is also there throughout. Gurudev and Guruji's blessings are seen throughout this book.

A sacred place is where you meet yourself again and again. It is in the world of words and in the space of Gurudev's thoughts on education that we dived and thrived for a year as we created this pātra (book) through the fictitious patrakāra (journalist) called Amrita. Gurudev was our Sūtrātmā, the heart and soul of the sūtras, which are his profound vision and thoughts. Amrita and Rishi, the fictitious ex-student of Chinmaya Vidyalaya, became the sūtradhāras, the ones who linked Gurudev's thoughts and uncovered the sūtras. And the phala śruti or the benediction at the end of this journey is a joyous vision and fulfillment.

Please note that the spelling and grammar in the text reflect American English as the book is published as a Mananam Series Publication. Facts and figures in this book are as on 30 September 2012. Wishing you a happy journey and a gentle transformation!

Storyline

Amrita Trivedi is a young journalist waiting desperately — in fact, praying for the story of a lifetime, a lifeline to keeping her job with the prestigious magazine 'Today's India.' Rishi Kumar is the success story, the young founder of a company that is making waves. 'Adif' is a conglomerate with interests in advertising, education, art, and herbal products. It aims at 'adding value to the life of all' and 'making a difference' in society. The meeting — Seat 2A and 2B on flight 5W 414 from Mumbai to Delhi…

Gosh! Aren't you Rishi Kumar? You are featured on the cover of 'Week.' You are amazing. What makes you tick? Did I not see you at the airport helping a man with crutches? That was so considerate. Do tell me what makes you so different?

Too many questions, young lady! Are you a journalist? I too saw you back there — why did you look so worried? Will worry change the situation? Relax.

You can change the situation and make a difference. I am Amrita Trivedi, a journalist, looking for a success story for a magazine feature. Can I interview you right away?

Ah … Ok!

Here's my first question. What or who has left the biggest impression on your life?

That's an easy one. My Guru Swami Chinmayanandaji, and my school Chinmaya Vidyalaya. Come to think of it, his life, work and teaching — indeed his unique approach to modern education — would be more inspiring and the ideal story you are looking for.

I

Making of the Master

CHILDREN ARE NOT VESSELS TO BE FILLED,
BUT LAMPS TO BE LIT.
| SWAMI CHINMAYANANDA |

Deep within each soul lies a potential that manifests and blossoms in and through our various interactions with the outside world. The very texture of our lives is shaped by the inner raw material meshed with the outer molding. Our upbringing at home as well as our school and college education blend to serve as significant external factors. Geographical, social, educational, and political conditions also play a pivotal role, but it is the contact with the truly great that brings about total transformation and fulfillment.

Let us explore what shaped Gurudev's life — his upbringing and education seen in the context of those times. We shall then see the subsequent work he did to invigorate India's education and culture.

Introduction to India's Modern Education

The British Rule — The East India Company was established in 1600 and India was officially under British Rule from 1757 to 1947. This had a very deep and far reaching impact on the very fabric of Indian life.

The British discovered in Bharat a land that was not only wealthy in resource, but also in values and culture. Its spiritual thoughts, religious beliefs, cultural traditions, and social norms were ancient and deep-rooted. This land of great might, mystery, and mystics, of diversity in every possible sphere — climate, language, customs, and traditions — was truly mind-boggling. And yet, the people shared a common way of life, culture, and values. It was indeed a challenge to subjugate the people of India and rule over them.

The British achieved what hundreds of years of Muslim rule in India was unable to; they were able to fracture India's ancient civilization. Their success can be seen in two major policies that were designed to suit their colonial needs. These remain unchanged more than sixty years after the British have left Indian shores and their legacy continues to create new cracks in this mighty edifice of Indian civilization.

The policy of 'divide and rule' fragmented Indian society into landowners and peasants, rich and poor, Hindus and Muslims, North and South, with each faction opposed and fighting the other. The second policy was the introduction of an 'Anglicized education system' set in motion by Lord Macaulay in 1835.

The Colonial Classroom — Lord Macaulay held India's ancient culture in low esteem and saw his as a civilizing mission. He recognized that 'the average intelligence and virtue is very high in this country...' but felt 'Indian literature is admitted to be of small intrinsic value ... language is barren of useful knowledge ... books give false history, false astronomy and false medicine as they are in the company of a false religion ... and so ... we ought to employ them (Indians) in teaching what is worth knowing, that English is better worth knowing than Sanskrit or Arabic ... the people should through education get Anglicized in terms of both cultural and intellectual attainments.'

> I have traveled across the length and breadth of India and I have not seen one person who is a beggar, who is a thief. Such wealth I have seen in this country, such high moral values, people of such caliber, that I do not think we would ever conquer this country, unless we break the very backbone of this nation, which is her spiritual and cultural heritage, and, therefore, I propose that we replace her old and ancient education system, her culture, for if the Indians think that all that is foreign and English is good and greater than their own, they will lose their self-esteem, their native self-culture and they will become what we want them, a truly dominated nation.
>
> Lord Macaulay's speech in British Parliament [often mis-attributed], 1835

The very aim of introducing modern education was to prepare Indian clerks for running local administrations wherein school education was taught in the vernacular medium and all higher education was compulsorily taught in English. Their educational effort was therefore directed towards the middle class.

> We must at present do our best to form a class who may be interpreters between us and the millions whom we govern; a class of persons, Indian in blood and color, but English in taste, in opinions, in morals, and in intellect.
>
> Lord Macaulay

A class of Indian intellectuals like Raja Ram Mohan Roy reared in this system of education believed modern education would improve the life of common man and conquer ignorance, hunger, poverty, and disease. It would do this while also unlocking the key to the treasures of Western scientific and democratic thought that could put an end to imperialism and tyranny. History has proved some of their thinking true, and the British did indeed thrust modernity into Indian life — but at what cost?

Some of the British were quick to realize that sons of gentlemen in England went to college from a desire of learning, whereas the Indians went to college only to earn a living — to obtain employment under the British Government. They also observed how 'British colleges are a growth whereas Indian schools and colleges are but an alien graft' (Fuller Report). In a roundtable conference in 1931, **Mahatma Gandhi** said in one of his speeches, **"The beautiful tree of education was cut down by the British. Therefore today India is far more illiterate than it was 100 years ago."**

THE EDUCATIONAL SYSTEMS OF THE LAST CENTURY THAT HAVE BEEN
THRUST UPON OUR CHILDREN ARE SLOWLY CRUSHING THEM
INTO UGLY TWISTED CARICATURES!
THE SYSTEM IS NOT GEARED TO THE NEEDS AND DEMANDS OF THE WORLD
WE HAVE PERVERTED FOR THEM TO LIVE, PLAY, AND GROW IN.
WE ARE DEFINITELY GROWING INTO A NATION OF HEARTLESS BRUTES,
EXTREMELY UNEDUCATED AND UNCIVILIZED.
| SWAMI CHINMAYANANDA |

The consequence of this particular British intervention was that an ancient system of education that had flourished in India for thousands of years, withered away. William Adam, a Scottish Baptist missionary turned journalist, observed in his first report (1835) that there were about 100,000 village schools in Bengal and Bihar alone. Before the British arrived there were thousands of gurukulas (traditional schools) flourishing in India. Now hardly a few remain. Indians became alienated from their cultural roots — their values, customs, languages, religion, and all that they held in great reverence.

Our English schools are flourishing wonderfully; we find it difficult to provide instruction to all. The effect of this education on Hindus is prodigious. No Hindu who has received an English education ever remains sincerely attached to his religion. It is my firm belief that if our plans of education are followed up, there will not be a single idolater among the respected classes thirty years hence. And this will be effected without our efforts to proselytize; I heartily rejoice in the prospect.

Lord Macaulay in a letter to his father. October 12, 1836

It is astounding to observe how successful Lord Macaulay really was in realizing his ambition. His educational policy and thoughts were deeply entrenched to become the very psyche of Indians and are being followed zealously even today.

What was the ancient education system that the British virtually eradicated?

Ancient Indian Education

> We owe a lot to the Indians, who taught us how to count, without which no worthwhile scientific discovery could have been made.
>
> Albert Einstein

The sages of Vedic India were great educationists concerned with life as a whole and the holistic development of the individual and society. Spirituality formed the basis of all aspects of life, including education.

Saṁskāras — Education was marked by ritualistic ceremonies (saṁskāras) that refined the individual by removing his weaknesses (doṣa apanayana), empowering him with virtues and capabilities (guṇa ādhāna), and making him a wholesome person (hina aṅga pūrti).

Prenatal Education — Education of the individual started even before birth. Mothers were given the special responsibility of imparting prenatal education by entertaining good thoughts, reading sacred texts, listening to holy chants and wise words, keeping the company of noble souls, and making auspicious resolutions for the child. Ceremonies like garbhādhāna, puṁsavana, and sīmanta unnayana reinforced this education, culminating in the birth of the child with the jāta karma (birth ceremony).

Preschool Education — The informal education at home in the loving and caring presence of the large joint family, given especially by the parents and the elders, nourished the child and became a strong support for his lifelong growth and progress. (Childhood neglect and abuse are major contributors for troubled and criminal adult life in the present.) Childhood was marked by rituals and family celebrations like the naming ceremony (nāma karaṇa), eating the first morsel of food (anna prāśana), leaving the house for the first time (niṣkramaṇa), piercing the ears (karṇa vedhana), and the first hair cut (cūḍā karma).

Initiation into Literacy (akṣara abhyāsa) — By the age of three-to-four years, the child was introduced to the alphabet by the family Guru. He held the child's finger and first inscribed the holy syllable 'Om' on a plate of rice. Om represents the imperishable Truth (akṣara Brahma). The very purpose of learning the alphabet (also called akṣara mālā, as they remain unchanging in all the words) was ultimately to know the imperishable Truth. Prayers were offered to Lord Gaṇeśa, the remover of obstacles, Goddess Sarasvati, the deity of learning and the family deity. The Guru wrote all of the above with a ring dipped in honey on the tongue of the child so that he would speak what he learned, speak the sweet name of God, and propagate the Truth alone.

School (Gurukula) Education — Between the ages of six-to-eight years, the child was taken to the gurukula — a residential school where he or she stayed between ten-to-eighteen years, immersed in continuous and rigorous studies without a single vacation.

School Induction Ceremony (upanayana and vidyā–ārambha) — Young boys and girls were initiated by means of an elaborate ceremony into the famous and powerful Gāyatri Mantra, a mantra repeated daily thereafter in their dawn and dusk prayers (sandhyā vandana). The mantra means, 'We meditate on the light of God/Truth (represented in the sun). May He illumine our intellect.' With this ceremony the student was called dvija or twice-born — born into the vast realm of knowledge and education, and thus was endowed with culture. The student thereafter was ceremonially introduced to the Vedas and first taught the Medhā Sūktam to further manifest the powers of his intellect.

The Guru and Guru-mātā (wife of the Guru) lived with the students, often within the same house. The relationship between the Guru and student was one of mutual love and respect.

This reverential attitude toward the Guru is the hallmark of Indian spirituality and culture.

gururbrahmā gururviṣṇuḥ gururdevo maheśvaraḥ,
guru sākṣāt paraṁ brahma tasmai śrī gurave namaḥ.

I salute the Guru who is the Creator (of knowledge), the Sustainer (of virtues), and the Destroyer (of all my weaknesses); and is verily the Lord Himself.

The Guru understood his responsibility of teaching as a sacred duty, a privilege, and an honor. He and his wife were role models, imparting lessons by example in simple living and high thinking, sacrifice, dedication, discipline, and service. The Guru was to the student a friend (kalyāṇa mitra), philosopher (Guru), and guide (deśika) — a person who would be his inspiration for life.

tvameva mātā ca pitā tvameva tvameva bandhuśca sakhā tvameva,
tvameva vidyā draviṇaṁ tvameva tvameva sarvaṁ mama deva deva.

You are my mother, father, relation and my friend. You are the knowledge and wealth — in fact, you are everything to me.

In ancient India, women were given equal rights in education and teaching. Renowned female seers like Gārgi or Maitreyī were prominent participants in educational debates and proceedings of 'pariṣads' (assemblies). Students would reside together as equals, irrespective of their economic or social standing. All had to perform household chores and serve others. This paved the way for mutual camaraderie and respect, which continued long after graduation when each assumed their respective roles in society — be they a king, a king-maker, or a hawker.

I have heard as a child that even the divine incarnations, Śrī Kṛṣṇa and Śrī Rāma went to the gurukula and received knowledge from Guru Sāndīpani and Guru Vasiṣṭha. We hear of the wonderful friendship between Śrī Kṛṣṇa as the king of Dvārakā and Sudāmā the poor brahmin who was given a royal welcome in His palace and gifted with riches. It seems utopian — for all to be treated as equals in school.

The teaching-learning process involved chanting, discourses, reflection, independent thinking, group discussions, research, demonstrations, and hands-on experimentation. Classes always started and ended with peace invocations. The students were not divided age-wise into classes but as per their individual progress.

Opening prayer:

saha nāvavatu, saha nau bhunaktu, saha vīryaṁ karavāvahai,
tejasvināvadhītamastu mā vidviśāvahai. Om śāntiḥ śāntiḥ śāntiḥ.

May we be protected, may our knowledge be protected. May we both enjoy the teaching-learning process and enjoy the result of knowledge. May we both put forth our best efforts. May our knowledge be bright and brilliant and available when needed. May we never have ill feelings towards each other. May there be no obstacles from unseen sources, surroundings, or from within us. May peace prevail.

Besides studies and routine chores, daily life in the gurukula involved spiritual practices like fasting, worship, fire rituals, dawn and dusk prayers, yoga and meditation. All these opened the door to a unique way of learning — intuition.

Tuition and Intuition — Tuition is acquired knowledge from outside, learned in steps and followed by study and practice. Intuition is revealed knowledge that springs forth from within, spontaneously, when the intellect is fine-tuned to the higher source of knowledge. Great scientific discoveries or masterpieces of art and literature also happen when the self is at abeyance and the flash of intuition occurs. The entire Vedas are such 'revealed knowledge' of eternal truths that govern the world, discovered by Sages (Ṛṣis) in their seat of meditation.

I must say, this all sounds like a really neat way of learning. No books, no homework, no projects ... just sit down — pray and meditate!

No such luck. Intuition works only when coupled with tuition. Guruji says there is no gain without pain. Hard work is also required.

The students studied both secular and spiritual knowledge which were never divided into watertight compartments, as we see today. The spiritual scriptures of India like the Vedas, Rāmāyaṇa, and Mahābhārata, covered an array of subjects like geography, history, sociology, geology, astronomy, geometry, astrology, and so on. Scriptures on non-spiritual subjects like medicine (Āyurveda), the art of warfare (Dhanurveda), economics (Artha Śāstra), politics (Nīti Śāstra), architecture (Vāstu Śāstra), and performing arts (Nātya Śāstra), elaborated upon ethical values and their role in our spiritual evolution. The scriptures which were mostly in Sanskrit, covered everything — from living a healthy life and avoiding social evils, to improving concentration, tenets of behavior, and so on. Education in ancient India covered all aspects of life, thus making education holistic and relevant at all times.

> **The Sanskrit language,** whatever be its antiquity, is of a wonderful structure; more perfect than Greek, more copious than Latin, and more exquisitely refined than either, yet bearing to both of them a stronger affinity, both in the roots of verbs and the forms of grammar, than could possibly have been produced by accident; so strong indeed, that no philologer could examine them all, without believing them to have sprung from some common source.
>
> Sir William Jones, British Philologist, 1786

An Exquisite Example — This unbelievable Sanskrit verse (936) from Pādukāsahasram of Śrī Deśikan, of thirty-two syllables uses only one consonant (ya) and one vowel (ā) in the entire verse.

यायायायायायायायायायायायायायाया।
यायायायायायायायायायायायायायाया।।

It is to be read in the prose order:

yāyāyā, āya, āyāya, ayāya, ayāya, ayāya, ayāya, ayāyā, yāyāya, āyāyāya, āyāyā, yā, yā, yā, yā, yā, yā, yā, yā.

The meaning of the verse is:

The sandals (pādukā) which adorn the Lord, which help in attainment of all that is good and auspicious, which give knowledge, which cause the desire (of having the Lord as one's own), which remove all that is hostile, which have attained the Lord, which are used for going and coming from one place to another, by which all places of the world can be reached, these sandals are for Lord Viṣṇu.

A love for knowledge and a zeal for constant self-improvement were embedded in the ancient Indian approach to learning. It was passed from generation to generation through the teacher-taught lineage.

I have heard of family lineage but never of a knowledge lineage. What is that?

Guru Paramparā — In Indian culture it is not only 'who you are' that is given importance, but also 'whose you are,' your lineage or paramparā.

Bindu paramparā is your family lineage that molds you with its heredity, history, and culture. Nāda paramparā is the learning and knowledge lineage — be it secular or spiritual. The teacher taught the student who in turn verified his learning with his own experience and passed it on to his student.

The artisan is known by whom he apprenticed with, the musician is recognized by the teachers who taught him, the student is respected by the university he graduated from, and the disciple by the Guru under whom he studied.

The teacher-taught lineage is a most valued and time-tested Indian way of conveying knowledge and wisdom. The student therefore always salutes not just his Guru, but also the entire knowledge lineage — vande guru-paramparā.

Knowledge was considered sacrosanct and could not be bought or sold. Traditionally, there was never a fee or donation taken from the students for their education, boarding, or lodging. The kings acted as patrons of the gurukulas and society supported them. This tradition helped maintain a spirit of humility and respect for both knowledge and the Guru amongst the students and society.

This is like a social state. But presently, in government schools, which give free education, neither the students nor the teachers are inspired to learn or teach. How did they tackle this problem?

The Guru taught because of his love for knowledge and the student learned what he was inclined to. Education was not a burden and each one learned selecting subjects according to his aptitude. A goldsmith's son nearly always became a goldsmith. Upon graduating, the student offered Guru dakṣiṇā according to his capacity to the Guru. Offering Guru dakṣiṇā is a traditional gesture of acknowledgment and gratitude for the knowledge, love and care that a student receives. This may be monetary in nature, or as a special task that the teacher wants the student to accomplish. For example, Guru Sāndīpanī had asked Śrī Kṛṣṇa to bring back his lost son as Guru dakṣiṇā. In short, students were taught how to live as ideal citizens of society.

The Graduation Ceremony and Convocation Address (samāvartana) — At the end of the course of study, a ceremony would take place after which the Guru delivered a Convocation address — his final words of inspiration and guidance. The convocation address (śiṣyānuśasanam) from Śikṣā Valli, Taittirīya Upaniṣad is relevant even today.

Having taught the Vedas, the preceptor (teacher) enjoins the pupils:

Speak the truth, do your duty, never swerve from the study of the Vedas.

Do not cut off the line of descendants in your family, after giving the preceptor the dakṣiṇā he desires.

Never err from truth, never fall from duty, never overlook your own welfare, and never neglect your prosperity. Never neglect the study and propagation of the Vedas or swerve from your duties toward deities and departed souls.

May the mother be to thee, God. May the father be to thee, God. May the preceptor be to thee, God. May the guest be to thee, God. Let only the actions that are free from blemishes be done — and not others. You must follow only those virtuous actions that are irreproachable — and not others. You must not even breathe a word when those who are more distinguished than you are in discussion on spiritual matters (or, you must offer a seat to superiors and worship them with acts of reverence and love).

Charity should be given with faith; it should never be given without faith; it should be given in plenty, with modesty, and with sympathy. Let there also be agreement in opinion (or friendly feelings) when charity/gifts are offered.

Now if there should arise any doubt regarding your acts, or any uncertainty in respect of your conduct in life, you should act in those matters exactly as those noble souls who are present there, who are thoughtful, religious (experienced), not set on by others, not cruel, and are devoted to Dharma.

This is the command. This is the teaching. This is the secret of the Vedas. This is the commandment. This should be observed. Verily, having understood this fully, one must act in the way taught above, continuously till the last — and not otherwise.

The majority of graduates would return home to develop professional careers, get married, and live in accordance with dharma. There were some rare students who chose either to remain at the gurukula or retire to the forest to dedicate their lives exclusively to the pursuit of spiritual or secular knowledge.

So if I understand correctly, you think education was more sophisticated in ancient India than it is now?!

The evidence speaks for itself! People traveled from across Asia to undergo higher education in ancient India, because it was considered so advanced.

The historical epics Mahābhārata and Rāmāyaṇa, Manu Smṛti, and Upaniṣads all reveal the long and rich history of pioneering education that flourished in ancient Indian civilization.

The schooling system may have been advanced — but I can't imagine that universities of those times could rival the modern standards of today!

You obviously haven't heard of Takshashila, the ancient IIT and MIT of the world, where students from around the world came to gain specialization in more than sixty-four different fields of study like the Vedas, grammar, philosophy, āyurveda, agriculture, surgery, politics, archery, warfare, astronomy, commerce, futurology, music, and dance. And can you believe, one subject offered was the art of discovering hidden treasure!

That's amazing! How do I get to Takshashila? I am signing up right now!

Nearly 3,000 years ago flourished the great university of ancient India, **Takshashila**, which is located in present-day Pakistan and now sits in ruins. More than 10,000 students from around the world were educated in this famed University. Star graduates of Takshashila University remain legendary historical figures.

▲ RUINS OF TAKSHASHILA

Pāṇinī, a master of language and grammar, authored one of the greatest works on grammar ever written, called *Aṣṭādhyāyī*. It defines the features and rules of Sanskrit grammar in eight chapters, hence the name.

Jīvak was a genius doctor and an expert in understanding the health of the body by pulse reading. He studied āyurveda in Takshashila University for seven years. His areas of specialization included pañcakarma, marma, and surgery. There are over 15,000 handwritten manuscripts of Jīvak's available even today.

Nalanda in the state of Bihar was another one of ancient India's learning treasures, cited as one of the first great universities in recorded history. It was a university for higher learning, which attracted pupils and scholars from Korea, Japan, China, Tibet, Indonesia, Persia, and Turkey. Prospective students had to be at least twenty-years old, and undertake an oral entrance exam.

Like today's most sought-after universities, only a quarter of applicants were admitted, and upon entering Nalanda, they were promptly humbled by the caliber of their teachers and co-students. Students could opt to study philosophy, fine arts, medicine, mathematics, astronomy, politics, or the art of war among other subjects. Interfaith debates were also encouraged and at its peak, Nalanda University could accommodate over 10,000 students and 2,000 teachers.

▲ RUINS OF NALANDA

Āryabhaṭṭa (476–550 C.E.), the great mathematician-astrologer, set up an astronomy observatory in his birth place Taregna in Bihar and wrote the very famous *Āryabhaṭṭīya* (a compendium of mathematics and astronomy) when he was just twenty-three years of age. He studied at Pataliputra (near Patna) and became the head (Kulapati) of its famous Nalanda University.

The University was considered an architectural masterpiece. In 1193, Bakhtiyar Khilji, a Turkish Muslim invader who pillaged and burned the prolific institution, brought the University to a brutal and decisive end. Legend has it that the three libraries of Nalanda were so large that they smoldered for six months.

Vikramshila in Bihar, **Varanasi** in Uttar Pradesh, and **Ujjain** in Madhya Pradesh were locations of other famous, popular, and huge universities of ancient times.

Hearing all this makes me feel really proud to be an Indian. I've always felt the best only came from the West.

With this understanding of the ancient and modern Indian education, let us delve into the education that shaped Pūjya Gurudev and his thoughts.

Secular Education of Gurudev

Divine Entry — A child was born at 7.30 P.M. on Monday, May 8, 1916, at Ernakulam, Kerala, in a cultured, aristocratic, and wealthy family as the son of Kuttan and Parukutti Menon. The astrologer-priest who saw the horoscope of baby Balakrishnan Menon declared soon after he was born, that the position in Rājayoga indicated he would become a man of worldwide repute.

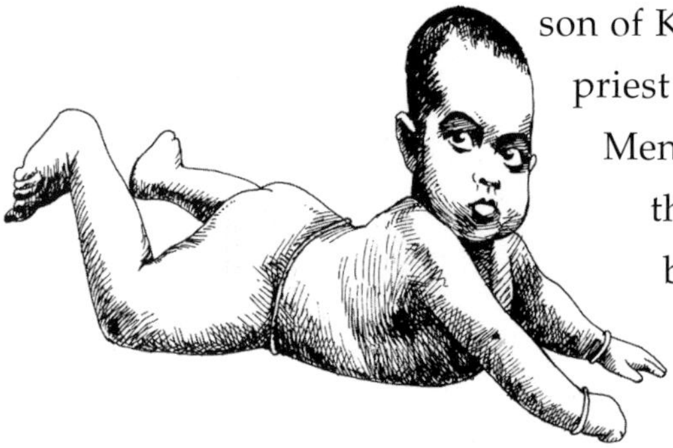

If we are destined to become great, do external influences matter? Would we become great even if we didn't try?

Gurudev explained it this way: What comes to you is your destiny. And what you do with what you get is your self-effort. Let us see what he got and what he did with what he got.

A Loving Start — Balan grew up within a large, loving, extended family living in Poothampalli House. This deeply influenced his lifelong belief in the importance of showering a child with love and affection in the early years.

▲ GURUDEV'S EXTENDED FAMILY

THE HINDU JOINT FAMILY IS IMPORTANT TO THE CONTINUATION OF OUR CULTURE; IT AFFORDS THE MEMBERS ALL OF THEIR NEEDS IN CRISIS.

| Swami Chinmayananda |

Balan was always alert and inquisitive. One early fascination was airplanes. He loved to draw them. On the rare occasion when one flew overhead, he became ecstatic. "I am going to fly in a plane when I grow up," he assured his mother, and he did so most of his adult life.

Early Spiritual Seeds — Honoring birthdays of saints, Hindu festivals, seasons, and harvest time were all festivities that Balan actively participated in. He undertook all the rituals prescribed by the scriptures for a Hindu child.

Holy men or swamis often stopped for rest at Balan's home during their travels because of the pure and peaceful environment at the Poothampalli House. **Chattambi Swamigal**, a great yogi of the time, often visited the Menon household, paying particular attention to Balan. He had extraordinary powers (siddhis) and is said to have had the power to be in three places at the same time. Balan was drawn to the Swami, and often sat by his side pulling and twisting his long grey beard. On a visit, Chattambi Swamigal once remarked, "Don't worry, I've taught him everything." The Swamigal is said to have named Balan and presided over his initiation into traditional education (akṣara abhyāsa).

> Chattambi Swamigal has been one of the constant altars at which I have, day by day, surrendered and from whom I have invoked endless streams of power and strength. My capacity to serve the world, I owe to this unique Sage... It seems that I had a secret initiation at the hands of the Swamigal, who accomplished this marvel in a tiny baby, perhaps, then only a thousand days old in the world.
>
> Swami Chinmayananda in 'The Secret Initiation,' March 16, 1967

Indian tradition lays great importance on the power of initiation. I have heard it awakens the inner latent powers in a person.

Formal Education of Balakrishnan Menon

- Age 5-12 (1921 – 1928) : Sree Rama Varma High School, Kochi, Kerala
- Age 12-16 (1928 – 1932) : Vivekodayam School, Thrissur, Kerala
- Age 16-18 (1932 – 1934) : Fellow of Arts (FA), Maharaja's College, Kochi, Kerala
- Age 19-21 (1935 – 1937) : Bachelor of Arts (BA), St Thomas' College, Thrissur, Kerala
- Age 24-27 (1940 – 1943) : Master of Arts (MA) in English Literature and Bachelor of Law (LLB), Lucknow University, Uttar Pradesh

Chattambi Swamigal had also at one time mentioned that Balan would be famous, "But first he will have to suffer greatly." Tragedy struck early in the idyllic life of young Balan; soon after giving birth to his younger sister, their mother died unexpectedly when he was just five years old. The women of the household took charge and were determined to give him a happy and healthy start in life.

College at Four — Before his mother died, at the age of four, Balan was a challenge to his mother and aunts, who began to struggle to keep him

entertained while his older cousins were in school. His youngest aunt solved the problem. Being a teacher in the nearby St. Theresa Convent College, she took the four-year-old along to her classes each morning. He looked forward to these visits because he loved the attention showered on him.

Four years is pretty young to start college! He must have felt funny going to school thereafter.

Balan started his formal education at the age of five. Like many other children across India, he studied in the medium of English, with his mother tongue, Malayalam, as a second language. Being patterned after the British system, even the textbooks displayed English children in English homes with English pets; even the farms, countryside trees and plants were from England. India's abundance of flora, fauna, heroes, and history were completely ignored.

Early school years presented no problems for Balan even though it was a regimented life, with an occasional caning by the headmaster for anyone who failed to conform to the regulations. He was intelligent, had a natural love for reading, completed his lessons easily, studied well, and spoke with confidence. He was considered a well-disciplined, happy, and ideal student.

Learning Sanskrit — Balan studied Sanskrit under the tutelage of a brilliant scholar who had a knack for making this classical language easy by demonstrating its similarities with Malayalam. "He is one who would be considered among the illiterate because he has received no English-styled education," Swami Chinmayananda would later lament when criticizing India's modern standards of education.

Gurudev's Beloved Sanskrit Teacher — My father, a teacher in a government high school in Irinjalakuda, recommended **Śrī Kartha**, a retired and eminent scholar, to teach Balan Sanskrit. He was a good teacher, popular with other children for his jolly nature and jokes. Years later, Gurudev expressed a desire to meet Śrī Kartha. By this time he was 95 years old, and seemed to have lost his memory. Nevertheless, my father explained to him slowly that Balan was coming to see him. He suddenly began giving instructions to everybody ... "Do this, do that ... Balan is coming to see me after a long time. Now I hear that he has become a sannyāsī! At last that day has come!" Upon meeting, Gurudev and Śrī Kartha embraced each other and tears of joy rolled down their eyes. It was indeed a memorable moment.

Smt. Nalini Menon, childhood friend of Gurudev,
spent her school days in Thrissur with him. An ardent devotee,
presently Trustee of CM Thrissur.

Balan was a caring older brother who would help his sisters with their homework and a loving grandchild who would sit with his grandmother, entertaining her with jokes. He was also a large-hearted friend. He would often pay the fees of Shankar Narayan, his best friend at school, who was an orphan.

Even though he was exposed to a religious culture, his spiritual sādhanā began as a game — a game devised to avoid boredom.

The Visual Game — "It was during those days of waiting for the conclusion of the evening worship service that Swami Chinmayananda was born in Balan, then only a frail child," Gurudev later explained. "Somehow Balan had stumbled onto this new game: He would look at the picture of the Lord, then would shut his eyes to see the same Lord Śiva in the darkness within. This gave Balan a game so sweet and pleasant that it became a habit to recall this picture onto his mental screen. It came readily as soon as it was ordered; and his wonder grew at this success."

Inadvertently, Balan had discovered a technique of meditation — mental visualization of God (rūpa dhyāna/upāsanā). This not only uplifts and purifies the mind but also makes it serene and single-pointed.

Rebellious Adolescence — As Balan entered his teens, he lost enthusiasm for his studies and became an outspoken and boisterous student. Bored in the classroom, he often passed time cracking jokes and pulling pranks and imitating the teachers, which sent all into peals of laughter.

▲ VIVEKODAYAM SCHOOL REGISTER

Balan's nonchalant attitude toward his studies finally got the better of him and being unprepared he sat for a science paper, and failed. Soon after, his exasperated father enrolled him in college at Thrissur.

CHINMAYA BLOCK
FOUNDATION STONE LAID BY
H.H.SWAMI CHINMAYANANDA
ON
24-11-1975

▲ VIVEKODAYAM SCHOOL

I had been a student of Vivekodayam Boys High School, and from my own personal experience, I must admit that, if I have fulfilled my life and benefited by education and successfully transformed my personality, the early foundations were laid in the Geeta Classes that I attended in the school, and also due to the religious and spiritual atmosphere that was liberally available in this Gurukula Institution.

Chinmayananda

Message for School Souvenir

An Agnostic Becomes an Atheist — Balan then abandoned the daily temple worship that had formed an integral part of his childhood. In fact, he had begun to ridicule his religion and its practices, taunting his sisters for prostrating at the feet of holy men who would visit the family home. He dressed in style, oiled and combed his hair 'till his head would get bald' as claimed by his father, and was called 'Silk Balan' for his love for wearing silk clothes. He considered himself quite an intellectual, rejected God, and brandished all rituals as superstition rooted in blind belief. Strangely enough, he continued to do his japa secretly in bed, and his early relationship with Lord Śiva persisted in spite of his rejection of God — typical contradictions of teens.

How did one who was almost a school dropout become a Swami?! I've heard that he spoke excellent English ... from where did he pick that up? — in the Himalayas?

No. He did actually go to University where he earned a Master's degree in his favorite subject, English Literature, as well as a secondary degree in Law. And just like you he was also a Journalist.

That is great. Now I really want to know your Swami!

The University Student — In 1940, Balan joined Lucknow University immersing himself in English Literature, unenthused by the prospect of also studying Law, which he pursued to oblige his father. Pandit Jagmohanath Chak, the Dean of the Faculty of Law, was his professor. He was the favorite of many of his teachers like Prof. N. K. Siddhanta and Prof. V. K. Nanda Menon the HOD of political science.

▲ PANDIT JAGMOHANATH CHAK

Ali Muhamad was a close friend with whom he shared many a meal from the Hindu canteen during his college days. Once, as a bet with his friends, he walked straight into the office of a very eminent barrister. When questioned about his uninvited intrusion, he said, "I am a law student and would like to know the secret of success." Barrister Tej Bahadur Sapru replied, "**Work like a horse and live like a hermit,**" little realizing that this youth was to become the hermit, Swami Chinmayananda, work 24/7, and speak to thousands on the topic 'Secret of Success.'

How did Swamiji ever manage to pass the courses he wasn't interested in?

Initially he managed, then struggled, and in time left the course for a lofty cause, but finally emerged gloriously — with Honors.

▲ LUCKNOW UNIVERSITY

Activist to Journalist — In 1942, the struggle for India's independence intensified as the leaders of the Indian Congress were imprisoned. Everyone, especially university students, took to the streets demanding the release of Mahatma Gandhi. Balan was one of them.

He left university to join other student activists who were writing and distributing leaflets. As one of the more vocal participants, he gave public speeches to stir up national pride. As he became more involved in the freedom struggle, the British even jailed him, but he rejoined with greater fervor on his release. The authorities were now seriously after him, and he found a perfect hideout for the hunted — right in the middle of the enemy camp! He took up a job working as a machine operator in the military quarters of a British intelligence communications center in Abbottabad. Having been away from his studies for over two years, he had a lot to catch up on, but was determined to complete his university degree. So he prepared for the last round of his exams at Abbottabad. He returned to Lucknow and completed his Masters in English Literature and Bachelors in Law with honors. Convinced that newsprint was the best and easiest means to reach the public, he then took several courses in journalism.

Other Influences: Sports — As a child, Balan loved playing soccer or tennis after school. Later, as an undergraduate he was part of the university tennis team. He was pitched in singles against Ghaus Mohammad, the first Indian competitor ever to play at Wimbledon. He continued to avidly watch tennis matches on TV all his life and jokingly remarked, "If I had not become a Swami, I would have been a Wimbledon champ!"

I wish he had continued with a tennis career... He would have been the only singles Wimbledon champion in Indian history! But I guess he served the country more as a Swami.

Young Balan also loved to swim, an enjoyment that remained throughout his life. Even as a Swami, he would startle devotees by diving into a holy river or the sea, swimming out far until he was just a speck in the distance.

Other Influences: Fine Arts and Performing Arts — Balan actively participated in university theatrical activities and appeared in several performances. In his early days as a journalist, some friends invited him to Mumbai to act in a film they were producing. He went along, partly for the amusement of working on a film, but more so to pursue his chosen profession of a journalist.

Balan used to sketch profusely, and even as Swami Chinmayananda, his letters to devotees often had cartoons or sketches of the design of a school flag or the master plan of a site.

Later, as Swami Chinmayananda, he was a patron of performing arts and inspired many renowned classical dancers, musicians, and painters in India.*

Other Influences: Literature

LOVE IS THE HEART OF ALL RELIGIONS; THE THEME OF ALL CLASSICAL WORKS OF ART AND LITERATURE, THE SONG OF ALL DEVOTEES. SCIENTISTS KNOW ONLY WHAT LOVE DOES, NOT WHAT LOVE IS.

| SWAMI CHINMAYANANDA |

Balan displayed a love for literature from his very early days. As a rebellious teenager, he would skip class to read a book. At university, he was on the literary committee and the debating team. Shakespeare, Shelley, Swift, Shaw, and Milton were among his favorite writers, and he would relish discussions with his professor of literature, the distinguished scholar, Śrī Vilasan Nair.

His love for literature blossomed with his spiritual unfoldment. His innate flair for mastering the spoken and written word would mature into delivering discourses to the masses around the world, and writing hundreds of books and commentaries of pivotal significance to mankind. His noble thoughts often expressed as thousands of letters to his devotees — each a piece of art, and as beautiful poetry.

*See Chapter VI for Swami Chinmayananda's thoughts on the arts and culture.

I know not by what magic
How or where
What or when:
He answers my prayers ...
I need not know when He answers
what He does,
where He fulfills,
How He accomplishes
But this I know
He answers my prayers ...
I leave all care
With Him above
Whose love for me
Is endless and true.

A True Wordsmith — As a journalist, Balan quickly gained a reputation as a controversial writer willing to speak out against anyone, even the news media that supported his livelihood. He became chief reporter of the National Herald in Delhi and commented critically and boldly on many social and political issues.

Inspired Media Guru — Śrī K. Rama Rao, an eminent editor, noted freedom fighter and member of the first Rajya Sabha, was the only journalist of his era who worked in over twenty-five newspapers in metropolitan cities of undivided India, including Lahore and Karachi. He was jailed for his editorial in the National Herald, Lucknow (titled 'Jail or Jungle' in which he attacked the British government for torturing Congress satyāgrahis in the Lucknow jail). He trained a large number of journalists. Balan was one of his inspired and eager students. Recognizing the natural flair in Balan, Śrī Rao gave him his very first job as a journalist — sub-editor at the National Herald initially in Lucknow, and later in Delhi — a big jump for a novice.

IN MATTER OF
EDDING REQUIRMENTS
LET US BE YOUR
RUSTED CONSULTANT
KING OF SAREES
AYARAM & Co.
TA LUCKNOW MUSSOORIE

NATIONAL HERALD

LUCKNOW: SUNDAY MARCH 10, 1946

FOR
THE BEST RETURN OF YOUR MONEY
STAY & DINE
AT
CAPOOR'S
THE NOVELTY RESTAURANT OF THE PROVINCE
Hazratgunj Lucknow.

VIGNETTES

PRAISE OF THE POSTMAN

strange truth. All things
orld that serve Man,
to the degree of their
, got injured, broken
oyed, but in their very
they serve the best.
en, in serving society
ul devotion, are the lit-
ts of our age.
tomorrow onwards, they
e struck work had it
for the wiser among the
thinking better of it.
hreat is no more. But
that it could have err-
they struck work is a
f their usefulness. The
ety would have come to
ill; the springs of affec-
ove would have got
ven the nearest village
ve been rendered miles
o short we should have
d to realise that a post-

ger of sympathy and
love,
of parted friends,
r of the lonely,
scattered family,
r of common Life".
an be but a rare few
now who do not feel the
t the proposed strike is
. I for one dread to live
ty sans postmen.

he moment a dak
ost-office till the
ct, postmen are
arrying, enquiri
ng the innumerab
hey get no rest.
e last letter and
ffice only to find t
ady for them to
Without a
Cerry gather the
nd cheerfully star
rounds,
man his dak
sorts of people
and the worried, th
the desperate, the
the careless. To
dress in sealed

today an accomplished artist. With callous indifference, copied directly from the Civilisation around him, he brings hopes, blessings and compliments to one, curses, despress and sorrows to another. It is not his habit to compliment or to condole. He is a product of our ill-conceived Progress: beneficial and a thousand times evolved from his messenger days, and yet, pitiless and ugly, empty and soulless.

Whatever be the nature of the message he is delivering, the postman bears a habitul well-poised outlook on life and a face beaming serene in his immutable nonchalance. Professionally he refuses to look beyond the address.

Gopal is my postman. In the course of his duties he has been bringing consolation in my loneliness, hope into my dark despair. Yet never has Gopal, even for once, paused to watch my gratification and smile. When it is a money-order he counts the amount more than once, examines my signature, hands over the

ent Mercu
hup wast
was. There
tals who e
duties exe
postman.
nimity, wh

AZAD HIND FAUJ QAUMI TARANA

Solo Clarionet in
Allegro 6

IN PEDLARISTAN

Today, everyone of us is a pedlar in life. In feverish hurry we sell among ourselves our honest or assumed potentialities. Each strives hard to deceive all others with looks of assumed sincerity and faithfulness. We glorify this dire humbug as healthy competition. In the name of propaganda everyone shrieks and howls; in the name of religion we preach and perish. In the name of liberty and freedom we release annihilating elemental forces to kill each other. And this is the Commercial Civilization in an Age of Propaganda, among a World of Pedlars.

Thus, we see Balan's growth from an endearing and obedient child to a mischievous and rebellious teen and from a purposeless cocksure youth to a passionate political activist, as he went from his schools in the South to university in the North. This education culminated in the making of a prolific writer and courageous journalist with a deep sensitivity towards his fellow men. These myriad experiences from his school, college, university, and professional life profoundly influenced his perspective of the ideal education.

Swami Chinmayananda's Spiritual Education

Much like the Ṛṣis of ancient India, Gurudev believed secular education is important ... but gains fulfillment only when coupled with spiritual knowledge. This he spoke from his own experience.

Balan's own education finally found fulfillment in Rishikesh and Uttarkashi. It was here that his life's path shifted dramatically after coming in contact with two great Gurus, Swami Sivananda and Swami Tapovanam.

I cannot imagine an agnostic like him going to a Guru. How did that happen?

He went as a skeptical journalist to the ashram of Swami Sivananda at Rishikesh, ready to expose the 'bluff of the Himalayan ascetics.' But as you will see,... things turned out quite differently.

Swami Sivananda requested him to stay for as long as he wished and write whatever he saw. Balan's furiously curious mind found inspiration and answers in the lofty ideals he witnessed at work in this

◀ SWAMI SIVANANDA

great Guru. He stayed and studied the great philosophy enshrined in the scriptures — from books, the Guru, as well as other monks. The skeptic became a believer. It was on the auspicious day of Śivarātri, Tuesday, February 25, 1949, that Swami Sivananda initiated Balan into the holy order of sannyāsa — and thus was born Swami Chinmayananda Sarasvati — the Master who revels in the bliss of pure Consciousness.

Most swamis seem to have an 'ānanda' in their name, but I have not heard of a Sarasvati. What does it signify?

Just as a 'Ramesh Patel' would belong to the 'Gujarati Patel community' similarly 'Sarasvati' indicates Swami Chinmayananda's knowledge lineage (jñāna paramparā).

Swami Chinmayananda Sarasvati's Knowledge Lineage — He was initiated into the holy order of sannyāsa by Swami Sivananda Sarasvati and belongs to the lineage of the Advaita Vedānta of Ādi Śankaracārya. It is the order of the Śāradā pīṭha at Śṛṇgeri in South India whose first pontiff was Sureśvarācārya, one of the four main disciples of Ādi Śankaracārya. The order is the custodian of the Yajur Veda and mahāvākya 'ahaṁ brahmāsmi,' from the Bṛhadāraṇyaka Upaniṣad. The presiding deity of the order is Ādi Varāha, the sacred river is Tungabhadra, and the title is Sarasvati, one of the three titles given in the Śāradā pīṭha.

Swami Sivananda later directed him to Swami Tapovanam at Uttarkashi, and it was at the feet of this great Master that Swami Chinmayananda spent ten years learning the real essence of life.

So who is his real Guru?

In India, we believe that the mother is our first Guru. The father and all the others in life who teach and mold us are also considered Gurus. In the spiritual field, Swami Sivananda was Gurudev's dikṣā (initiation) Guru, and Swami Tapovanam was his śikṣā (knowledge) Guru. Swami Tapovanam was Gurudev's Sadguru — the one who taught him the knowledge of the Ultimate Truth and set him on the path to Liberation.

His Master — Swami Tapovanam was a true man of renunciation, wandering in the Himalayas long before his initiation into sannyāsa. It was clear that this pure-hearted monk saw God in everything. He would often stop in his wanderings to point out the majestic scenery saying, "Why can't man see Divinity behind the ecstatic Artist who has painted this inspired beauty?" His love for nature is seen clearly in his writings.

His devotion to the holy river Ganga — which he considered as the Ultimate Truth in liquid form — drew him to always live within hearing distance of its sweet rumblings, either at Uttarkashi or Gangotri. Many a time, this great soul spent months on end high above the Gangotri glacier lost in meditation. That place is now named Tapovanam after him. He was considered as the 'glory of the Himalaya — Himavat Vibhuti.' A local sannyāsi remarked, "Gangotri and Uttarkashi lost their glory when Swami Tapovanam left his mortal coil."

At the Feet of the Master — Swami Tapovanam rarely accepted disciples and few could cope with what this great disciplinarian demanded of the students he deemed fit for Vedānta. He told the curious 'Chinmaya,' as he was called by Swami Tapovanam, that he would say everything he had to teach once only, and Chinmaya would have to repeat it the very next day; if he forgot anything, he would have to leave. In and through all this strictness, Swami Chinmayananda remained fully alert to all he needed to learn and know. Swami Tapovanam believed that the highest Knowledge was not for everyone, but only for those who yearned and searched for it.

Headmaster's Disciple — Immortality is attained by tyāga (renunciation) (tyāgenaike amṛtatvamānaṣuḥ). — Kaivalya Upaniṣad 1.2

Born in an aristocratic family (in fact from Gurudev's own paternal family) as V. K. Krishna, Gurudev's Headmaster at Vivekodayam School was a great scholar and a living example of simple living and high thinking. He was a role model for selfless service and lived in a thatched hut all alone on the school campus. His spiritual pursuits continued side by side and in the later years he set up Sri Ramakrishna Ashram and the attached gurukula at Puranattukara, Thrissur. (In 1934, Mahatma Gandhi, visited this gurukula.) Direct disciples of Sri Ramakrishna Paramahamsa initiated him into the holy order of brahmacarya and sannyāsa and named him **Swami Tyageeshananda**. Interestingly, Swami Tapovanam used the name Swami Tyagananda when he took on ochre robes himself (vidvat sannyāsa). This spirit of renunciation seen in both his Headmaster and spiritual Master left a deep impression on the mind of Gurudev.

The Master's Disciple — In the hot summer season, Swami Tapovanam would retreat fifty-six miles further up the Himalayas to Gangotri, to remove himself from the influx of pilgrims who flooded to lower ranges during the warm weather. As one of his disciples, Swami Chinmayananda accompanied him.

Living conditions in Gangotri were tough. Removed from the comforts of civilization, there was no nutritious food, warm clothing, adequate shelter, or electricity for reading; and no talking was allowed among disciples, not with a disciplinarian for a Guru. With an intense desire for knowledge of the Supreme, Swami Chinmayananda braved the difficulties without complaint.

Each day began with an icy cold bath in the Ganga, waking up the body for morning class at 6 A.M. Following the Vedic tradition, class would begin with a prayer and continued for a few hours daily. The rest of the time was spent in reflection, prayer, meditation, and service of the Guru.

The Master Disciple — During scriptural study, Swami Tapovanam would read out one verse of the text, then give the equivalent meaning in Hindi. Word by word, he explained the Sanskrit, giving the rules of grammar, as well as possible interpretations and misinterpretations of the meaning. As the Guru spoke in Hindi, Swami Chinmayananda meticulously translated everything into English because he wanted all of his notes in the language most familiar to him.

Swami Chinmayananda's gurubhāī, Swami Govindagiri, himself a master of the scriptures, remembers those first classes with the eager new student of Vedānta; "At that time I had studied several texts with Swami Tapovanam and had not once dared to question him during class, but not this Chinmaya — he would put so many questions to Swami Tapovanam. He was not willing to move to the next topic until every doubt on the present subject was removed by the teacher."

His Master's Voice — The Master once explained, "The Truth is the mind of the mind, without the conditioning of the mind." "Then why do you not explain the Truth without the conditioning of the mind?" questioned the disciple.

The Master responded, "Chinmaya, get me water to drink." The disciple was somewhat surprised because it was unusual to be thirsty in the cold climate of Gangotri at such an early hour. Nevertheless, he quickly brought a glass of water and placed it in front of the Master. Swami Tapovanam said, "I asked you to get just water, not water in a glass." But how can I bring it without a container?" questioned the perplexed disciple. The Master replied, "Nobody can carry water without a vessel. It is the same in conveying knowledge of Truth. The Absolute, which is beyond speech and mind, is explained in words and grasped by the mind. But just as the glass is not drunk, only the water, the conditionings are left behind when the Truth is realized."

What sublime Knowledge ... conveyed in such a simple way.

Master Lessons — Aside from scriptural study, there were lessons learned daily from the austere life and living example of the Guru. Swami Tapovanam never missed an opportunity to teach the ideals of spiritual life and discipline in practical situations. His goal was to turn the student's mind beyond material concerns even in their daily routines.

The Master Stroke — Swami Chinmayananda spent long nights contemplating on the words of his Guru and meditating on the Truth. It was evident among the other disciples that he displayed all the qualifications of one ready for the final plunge — the dive into Self-Realization. "Never forget, the peace you are seeking is within," his Guru cautioned him, and it was there, deep within that he realized his oneness with the Supreme.

How did he ever manage to leave a place of such beauty and serenity?

Master Plan — One afternoon while he was sitting on a large boulder on the banks of the Ganga at Gangotri, Swami Chinmayananda had a

vision ... some would say a divine saṅkalpa — the will of God. 'The Ganga flows to bless mankind. Leaving the pristine beauty of the Himalayas, it flows into the heat and sweat of the plains allowing the gutters to flow in and the dams to slow its path. Millions over the years have sipped and dipped in its sanctifying waters. It blesses all as it widens in influence before it attains its confluence with the infinite ocean. I too must take this divine Knowledge that has fulfilled me to the hearts and hearths of each and every man, woman and child of India, whose very inheritance is now lost to them.'

This was the birth of Chinmaya Mission ... the afternoon dream of a wandering monk, the vision of a Realized Master, the Master plan of his life, that of taking the eternal flow of divine Knowledge to the masses and fulfilling the thirst of a nation and its future generations ... it heralded a cultural and spiritual renaissance of India's ancient wisdom. The various spiritual, social service, cultural, research, educational activities and projects of Chinmaya Mission have transformed the lives of millions directly or indirectly the world over.

That is quite a story — the Making of a Master. But what led a Swami to start a school — his own experiences in education?

The 'Chinmaya' experience of education started off as an 'experiment in education,' matured into the 'Chinmaya Vision of Education' and concretized as the 'Chinmaya Education Movement.'

Have a great day. Let's continue this story on my return trip tomorrow on flight 5W 415. Hari Om!

II

An Experiment in Education — Chinmaya Vision Programme

IT ALL STARTED AS AN EXPERIMENT; IT IS EVEN NOW AN EXPERIMENT, AND I AM SURE IT WILL EVER CONTINUE TO BE AN ENDLESS PROCESS OF EXPERIMENTATION. WE MUST SUCCEED. WE SHALL NOT FAIL THE SILENT DEMAND OF INNOCENT CHILDREN GROWING UNDER OUR CARE TO MAKE A CULTURAL HISTORY OF THE MORROW.

| Swami Chinmayananda |

Man has made unprecedented outer progress in the last century. Technological and scientific strides in transportation, communications, housing, and infrastructure have transformed the global modern lifestyle at a rapid pace. The primary concerns of the early twentieth century, such as epidemics and infant mortality, have been virtually eradicated in many countries. But is the world a better and happier place to live in?

Old problems have been replaced by new ones. The industrial revolution has tipped the ecological balance to critical levels; wars are fought in more complex ways; relationships are breaking down rapidly, and violence and aggression persist even within nations that are not at war.

Progress is the outcome of knowledge generated through our education. And knowledge-sharing has never been greater than what we see in today's world, and we appear to have amassed vast amounts of knowledge. On the Internet we can find just about any information from fixing a date to making a bomb!

Knowledge has become a major commodity. CKOs (Chief Knowledge Officers) are sought after in large companies, and email databases and genetic codes are sold at a high price. We have advanced in every field of knowledge, especially science and technology, and we see that thousands of new fields of knowledge have been created, such as nanotechnology and cyber-security. Yet countless unanswered problems persist. Today it is commonplace for humans to prefer the company of a dog or a mobile phone to a fellow family member, and we find guided missiles in the hands of misguided people. Jet-setting executives with peptic ulcers travel in superfast cars on smooth roads in super luxury — at crawling speeds in traffic jams.

THE TRAGEDY OF HUMAN HISTORY IS DECREASING HAPPINESS IN THE MIDST OF INCREASING COMFORTS.

| Swami Chinmayananda |

Hari Om! We meet again. You managed to get upgraded to first class. Good. We can continue the story.

Is not the aim of education to empower us to face the challenges of life? I have interviewed some of the most educated professionals, and many of them feel more inadequate, stressed, frustrated, and dejected than ever. Shouldn't modern education and the advancement in knowledge have made us happier?

Nārada was a master of sixty-four fields of knowledge yet he lamented to his brothers, "I am only a knower of words, but not a knower of the Self. I have heard that only the knower of the Self goes beyond grief. Please give me Self-knowledge." — Chāndogya Upaniṣad 7.3

What Is Wrong with Our Schools

We seem to find it necessary in our schools to teach about the lives of the kings, generals, and camarillas, which should be reserved for those who take an interest in political criminology; we teach a hundred names of plants they will never see, while they can't distinguish an apple tree from a cherry tree and don't know if lemons grow on a bush or a tree, adding only to the great body of useless information acquired in school and promptly left there at graduation. One of the most important subjects, how to get along with fellowmen, is left to chance and worse.

It isn't what you put into the student that matters so much as what you bring out of him. You may pour into his brain with a Nuremberg funnel all the seven wisdoms, up to the rim; but if you can't get out of him the spark of human kindness and the yearning to raise the standards of mankind, you may have given him a whole array of honors and medals, but you have rendered no service to the youth or to society.

Chinmayananda

It matters little what a person knows; it is what a person is able to do, that counts. Modern education is producing human beings who are increasingly intelligent, knowledgeable, hardworking, disciplined, smart, and successful. Man is more intelligent than ever before! However, Hitler, too, was very intelligent and smart! The holocaust was perpetrated in a country that had some of the most highly developed science, art, music, and culture of the twentieth century. This indicates that there is a real need to rethink what we call true education.

THE VISION OF THE VISIONARY

> The need is not for new horizons, but new spectacles to see the existing horizons.
>
> Anonymous

'Oh, East is East and West is West and never the twain shall meet.' "Why not?" questioned Gurudev.

The world is full of opposites — pleasure and pain, heat and cold, profit and loss, failure and success — yet dharma unifies all. (Dharma is that which unites, integrates, and supports the entire universe — dhāryate iti dharmaḥ.) Is it not possible for the ancient to complement the modern, and the East to meet the West in the benign presence of dharma? Should not the best and the most relevant aspects of two opposites integrate into a whole, as seen in the yin and yang of ancient Indian life and lifestyle? Integration has always been the Indian way of dealing with opposites.

Is it not possible to infuse modern education with ancient Indian educational principles to form a holistic yet relevant system of study, best suited to the needs of today? This was the thought that prompted the great Master, Swami Chinmayananda, to initiate his experiment in education.

What is Education? — Animals train their young ones with the knowledge and skills to stand on their own feet. Surely education is more than mere training? The sole aim of education cannot simply be the pursuit of higher marks for better jobs.

THE PRESENT INDIAN EDUCATION SYSTEM IS A STRANGE METHOD
BY WHICH THE KNOWLEDGE FROM THE TEXTBOOK OF THE TEACHER
IS TRANSFERRED TO THE NOTEBOOK OF THE STUDENT
WITHOUT EITHER OF THE MINDS BEING INVOLVED.

| Swami Chinmayananda |

When Dr. Karl Compton, the famous physicist, was in India, a native electrician constantly came to him for instructions on fixing the electric connections. In irritation, Dr. Compton said, "You know what I want; just use your common sense and do it," to which the electrician politely replied: "Sir, common sense is a rare gift of God. I have only a technical education."

Just as a dog's nature is to be a dog, the least expected of a human being is to be humane. The first aim of education is to make us humane. True education is thus the 'art of man-making.' So how can that be achieved in the present day?

DON'T JUST INVEST **ON** YOUR CHILD; ALSO INVEST **IN** YOUR CHILD.
| SWAMI CHINMAYANANDA |

Investment 'on' (modern education) does give outer prosperity, but it is investment 'in' (ancient Indian education) that will lead to inner unfoldment and lasting prosperity. Modern education can make us very able and capable, intelligent and smart, efficient and proficient; whereas the ancient Indian education system nurtured a holistic vision and created an ennobling attitude, which made a discernible difference in society. Gurudev sought to complement the positive aspects of modern education with ancient wisdom. He made a bold attempt to create a system of education that integrates the best of both.

Great people do not do different things; they do things differently.
Anonymous

The wise man does not topple the cart. He draws it toward its destination. During his lifetime, the personal guidance Gurudev gave, and the many letters he wrote to those who started schools under the Chinmaya umbrella, kept this holistic vision alive. Later this vision of Gurudev was concretized formally in 1996 as the **Chinmaya Vision Programme (CVP).**

Ability is what you are capable of doing, motivation determines what you do, attitude determines how well you do it, but it is the vision that determines how much you unfold as you do it. The stronger the motivation, the nobler is the attitude, and better the manifestation of our ability. The higher the vision, the greater is the blossoming of the personality.

History of Chinmaya Vision Programme (CVP) — Swamini Vimalananda (CVP Director) recollects: "It was the Silver Jubilee of the Chinmaya Vidyalaya, R S Puram, Coimbatore. Pūjya Guruji Swami Tejomayananda asked me to guide the celebrations. I started thinking, 'What is Gurudev's vision behind starting the Vidyalaya? Are we really implementing it? Is the Vidyalaya a school with a difference?' We then penned down Gurudev's vision into a program and I presented it on the occasion of the Anniversary Celebration. It received a standing ovation, the blessings of Guruji, the approval of Dr. Chhaya, a prominent educationist and the patronage of Central Chinmaya Mission Trust (CCMT) trustee Śrī Laju Chanrai. Thereafter, Radhika [Krishnakumar], Mytrae [Maganti], Viji [Vijaykumar], and I worked hard for months concretizing the four aspects of CVP, writing and compiling a manual, and introducing it to all the Vidyalayas and Colleges; all in a year's time! CVP always seemed Gurudev's will at work as it started with a bang, progressed at an unbelievable speed and was received whole-heartedly by thousands. Teachers, parents, management, all responded with words such as, 'need of the hour,' 'inspires the teacher in me,' 'real education,' and 'this is what Gurudev envisaged.'"

CVP was rolled out to Chinmaya Education Institutions (CEIs) across India in four phases — first, the principal, the management, and a couple of senior teachers were introduced to the program. It was followed by an orientation session for the entire staff. Later the parents were involved and finally students, too, became active participants in the program.

Swamini Vimalananda and Smt. Radhika Krishnakumar traveled and addressed management and teaching staff at hundreds of schools across India to deliver the CVP Seminar, guiding the implementation of Gurudev's vision. Through almost 200 seminars, the program has spread to 2,000 schools and colleges across fifteen states of India. It has also crossed the shores of India — the Sri Lankan government is supporting the integration of CVP into their system.

Why is a vision so important? — As the vision, so the world appears to us (yathā dṛṣṭi tathā sṛṣṭi). The world looks rosy to one with red-tinted glasses. If our vision is narrow and disturbed, the world seems filled with strife. But, if our vision is broad and love-filled, then our world, too, seems expansive and joy-filled.

The Chinmaya Vision Programme is not just a positive-attitude-inducement program, an autosuggestion to make the world feel good, despite what it seems to be. It is a holistic vision to see life and the world as a whole and to know the place and importance of each part of the jigsaw puzzle of life and the world. It is to appreciate and give more importance to the unifying essence underlying all the differences. It also means properly understanding the filters through which we see the world and cultivating a positive attitude in facing life.

> A narrow vision is divisive, a broad vision is expansive, and a holistic vision is all-inclusive.
>
> Swami Tejomayananda

In school, the lessons are taught first and the tests come later. But in life we see that the tests come first and the lessons are learned afterward. Should the aim of education be to prepare us to face school and college exams or to face the challenges of life?

I never thought of education in that way ... I always studied to pass exams and get good marks; otherwise I got remarks from the teachers that would set off sparks with my mother! I guess I really need to change my vision on education.

'Chinmaya' also means pure Knowledge. For an education program, this name is all the more appropriate. CVP is not just a vision. It offers practical ways to translate the lofty vision into a program that can be practiced.

It was after Gurudev's Mahāsamādhi in 1993 that CVP was formally developed, based entirely on Swami Chinmayananda's thoughts and advice. Back in 1965, he wrote:

> Children are the very cream of our generation and they are the rulers and makers of tomorrow. Upon them depends the future of the nation and the safety of our culture and tradition. Let us give them a healthy physical and mental atmosphere for growth (Integrated Development), ingrain in them respect for and love for all living creatures (Universal Outlook), team spirit and national fervor (Patriotism) and pride in our hallowed, divine culture (Indian Culture).
>
> Chinmayananda.

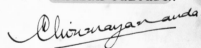

Let me introduce my favorite childhood friend Siddha the Leopard, who will take you through CVP.

The Four Aspects of CVP

1. Integrated Development (physical, mental, intellectual, and spiritual development)
2. Indian Culture
3. Patriotism
4. Universal Outlook

Integrated Development

SCIENCE IS MOVING IN SUCH A WAY SO AS TO MAKE US UNDERSTAND THAT EVERYTHING IS ONE. NATURE TOO, TEACHES US HARMONY; YET, WE HAVE MORE AND MORE DISINTEGRATED PERSONALITIES MOVING ABOUT IN A STRIFE-RIDDEN SOCIETY.

| Swami Chinmayananda |

When an aspect of the human personality remains unfulfilled, it creates a problem for the individual. Right food, clothing, and shelter address man's primal physical needs. Thereafter is the need for grooming, work, rest, and exercise, without which man suffers due to weakness and diseases. Emotionally we need to give and receive love and form healthy relationships, without which we suffer from insecurities, fear, loneliness, and clinging attachments. In addition, the intellect needs positive and stimulating thoughts, without which it becomes dull, frustrated, and stagnant. Spiritually we need inspiring goals, noble ideals, and virtuous deeds; otherwise life seems purposeless. A lopsided development of the head over the heart in the present time is the root cause for many professional and personal problems.

Integrated development aims at the overall unfoldment and gentle blossoming of the student at all levels of the personality, so that he becomes physically fit and well-groomed, emotionally balanced, intellectually alert and creative, and spiritually awakened.

Integrated Development — Physical Development

> The body is indeed the foremost vehicle for the performance of dharma (śarīram ādyam khalu dharma sādhanam). — Kumāra Sambhava 5.33

The goal of physical development is good health and proper growth of children. This leads to the optimum expression of their entire well-being, which includes physical security.

CVP IN ACTION **Emergency Training** — If we are not trained to handle emergencies, the mind gripped in fear may not allow us to respond quickly or correctly. CV Jamshedpur performs the fire evacuation drill twice a year so that children do not panic and know what has to be done in an emergency.

- **Physical Fitness**

In school, I hardly spent any time in the playground. It was all the time 'study, study, and study.'

In my school, playtime was sacrosanct. We also played traditional Indian games like kabaddi and even had a competition of creating our own game; the school actually adopted the game I created.

Medicine has advanced rapidly in the last century but health is still deteriorating. Childhood obesity is a problem in some of India's most developed towns and cities. "From my experience, I find that educated women are physically less fit, have a lower threshold for pain, and suffer greater difficulties at childbirth," observes Dr. Shyam Shah, a leading gynecologist.

A healthy body is more likely to house a healthy mind, so in this aspect of CVP, children and youth get accustomed to the joy of being

physically fit and making healthy living a lifelong passion.

"Nobody in my present college gets up early to do their morning exercise, except me." Namrata Ladsariya, CIRS alumni, pursuing Bachelor of Computing (Honors), National University of Singapore.

> **IN ACTION** **Fit to Teach** — Effective education can also transpire through emulation and imitation. Vidyalaya teachers are allotted time for physical recreation and fitness through games, yogāsana, and exercises and are encouraged to join in games with students in their free periods. This has created a greater bond and an opportunity to meet in a non-academic environment. Besides, such fit teachers take less sick leave!

- **Nutrition**

  The essence of what we eat and drink forms the body, senses, and mind and sustains life through the efficient functioning of the physiological functions (annamayam hi somya manaḥ, āpomayaḥ prāṇaḥ, tejomayī vāg iti).
  — Chāndogya Upaniṣad 6.5.5

"I do not know whether I live to eat or eat to live," confessed a youth. Understanding how food affects the body, senses, and mind, as well as cultivating the right food habits that are vital for growing children, is the aim of nutrition education.

> **IN ACTION** **Green Food** — Vidyalaya canteens avoid serving junk food and aerated drinks and provide wholesome and tasty alternatives. CVs do not

allow non-vegetarian food on the campus. CV Trichy has been propagating vegetarianism to students, parents, and others through its Karuna Club.

- **Hygiene**

Lack of a sense of hygiene is a national weakness and needs a collective effort, beginning right from childhood. The attitude of — 'it is my right to dirty and another's duty to clean' — contributes much to the mess that we create. The habit of keeping oneself and one's surroundings clean stays with children throughout their lives.

IN ACTION **Return Gift** — A student of CV Tarapur went around his housing colony as part of his hygiene project, politely returning to the owner all the litter he found outside each home. The secretary of the housing colony in a letter of appreciation wrote to the Principal, "Your student achieved what several notices could not."

- **Physical Grooming**

A cat grooms itself each day, as do many birds and animals. Dressing neatly and aesthetically and speaking clearly and pleasantly all contribute to an impressive well-groomed physical personality.

IN ACTION **Beauty Without Cruelty** — Children are made aware of the use of animal products in the food, cosmetics, and leather industries. Thereafter, they choose to practice 'beauty without cruelty' and take to the herbal or natural option. CV

Nagapattinam gave a list of products marked green, brown and red to its students to facilitate choices.

- **Health Education**

KNOW WHAT IS UNDER THE BONNET.

| Swami Chinmayananda |

In India, it is common to see a fifteen year-old illiterate boy at a service station setting the car right by simply tapping the vehicle in the right places. Health education involves knowing our body well enough to live a healthy lifestyle and dealing with minor health issues with a few timely adjustments, safety measures, and exposure to alternative medicines like āyurveda.

IN ACTION **Play Safe** — CV Tarapur has a disaster management cell to share practical ways to avoid accidents and injuries and safeguard the students' health, especially during playtime. They are also given training in self-defense.

- **Health Assessment**

Prevention is better than cure. Early detection of an ailment helps to set it right. Regular check-ups and expert guidance to both students and parents on health issues definitely prevent many health-related problems.

IN ACTION **Check Your Fat and Health Horoscope** — CV Chennai conducts obesity check-ups biannually and gives guidance regarding diet and exercise. The children of CVs in Coimbatore undergo a complete physical check-up, including ECG. Doctors offer guidance to parents on health issues and the school maintains health records. The parent of a child detected with a hole in the heart fell at the feet of the principal in gratitude for timely detection and action, which saved the life of her child.

At the age of eighty, my grandfather sits ramrod straight, remains full of energy, and has never suffered from a headache in his life! His simple and disciplined lifestyle is the reason for his fitness, something which none of his grandchildren have adopted. He is a very well-balanced person — strict, but very loving and lovable.

Integrated Development — Mental Development

> One who is disintegrated has neither right thinking nor right emotions. How can there be peace and happiness for one who has not developed emotionally? (nāsti buddhir-ayuktasya na cāyuktasya bhāvanā, na cābhāvayataḥ śāntir-aśāntasya kutaḥ sukham). — Gītā 2.66

ONE MALADJUSTED EMOTIONAL PERSON CAN RAISE A STORM ALL AROUND HIM.

| Swami Chinmayananda |

A human being without love is like a flower without fragrance. Mental development aims at making the student emotionally balanced. It helps him live in harmony with himself and the world. Conscious elimination of negative emotions and cultivation of positive emotions lead to the overall emotional well-being of the student.

IN ACTION **Appreciation Board** — CV Tripunithura has a Good News Bulletin where even small achievements — in all areas — are displayed. This has boosted the confidence of the students as they are congratulated and valued by everyone.

- **Emotional Expansion**

Bondage is to live for 'me' and 'my' comforts alone (ahaṁ mametyaṁ bandhaḥ). — Sadācāra 29

The wise revel in the well being of all (sarva-bhūta-hite ratāḥ). — Gītā 12.4

ALWAYS ENCOURAGE CHILDREN TO BECOME DYNAMIC 'GIVERS OF LOVE,' RATHER THAN SLAVISH 'BEGGARS OF LOVE.'

| SWAMI CHINMAYANANDA |

Children are taught to experience the joy of selfless actions, sharing, and caring, and they learn to rejoice in the joy of others. This makes them trusting, sensitive, accommodative, and kind.

IN ACTION **Big Brother and Give Up to Give** — The senior students of CV Koramangala, Bengaluru, produced learning aids for teaching math to nursery school students, thus displaying love and care for the tiny tots.

Students of CV Kannamally abstained from buying firecrackers for Divālī and donated the amount saved to purchase medicines for the people of an Ādivāsī (indigenous people) village near Vyanad.

- **Handling Emotions**

Frustrated desires lead to anger (kāmāt krodho'bhijāyate). — Gītā 2.62

DO NOT PUT ALL YOUR EMOTIONAL EGGS IN ONE BASKET.

| SWAMI CHINMAYANANDA |

Understanding emotions and living in love helps students to manage their emotions and enables them to strike a balance between the head and the heart.

CVP IN ACTION **Laugh It Out** — Humor helps us to better handle what comes in life. CV Bengaluru brought in experts who taught students the importance of humor. With this awareness, students visited a school for the physically challenged and brought love and laughter to their lives. The school started a laughter club and the students laugh away their bad moods.

- **Gender-specific Education**

Woman: I do not respect you because you do not love me.
Man: How can I love you if you do not respect me?

Love and Respect, Dr. Emerson Eggerichs

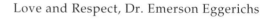

Understanding gender-specific mental make-up and forming healthy relationships with the opposite sex are important for teenagers and young people.

CVP IN ACTION **Sense in Adolescence** — Dr. Meera Krishna, a gynecologist and director of CORD Siruvani, conducts annual sessions at CIRS and CVs in Coimbatore for teenage boys and girls, discussing and guiding them on issues of adolescence.

- **Handling Relationships**

Be tender toward the faults of others and strict toward your own faults.

Swami Tejomayananda

> We stand as one family bound to each other with love and respect...
>
> Chinmaya Mission Pledge

Children who live in a virtual world of TV, computers, and mobile phones — with virtual friends on Facebook — find it difficult to live in the actual world and are often unable to relate to people of different age groups or handle situations or relationships effectively. Even in India, divorce rates are on the increase, along with single-parent homes with troubled children.

Learning to identify with all and value the good that others have, creates love and respect, which fosters harmony in relationships and makes for a happy life.

CVP IN ACTION **Tree of Togetherness** — For a vacation project, CIRS students made family trees and discovered the history and geographical locations of their ancestors. They learned about the customs, traditions, professions, and special achievements of their ancestors and family members. The family tree was painted aesthetically and enjoys a place of pride in the home.

- **Mental Assessment and Counseling**

> When the mind abides within (in peace, love, and joy), there is a natural sense of well-being (hṛt sthale manaḥ svasthatā).
>
> — Upadeśa Sāra 10

Evaluating the emotional well-being or the Emotional Quotient (EQ) of the student and guiding him toward greater emotional stability and strength is critical in these days of ever-increasing distractions, agitations, and addictions. We find high intelligence with low emotional maturity, ambitious youth with little staying power, and

hurting souls with hard exteriors. Regarding this aspect, the school takes responsibility and provides active care of the mental health of its students. The availability of ācāryas in the management and also as highly trained spiritual guides is a unique feature of CVs.

The Importance of a School Ācārya

ALL THE EDUCATIONAL INSTITUTIONS OF THE PAST HAD SPIRITUAL PEOPLE,
WHO RAN THEM WITH DEDICATION AND PURE LOVE.
BEING RENUNCIATES, THEY DID NOT RUN THEM FOR A LIVELIHOOD,
WERE NOT DISTRACTED AS MUCH AS OTHERS, AND HAD MORE NOBLE QUALITIES.

| SWAMI CHINMAYANANDA |

Strangely, a colleague of mine is a genius but never fared well in school. I guess most of our intellectual potential is never explored in school.

Integrated Development — Intellectual Development

God does not protect us like a shepherd with a stick, but by giving us intelligence and right thinking (na devā daṇḍamādāya rakṣanti paśupālavat, yaṁ tu rakṣitumicchanti buddhyā saṁvibhajanti tam).

— Vidura-nīti 3.40

Lack of thinking (avicāra), incomplete thinking (alpa vicāra), and wrong thinking (viparīta vicāra), cause problems. Complete and right thinking resolves the problem (avicāro kṛto bandhaḥ vicāreṇa nivartate).

— Pañcadaśi, Nāṭakadīpa 5

It is more important to learn 'how' to think, rather than 'what' to think.

Swami Tejomayananda

The intellect is the most powerful tool we possess. It can make us or mar us. The purpose of intellectual development is to kindle its infinite potential, explore its reach and depth, guide its direction, tame its waywardness, and develop qualities of subtlety and alertness.

> IN ACTION **Leading the Leader** — Student council members of CVs in Coimbatore were trained by professionals in leadership qualities, understanding roles and responsibilities, and problem-solving techniques. This gave them greater confidence in performing their duties as school leaders.

- **Independent Thinking**

What can books do for one who does not exercise his own intellect? (yasya nāsti svayam prajñā śāstram kimatra kariṣyati). —Subhāṣita

Higher than mechanical thinking and practice is doing with understanding, and higher still is independent deeper contemplation (śreyo hi jñānam abhyāsāt jñānāt dhyānam viśiṣyate). —Gitā 12.12

THROW AWAY YOUR BOOKS AND REFLECT.
[LISTEN WITH FAITH, THEREAFTER REFLECT INDEPENDENTLY.]
| SWAMI CHINMAYANANDA |

'Tomato is a fruit' is information, 'not to put it in fruit cream' is understanding, and allowing the child to discover what happens when she puts 'a tomato in her own bowl of fruit cream' is wisdom.

Taught knowledge is mostly forgotten, but learned knowledge never is. We live by what we have learned and not by what we are taught.

The teacher, therefore, kindles questioning and lateral, independent, out-of-box thinking. We become excited by what we discover, fulfilled by what we solve, and resolved and committed to what we are convinced of.

IN ACTION **Justice through Juvenile Jury** — Children resolve their own issues and disputes by creating a student jury. It provides an opportunity for senior students to manage their own problems and difficulties through careful deliberations.

- **Kindling the intellect**

> Have you learned that knowledge by which the unheard of becomes heard, the unknown becomes known and the un-thought-of becomes thought-of? — the Guru asks a disciple who had just returned from university after graduation (yena aśrutam śrutam, amatam matam, avijñātaṁ vijñātaṁ bhavati). — Chāndogya Upaniṣad 6.1.3

Even the most intelligent among us use only a minuscule part of our potential brainpower. Various areas of knowledge are meant to kindle our intellectual capacities and awaken higher, deeper, and subtler thinking. Mathematics kindles logical thinking and science, our power of observation.

Faith As a Way of Learning

> One with faith learns and knows (śraddhāvān labhate jñānam); whereas, the 'doubting Thomas' destroys himself (saṁśayātmā vinaśyati). — Gītā 4.39

FAITH IS BELIEF PENDING INQUIRY.

| SWAMI CHINMAYANANDA |

True faith is neither blind nor emotional. It is a deep conviction based on experience and reason, which gives to us a basis for further inquiry — which should continue until we 'know' what we believe in.

We need to have faith in the means of knowledge. I trust what my eyes see in order for me to understand what I read. In school and college, knowledge takes place due to trust in the books, teachers, and instruments and methods of teaching and learning.

Questioning is not opposed to faith. Unfortunately, in the present day, we have become 'men of little faith' right from school and are therefore plagued with doubts and confusions about most things in life. Instead of being critical thinkers, we have become criticizing thinkers. Instead of questioning, we are suspicious. We do not question what we want to do but question what we do not want to do. A truly inquiring mind is capable of greatness.

CVP IN ACTION **Serve through Science** — Students of CV Bokaro developed a unique low-cost water filtration system made of only a filter and a tap, which consumes just two watts of electricity. The invention was adopted by a multinational company that distributed them to thousands of villagers at a nominal cost.

- **Intellectual Assessment and Guidance**

People who choose professions according to their aptitude or inherent talents attain success (sve sve karmaṇi abhirataḥ saṁsidhiṁ labhate naraḥ).

— Gītā 18.45

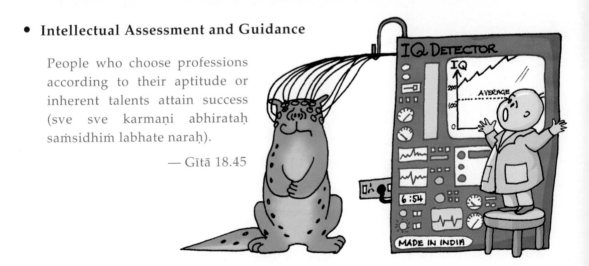

> The duty of the educational institution is to guide the student in choosing the right profession and also prepare him for life as a whole. It must show him higher goals that he can strive for.
>
> Swami Tejomayananda

It is most essential to assess the students' aptitude and intellectual capacities that will guide them into professions that enable them to work throughout their lives with motivation and satisfaction.

IN ACTION **Aptitude Guide** — Teachers of CV Chennai chart the natural inclination of the student right from kindergarten. Changes and development are noted and the parents and students are guided in choosing the right subjects in school and careers thereafter.

- **Aesthetics**

That which is ever fresh, new, and charming is beautiful (kṣaṇe kṣaṇe yannavtām upaiti tadeva rūpaṁ ramaṇīyatāyāḥ). Kavi Kālidāsa

> Your inner beauty gets reflected in the smiles of people around you.
>
> Anonymous

Beauty delights the senses, charms and attracts the mind, awakens and sensitizes the intellect, fills us with love and peace, and brings life and cheer to all situations. Students are therefore taught to bring beauty into all that they do — beautifying themselves within and without and spreading the fragrance of beauty in their surroundings.

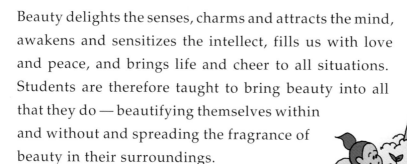

IN ACTION **Colorful Welcome** — At CV Hindupur making vibrant welcome raṅgolīs each day at the entry gate of the school gives students a chance to express and develop their aesthetic sense. It also helps them to begin the day with fun — adding color and beauty to everyone's lives.

I had a value education teacher in school who exhibited beauty in every action she performed. She made me realize the beauty in thoughts, words, and deeds, and also in nature, God, and myself.

Integrated Development — Spiritual Development

In the heart within us is the infinite Truth (hṛdaya kuhara madhye kevalaṁ brahma mātram).
Ramana Maharshi

Education is the manifestation of the perfection already in man.
Swami Vivekananda

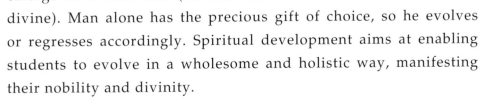

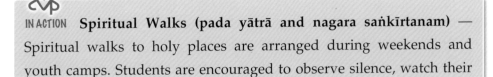

Outer progress is measured by what a man 'has' and inner evolution by what he 'is.' Man evolves from a stone-man to a plant-man (with little awareness), to an animal-man (selfish and brutish), to a man-man (humane and refined) to finally emerge as a God-man (selfless and divine). Man alone has the precious gift of choice, so he evolves or regresses accordingly. Spiritual development aims at enabling students to evolve in a wholesome and holistic way, manifesting their nobility and divinity.

IN ACTION **Spiritual Walks (pada yātrā and nagara saṅkīrtanam)** — Spiritual walks to holy places are arranged during weekends and youth camps. Students are encouraged to observe silence, watch their

minds and everything around them. They absorb the spiritual vibrations of the place and pen down their thoughts in prose or poetry and return, singing bhajans. It has changed the attitude of some of them toward themselves, nature, and the Divine.

Age-Development Plan — This graded system, when followed faithfully, will effectively impart to the growing generation the inner values of life.

3–5 years: Create an environment of affection, tenderness, concern for other living beings, appreciation for the good and noble, and recognition of beauty in things. Touch the children; tell them that you love them, that they are beautiful, intelligent, good, and noble.

5–10 years: This is the right time for the higher and nobler values of life to sink in. This can be done through Purāṇic stories, stories of great saints and sages, and mighty heroes of science and politics. They will learn how in the confrontation of good and evil, good always ultimately triumphs. Chanting and group singing are also effective at this age.

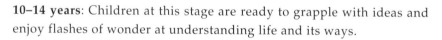

10–14 years: Children at this stage are ready to grapple with ideas and enjoy flashes of wonder at understanding life and its ways.

15–18 years: During these ages of questioning authority, previously taught values sink into the teenager's mind. They should be encouraged to question what they have studied. They must be encouraged to come out of their shyness, and be noisily complimented for what they have tried to express.

18–20 years: At this age youth have reached fuller growth in their minds. Now they need deeper understanding and definitely require regular spiritual practices like japa and meditation, to experience the possibility of controlling the mad onrush of their own wild and crazy minds. They will come to understand for themselves the importance of self-control and mind-control.

20–25 years: Now youngsters can readily be initiated into the highest. Without hesitation, they can be taught Upaniṣadic texts and chapters of the Gītā. Let them study the rest by themselves. Leave them alone to grow at their own pace.

Extracted from Gurudev's Talk at First National Conference of Principals, Headmasters, and Correspondents of Chinmaya Vidyalayas, Bengaluru, May 1985

- **Value Education**

The ornamentation of a human being is his virtues (narasya ābharaṇam guṇaḥ).

— Subhāṣita

IN OUR INSTITUTIONS, WE WILL NOT ONLY HAVE CLASSES ON VALUES, BUT WE WILL ALSO HAVE EXERCISES IN MEDITATION, JAPA, MANTRA, PRAYERS, AND EXPLAIN THE PSYCHOLOGICAL NEED FOR ALL THESE. THROUGH THESE, THE STUDENTS' MINDS WILL BE QUIETENED, POWER OF CONCENTRATION WILL INCREASE, AND CONSEQUENTLY THEIR PERFORMANCE WILL IMPROVE.

| SWAMI CHINMAYANANDA |

Values when lived become virtues.

Swami Tejomayananda

Valuables are valuable, but values are invaluable. It is only on the strong foundation of goodness that the edifice of greatness can be supported. The aim of Value Education is to lay this firm foundation of values.

CVP IN ACTION **Mini Chitraguptas** — Grade VII students of CV Bengaluru were asked to keep a record of their own good and wrong deeds. The teachers were pleasantly surprised to find a visible improvement in their behavior within a month of their daily record-keeping. Maintaining a spiritual diary has helped many Vidyalaya students assess themselves and change over the years.

- **Spiritual Assessment and Guidance**

Do not neglect study of the scriptures and self-introspection (svādhyāyān mā pramadaḥ).

— Guru to students, Taittirīya Upaniṣad

We seek the Lord's grace to keep us on the path of virtue, courage, and wisdom. May thy grace and blessings flow through us to the world around us...

Chinmaya Mission Pledge

The scriptures act as a mirror, which shows us what we are. Study of the scriptures, introspection, self-assessment, and teacher-assessment of the SQ (Spiritual Quotient) of the student as well as spiritual guidance help one to evolve.

Are You a Yogi — A four-way test for every seeker of secular or spiritual knowledge, whether student or teacher:

Jñāna yogi: Questions, seeks, searches, researches, tests, discovers, experiments, works for and works with knowledge.

Karma yogi: Acts on, is humble, accepts, obeys, puts forth unconditional and dedicated effort, does egoless work, accepts results without complaining, and works for high goals.

Bhakti yogi: Loves classmates and colleagues, loves knowledge, loves teaching/learning, loves God, and loves teacher/student.

Dhyāna yogi: Introspects, contemplates, dwells deep, focuses, quietens mind, is subtle in thinking, and seeks answers within.

- **Spiritual Techniques**

  Yoga is the technique by which one connects with the higher. Yoga purifies our mind, makes us dexterous in action, and gives peace and tranquility (yoga ātma-viśuddhaye, yogaḥ karmasu kauśalam, samatvam yoga ucyate). — Gītā 6.12, 2.50, 2.48

THE BRAHMINS OF YORE WERE FORCED TO DO JAPA; AND SO LONG AS THEY DID IT, THEY WERE THE MOST BRILLIANT IN THE ACADEMIC FIELD. IT WAS NOT FOR NOTHING THAT THEY WERE MADE TO CHANT THE GĀYATRĪ MANTRA.

| SWAMI CHINMAYANANDA |

Sādhanā (spiritual practices) makes the body, mind, and intellect trim, refined, and fine-tuned. It helps to harness our energies and direct them toward desired goals. Regular spiritual practices, such as japa, prayer, meditation, yogāsanas, prāṇāyāma, and chanting, increase one's willpower, bring discipline into one's life, offer solace in times of trouble, enrich our relationship with God, and connect us with the spiritual core in all beings. They manifest the extraordinary powers (siddhis) latent in us and also create the right conditions for intuition, enabling students to reach the higher goals of life.

CVP IN ACTION **Spiritual Practices and Memory Mantra** — Common spiritual practices like yoga, japa, havans, pādukā pūjā, and Gītā chanting are explained, taught, and practiced regularly in most Vidyalayas. The students of CVs in Coimbatore have seen the efficacy of Medhā Sūktam as a powerful memory mantra and chant it each day — especially on the day of exams!

I wish my school had thought about integrated development. However, we did have cultural events. I always took part in all cultural programs. I went to special Kathak classes after school hours and performed what I had learned there, during the school annual day function.

Folk or classical dance forms are expressions of culture. Culture unifies a society or nation more strongly than a geographical boundary or a common government.

Indian Culture

Nature is called Prakṛti — the creation of God (prakṛṣṭa kṛti). Vikṛti is created when we go against nature (viparīta kṛti). Saṁskṛti or Culture is to create something aligned with nature, which is beautiful and refined (samyak kṛti).

WHEN A GROUP OF PEOPLE LIVE TOGETHER FOR A LONG TIME
IN A PARTICULAR GEOGRAPHICAL AREA
AND RESPECT CERTAIN FUNDAMENTAL VALUES, THE FRAGRANCE, GRACE,
OR GLORY THAT EMANATES FROM THAT SOCIETY IS CALLED CULTURE.

| Swami Chinmayananda |

The majority of educated Indians have become increasingly alienated from Indian culture, and more so since India's independence. Many have developed an inferiority complex toward anything Indian, because it is not considered 'modern' or 'Western.' Educational institutions carry the responsibility to address this issue.

Spiritual and secular subjects were never segregated in ancient India. With the demise of gurukulas during the British rule, pāthaśālās came into existence, which taught Indians their languages, religion, and culture. But these pāthaśālās also declined into obscurity post-independence. In the name of secularism, all spiritual, value-based and culture-oriented knowledge was discouraged by the government. This was one of the reasons that India has shifted from upholding its spiritual culture to promoting a materialist culture.

Ancient civilizations, such as Egyptian and Greek, are known today only through books in libraries or from ruins. Indian civilization traces its origins further than both Egyptian and Greek, yet remains a living culture despite attempts to destroy it from outside and from within. Its longevity lies in its ability to adapt and accommodate other cultures and religions without losing its eternal essence that has enabled it to survive. Spirituality is the very core of Indian culture. The belief in the universality of life, essential divinity in all, and respect for all lead to the enduring vivacity of Indian culture. Life's eternal values are easily communicated through India's rich culture.

In Michigan in 1992, I had the opportunity to cook and serve food to Gurudev. While serving 'yogurt,' he said, "This is made from American culture. If we continuously expose this to the Indian way of culturing, it will become Indian culture and we will get 'curd.' American is transformed to Indian." I learned my lesson.

Narrated by Sugeetha Rajan, Founder-Principal, CV Kannur

The student is given wide exposure to the various aspects of Indian culture. The teacher creates a cultural awareness and an appreciation of the vast literary, scientific, and artistic heritage of India, with explanations of customs and traditions. Knowledge of cultural roots enhances self-esteem. Whether through epics, or stories, values such as love and nonviolence are embedded in children's minds and remain with them throughout their lives.

CVP IN ACTION **Drop In** — Indian Culture encourages people to drop in rather than drop out. CV Kannur is an accredited center for National Open School, and it helped a large number of school dropouts to continue their education and complete their course of study without losing a year. Being associated with the best school in town boosts the students' confidence and encourages them to perform better.

- **Cultural Exposure**

  An uncultured person (prākṛt puruṣa) is unaware of himself and his surroundings, and he does not try to change or progress. A selfish person (vikṛt puruṣa) is aware but does not care enough to do anything for others. A cultured or refined individual (samskṛt puruṣa) is aware, sensitive, and cares and therefore dares to become different and make a difference.

Swami Chinmayananda was acutely aware of the masses in India who lived in total ignorance of their own cultural and philosophical heritage. He cared deeply for this cause, and therefore started the Chinmaya Mission, under whose umbrella unique learning institutes like Chinmaya Vidyalayas and Sandeepany Sadhanalayas flourish.

The first step in becoming cultured is to become aware — to get exposed to the richness of one's culture. In this aspect of CVP, children are first exposed to basic and common aspects of Indian culture, such as festivals, customs, rituals, chanting, and symbolism.

Pūjya Gurudev did not miss a single opportunity to make people aware of our culture. He once asked the teachers of CV Delhi, "Do you know why you put the red dot on your forehead?" "It is the seat of wisdom. If you understand its significance and place it there with the right attitude and intention, your third eye really opens up!" he explained.

Festivals, Ceremonies, Rituals, Customs, Traditions, Chanting, and Symbolism

That which is celebrated with fun and enthusiasm (utsāha) is called a festival (utsava). Man loves to celebrate. **Festivals** are religious and social occasions where the community comes together to celebrate special occasions like the incarnation of the Lord (Kṛṣṇa Janmāṣṭami).

An individual passes through various stages of growth and maturity in life. **Ceremonies** (saṁskāras) mark each stage, making us aware of our responsibility and preparing us for the next stage of growth and achievement. These special personal occasions like birthdays and marriages are celebrated with family, relations, and friends.

Whatever we do with faith and reverence leaves a deep impression on our mind. **Rituals** like havan (fire worship) or pūjā (idol worship) leave noble impressions within us, which then guide all our actions.

Chanting of sacred mantras, such as the Gāyatrī mantra or verses of the Bhagavad Gītā, offers direct online contact with the Supreme. The divine sounds create vitalizing vibrations in the body and one's surroundings, which purify, rejuvenate, and energize everything, including the mind. Chanting verses in Sanskrit, the mother of all Indian languages offers access to the vastness of great literature and scriptures of the Indian tradition.

Traditions and Customs are handed down from one generation to the next, for example, touching the parents' feet each morning or on special occasions, greeting everyone with folded hands (namaskāra). It takes years and generations to form traditions but no time at all to break or destroy them.

Each of the above also has a deep **symbolic meaning**. For example, feet symbolize what we stand for, so we touch the feet of people as a mark of respect for the age, maturity, knowledge, and nobility of the other person. However, most do not know the significance and purpose of such customs. For many, traditions have lost their beauty and sanctity (for instance, wearing footwear while performing the marriage ceremony). Traditional gatherings have become mere occasions to eat, drink, and be merry. Behavior that is contradictory to our cultural beliefs has crept into celebrations, such as blowing out candles on a birthday cake — as extinguishing light is considered inauspicious as it symbolizes the ebbing away of life.

IN ACTION **Traditional Cures** — Research projects on Vaidya families with Āyurvedic lineage were taken up by students of CV Kalladathur. In the process they discovered an Āyurvedic remedy for 'chikungunya' [a viral infection which results in severe joint pains for months] that had been used years back. This rediscovery gave relief to the terrible pains of many.

- **Cultural Heritage and Appreciation**

Western-based sciences and literature are taught in virtually all schools in twenty-first century India. But Indian literature and art forms, Vedic mathematics and sciences also carry deep knowledge to enrich our lives. Great epics such as the Rāmāyaṇa and Mahābhārata, demonstrate the highest and noblest characters, ideals and values in man, elaborating upon their social and religious duties. Through symbolic meaning, they convey an underlying subtle philosophy. It is also vital that Indian history be retold so as to remove all false interpolations, such as the Aryan invasion theory, that only serve to divide the nation.

IN ACTION **Sanskrit Made Easy and Rāmāyaṇa Month** — CV Tripunithura produced a musical rendering of the legendary Sanskrit dictionary. This has made learning easier and also enriched the vocabulary of the students. The school also released a CD titled Amara Kosha (Sanskrit dictionary) as part of this laudable project.

Rāmāyaṇa Month is celebrated by all Vidyalayas in Kerala in various ways, including the rendering of its verses in assembly every morning.

- **Explaining Cultural Traditions**

  A genuine tradition has three components. It originates from a divine or authentic source. (śāstra). It is handed down unbroken up to the present (paramparā), and it must be verifiable by logic and experience (yukti and anubhūti).

Students are taught the origin and social development of various traditions and customs that exist within the Indian tradition, and their validity and applicability are discussed.

CVP IN ACTION **Young Āyurvedic Doctor** — An enthusiastic student of CV Kalladathur, assisted by her grandmother, prepared an āyurvedic medicine from herbs commonly grown in homes in Kerala for the prevention and cure of the common cold. All students and teachers drank this bitter concoction and learned the recipe. Since then, it has become a popular medicine especially during the monsoon season.

- **Cultural motivation**

  A cultured person entertains himself with literature, arts, and scriptures, whereas the uncultured while away their time in gossip, quarrel, pleasures, and addictions (kāvya śāstra vinodena kālo gaccati dhīmatām, vyasanena tu mūrkhāṇām nidrayā kalahena vā).

  — Subhāṣita

NEVER CAN A CHILD'S EDUCATION BE COMPLETE UNLESS WE IMPART TO THEM A TRUE APPRECIATION OF THE ETERNAL VALUES OF LIFE AND ALSO HELP THEM TO OPEN UP THEIR SENSE OF BEAUTY, RHYTHM, ETHICS, AND AESTHETICS. WE MUST GIVE THEM A CHANCE TO DISCOVER AND DEVELOP THEIR TALENTS AND EXPRESS THEM THROUGH MUSIC, DANCE, PAINTING, AND SO FORTH.

| SWAMI CHINMAYANANDA |

Students are encouraged to take up hobbies like folk arts and pursue careers in arts, classical dance, music, and drama.

IN ACTION **Reviving skills** — An IIT graduate took up the task of promoting bamboo basket-making in Chennai to revive this dying skill. Students of CV Annanagar participated in this project with great enthusiasm.

I definitely feel proud of India after learning about her great culture. Isn't patriotism the next aspect of CVP? Being a freedom fighter himself, Swami Chinmayananda must have been quite a patriot.

Patriotism

> For me, India is the best in the world (sāre jahān se acchā hindustān hamārā). Serving my mother and my motherland is greater than the pleasures of heaven (janani janma-bhūmiśca svargāt api garīyasī).
>
> — Patriotic song, Vālmīki Rāmāyaṇa, Yuddhakāṇda 6.124.17

Patriotism is love for and pride in one's motherland. It is a deep-seated emotion that enables one to put one's motherland before oneself and one's family.

Awakening the Abeyant

I cannot blame my youngsters for not having love for the country, or an awareness of what is happening around. They are the products of the education that we have been giving them even after independence. After centuries of condemning our country, we have now come to a point where we have no respect for the nation.

Without knowing the glory of the country, how can I love the country? If the younger generation is not prepared to sacrifice in order to build it, who is to do it?

The educated ones who come to the city just want a cushy job in an air-conditioned room. Where is the concern for the nation? Who is to sweat for it? Without any sacrifice, can we create anything?

Chinmayananda.

The influence of the West seems to threaten the very roots of our 'Indian-ness.' In this aspect of CVP, students develop a sense of pride in their country and are also made aware of its weaknesses. This inspires the youth to tackle the injustices and evils of society. Each student is rooted in the conviction that he or she is an Indian first and foremost, irrespective of differences of caste, community, religion, state, or race. CVP aims at creating dedicated and committed citizens who are proud of serving the nation. It encompasses citizenship, civic consciousness, fostering pride in being Indian and understanding vital national concerns such as unity in diversity.

IN ACTION **Arise, Awake** — All India Chinmaya Yuva Kendra (AICHYK) conducted a quiz across India called 'Awakening Indians to India' which included hundreds of students of CVs and achieved a world record for maximum participation in a quiz taking place simultaneously at many locations across India.

Along similar lines, students of CV Delhi organized an exhibition on 'Discover India.' Weekly and monthly quizzes on 'Incredible India' and 'Vision 2020' are also conducted by CV Delhi, CIRS Coimbatore and other schools inculcating patriotism.

Another national quiz on Transforming Indians to Transform India (TITI) in honor of Gurudev's birth centenary year is based on CVP and is now underway. It targets to reach out to one million families.

- **Education in citizenship**

> Ask not what your country can do for you; ask what you can do for your country.
>
> John F. Kennedy

> We live honestly the noble life of sacrifice and service producing more than what we consume; and giving more than what we take...
>
> Chinmaya Mission Pledge

Students are encouraged to develop social or civic consciousness and are provided an education that produces social cohesion. India has traditionally always been a 'duty-based' rather than a 'rights-based' society. Students are empowered to strive to create jobs, rather than beg for jobs. Individual development cannot happen at the cost of the country. There is no free meal (except for people with disabilities and those who are sick), and each one learns to earn and make the country self-sufficient in fulfilling its basic needs of food, clothing, shelter, education and basic health for all.

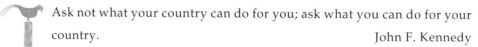

IN ACTION **Consumer Awareness** — With the aim of making children aware of the rights and responsibilities of consumers, how consumers are exploited, how to seek redressals against unfair trade practices, and study of the various quality standards of other countries, CIRS organized a consumer awareness program and workshop. It included a competition on labeling and packaging, a quiz on consumer protection, and a visit to a local consumer court.

- **Education in citizenship**

Lives of great men all remind us,
We can make our lives sublime
And departing, leave behind us,
Footprints on the sands of time.

— H.W. Longfellow

We serve as an army, courageous and disciplined, ever-ready to fight against all low tendencies and false values, within and without us.

We believe that the service of our country is the service of the Lord of Lords; and devotion to the people is the devotion to the Supreme Self...

Chinmaya Mission Pledge

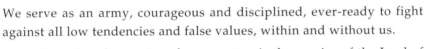

India has been the birthplace of countless great men — saints and sages, poets and artists, scientists and logicians, patriots and warriors. Not only does India have a glorious past, but even today, Indians both in India and scattered all over the world are continuing to create history. Many discoveries in various fields, be it town planning, agriculture, medicine, or fashion that are now attributed to foreigners, were actually made by Indians many thousands of years earlier.

Under this aspect, students learn about the glory of India and also understand its national weaknesses that are obstacles to progress, such as lack of unity, absence of civic and social sensibility, population explosion, poverty, herd-mentality, pseudo-secularism, and corruption.

CVP IN ACTION **Run for India and Match Your Step** — Marathons and Cross-country runs are an enriching experience for children. CV Kalladathur organized a 'Run from Drugs – Run for India' event on Independence Day, for students. As an additional outcome, the shop adjoining the Vidyalaya stopped selling pān masālā!

On Independence Day, students of CV Vazhuthacaud participated in a 'Run for Health' program involving senior citizens. This inspiring activity benefited both — children and senior citizens — invoking love for the country and its citizens.

- **Unity in Diversity**

> A noble vision is to see unity in diversity (avibhaktam vibhakteṣu tad jñāanam viddhi sāttvikam).
> — Gītā 18.20

Unity is strength. All should unite to stand against the forces that seek to weaken or divide the nation, threaten or dilute its identity, exploit or misuse its resources, transgress or infiltrate its borders, or belittle and ridicule its culture and values. Students are given the right understanding of secularism. Taking pride in being Indian above all differences is an important part of being patriotic.

CVP IN ACTION **Language Link** — Students of CVs are encouraged to learn different Indian languages through songs. At CV Thrissur, a weekly assembly is conducted in Sanskrit (the mother of all Indian languages) and Hindi (national language).

- **Understanding secularism**

Mahatma Gandhi was once asked that since he had read the Bible and showed respect toward Muslims, why did he practice only Hindu Dharma? He said, "I love and respect all mothers, but my mother is my mother and I love her the most."

Secularism, in its truest sense, is following one's own dharma or religion with understanding and depth, while respecting all religions and the rights of others to practice their religions with dignity. A religion cannot encourage actions opposed to the good of the nation. A religion cannot be given rights and privileges denied to others and at the expense of the religion of the majority due to political greed. In modern India, many have become irreligious in the name of secularism or are manipulated into adopting a different faith. Hindu Dharma is secular by its very nature (bin-sampradāyik) and has given rise to many religious sects (sampradāyas), such as Sikhism, without losing its essence. The perpetuation of this very essence is being threatened and perceived as communalism by the so-called irreligious intellectuals. Taking all this into account, teaching children the spirit of true secularism is an important aspect of developing patriotism.

Interfaith Interface — It's good that the celebrations in my college give due importance to all religions. I come to know about the culture and ethics of others — something we are not at all exposed to at home.

Shan Abdul Rahman, BBM, Chinmaya Arts and Science College, Kannur

I now see the logic of the four aspects of CVP. Integrated Development integrates the individual; Culture integrates one with society; Patriotism with the country, and a Universal Outlook with the world. Tell me more about what it means to adopt a Universal Outlook.

Universal Outlook

The wise see the one Truth in all — the whole universe — and all existing in the one Truth (yo māṁ paśyati sarvatra, sarvam ca mayi paśyati).

— Gītā 6.30

May thy grace and blessings flow through us to the world around us...

Chinmaya Mission Pledge

THIS LIFE OF HARMONY WITH A WIDER VIEW OF THE COSMOS BRINGS TO OUR HEART AN INWARD PEACE AND POISE. WHEN THIS UNIVERSAL VISION IS MAINTAINED WITHIN US, PROBLEMS VANISH LIKE MIST BEFORE THE RISING SUN.

| Swami Chinmayananda |

A universal outlook is the appreciation, sensitivity, and commitment to universal issues. After years of mindless pillage of nature, the world needs to come back to a universal holistic view of life. A universal outlook helps students see themselves as responsible citizens of the world (including understanding world issues), live in harmony with creation (environment education and the synthesis between science and religion), and to elevate their relationship with God as a universal force. CVP looks at the universal outlook from an economic, technological, philosophical, and cultural angle. Students discover the unity and relationship between the universe, man, and God and begin to wonder at the beauty and vastness of creation.

Hindu Dharma and Indian Culture have always been rooted in a universal outlook. In fact, the whole universe is considered a divine expression of God. Thus, everything is seen as sacred and worshipful. Every day is Earth Day, Sun Day, Tree Day, Cow Day, and so on. There was and is no question of exploiting nature.

Conquering Nature? — When Edmund Hillary reached the summit of Mount Everest, he planted a flag of his country and said, "I have conquered Mount Everest." Sherpa Tenzing, his Hindu co-partner, prostrated and prayed, "O Goddess 'Sagarmatha' (Goddess of the sky), I beg forgiveness for placing my feet on your head. You allowed me to reach the top. Do bless me." Man cannot seek to conquer Nature but learn to live in harmony with nature. Years later Hillary realized, "I did not conquer Everest, I conquered myself."

> We know our responsibilities; give us the ability and courage to fulfill them.
> Chinmaya Mission Pledge

CVP IN ACTION **Feeling Green** — Plants are alive, have feelings, and require our love and care. Grade V students of CV Thiruvananthapuram were asked to locate healthy and unhealthy plants and trees, in and around the school premises. Thereafter, signs such as, "I am happy at Chinmaya Vidyalaya," "Take care of me, I am sick," and "I need your love — water me," were placed in front of the trees. This increased awareness among students, staff, parents, and locals, creating empathy for the plants.

- **The Child as a Citizen of the World**

> To the one with a universal outlook the entire world is one family (udāra caritānām tu vasudhaiva kuṭumbakam). — Subhāṣita

It is the tendency of man to focus on trivial differences, such as color of skin and accent. Students are trained to see the commonalities in and through all differences, to avoid mistaking the part for the whole or the means for the goal, and to recognize the danger in politically correct statements which appease certain sections of society or following populist views. This type of favoritism is potentially harmful to the welfare of the world.

Through this aspect of CVP, students are exposed to other cultures and philosophies, adopting the positive aspects in them without losing their roots. World issues such as poverty, population, world peace, literacy and so on, are discussed in a meaningful and thought-provoking manner. Ultimately, the vast vision that the whole world is one family, is cultivated from a young age.

IN ACTION **Go Global, Grow Universal** — Many Vidyalayas, such as the CV Virugambakkam and CIRS, undertake interesting projects as part of the International School Award (ISA), a British Council accreditation scheme. Celebrating festivals of other countries, learning their local music, folk art, dance, and traditional games, and understanding their social, economic, and political challenges help students become global thinkers, who are better able to understand local, national, and international issues.

Some of my friends think that patriotism is opposed to a universal outlook. They believe that patriotism causes a conflict of interest and wars. They speak of a global village, global religion, global economy, global currency, and policy. Only then we would have a world free from the arms race, nuclear holocaust, or distinctions of developed and poor nations.

It sounds utopian and apparently the solution for all world problems. But have you noticed ... man speaks of world citizenship yet doesn't like anyone entering his home, sharing his TV, speaking to his wife; and he even finds it a struggle to contribute to charity! I would argue: Is loving my mother opposed to loving others? Is it not possible to harmonize differences? Hindu Dharma teaches us to live in harmony with the entire creation.

May all be happy. May all be healthy. May all see auspiciousness everywhere. May none be in grief, stress, or fear (sarve bhavantu sukhinaḥ, sarve santu nirāmayāḥ, sarve bhadrāṇi paśyantu, mā kaścid duḥkham āpnuyāt). — Prayer for universal well-being

When a child realizes every action has a cosmic effect, he develops a vast vision of the universe, a deep sense of responsibility to the cosmos, and control and thought in all he does. Maria Montessori

TO LIVE A LIFE OF HARMONY IS TO RECOGNIZE ONESELF AS A MEMBER OF ALL HUMANITY, LIVING IN A COMPOSITE UNIVERSE, AND A PART OF A FASCINATING MELODY OF EXISTENCE.

| SWAMI CHINMAYANANDA |

By living in harmony with all, students start understanding that 'all things contribute to all things.' They understand their role in the whole drama of life and do their part on the world stage.

The Part–Whole Harmony — Every part of our body works for the well-being of the whole body. All systems are in sync with all others (digestion is not opposed, but complements and supports circulation). The tongue forgives and cleans the teeth, which inadvertently bite it, and the feet are not jealous of the face that is pampered. It carries the load of the body and gets massaged by the hands when tired. The inner skeletal system holds the body upright and the glands secrete extra adrenaline so that the body can take to fight or flight when in danger. All beings seem to understand their role, adjust to the changing world, and are seen to live in harmony with nature, except for man!

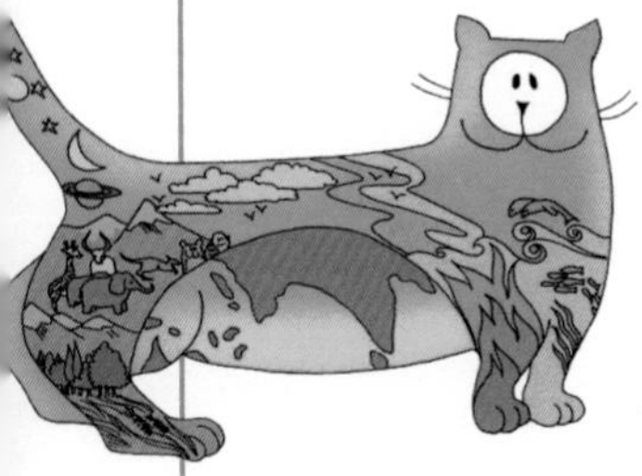

IN ACTION **Carbon Footprint** — 'Be the change you want to see in the world.' This motto is being followed by CV Naruvamood. For the fourth consecutive year, the Ministry of Environment and Development has sanctioned a climate change project initiated by the school. The Vidyalaya management sponsors 'smokeless cūlās' (cooking stove) in the neighborhood at half-price and has installed a bio-gas plant in the Vidyalaya for effective waste disposal. The school also measures its carbon footprint so that students can understand the amount of energy they consume.

- **Relationship between Science and Religion**

Śrī Kṛṣṇa tells Arjuna, "I will speak to you about jñāna and vijñāna (spiritual knowledge and secular knowledge, religion and science, pure science and applied science, theory and practice). On understanding their essence, there will be nothing more left to be known" (jñānam te'ham savijñānam idam vakṣāmyaśeṣataḥ yajjñātvā neha bhūyo'nyat jñātavyam avaśiṣyate). — Gītā 7.2

Well known scientist Albert Einstein was of the opinion that philosophy begins where science ends. Science is the study of the experienced world. Philosophy and religion on the other hand are the study of the experiencer of the world. For a complete understanding of life, students are given the knowledge of both. In India, great sages, such as Vaṣiṣṭha, Āryabhaṭṭa, and Carak were great philosophers and scientists, who, in their seats of meditation, discovered eternal truths governing creation. It is only in the modern 'scientific age' that a separation is perceived between science and philosophy — hence the need for re-synthesis. Without a foundation of values rooted in truth, science can be misused, to harm or even destroy the world.

How We Know What We Know — Every 'area of knowledge' has its own 'way of knowing.' We need practice to learn a skill like swimming and use emotions to appreciate the beauty of poetry. Literature is not illogical just because it does not use logic like mathematics, and history is not unscientific just because history cannot repeat itself like a scientific experiment to prove its results.

Science deals with perceptible, measurable, and conceivable objects and its concepts of the world. Spirituality ultimately speaks of the Truth, which is beyond sense perception and the purview of the mind. That does not make it and its way of knowing 'unscientific' or 'illogical.' The fact that one cannot show the infinite Truth in a laboratory test tube does not mean that Truth does not exist.

Religion uses faith, scriptures, reflection, and meditation as the means for gaining spiritual knowledge.

IN ACTION **Trees That Touch the Sky** — Learning through integration of different subjects strengthens the web of knowledge. CV Kollam integrated science and religion by creating a 'Nakshatra Vanam' — a forest of stars — by planting twenty-seven trees related to the twenty-seven birth stars spoken about in Hindu scriptures.

- **Relationship with God as a Universal Force**

> God or Truth walks through all legs, works through all hands, sees through all eyes, speaks through all mouths, hears through all ears, and pervades the whole universe (sarvataḥ pāṇi-pādam tat-sarvato'kṣiśiromukham, sarvataḥ śrutimalloke sarvam-avṛtya tiṣṭhati).
>
> — Gītā 13.15

Students are guided from a young age to view God as a universal presence, to wonder at the universe, and to feel the divine oneness in creation. It is much easier for younger students to develop faith and feel the presence of God, and this faith can be effortlessly achieved through simple stories from the scriptures. Later, with a deeper study of the scriptures and discussions, the practical application in daily living is seen and understood. An example is a student observing how prayer reduces tension before exams.

IN ACTION **Chant for Śānta World** — Mass chanting creates a strong feeling of universality and has a great impact on the mind. Every year, CM and CVs in Chennai commemorate Pūjya Gurudev's Samādhi Day by Mass Gītā Chanting for world peace. On one occasion, there were 20,000 students chanting the Gītā on Marina Beach!

CVP is comprehensive. To implement CVP is compulsory in all CEIs. However, the CEIs are not carbon copies of each other, as each institution implements CVP in its own unique way. Some are passionate about patriotism, and some embrace the vision of adopting a universal outlook, and most do a little of everything. To the extent they implement the program, to that extent the difference is seen.

Everyone is talking about being different. Companies sell their products claiming they are different from what is already available. Youngsters want to do things differently. Teenagers want to look different. You also aim to make a difference. But you really are different. I definitely see that your school, too, must have been different.

Yes! It truly had its own SWAD — flavor. **That is why Pūjya Gurudev called all Chinmaya Vidyalayas, 'Schools with a Difference.'** CVP makes the difference.

The student is the focal point of the program. The fragrance of CVP has spread to the family, society, country, and the world at large. Imagine 1.5 million ex-students of Chinmaya Vidyalayas and Colleges making a difference all over the world.

CVP IN ACTION **A South Indian in Scotland** — Jwala Krishnan, a former student of CV Taylors Road, Chennai (graduated 1989), today lives and works in Scotland as a high-profile Criminal Intelligence Analyst, with the police authority. Her area of interest revolves around understanding and providing a meaningful explanation of offender behavior and their propensity to repeat violence. A star athlete at school with a law degree from Madras University, today Jwala also serves as the chairperson for a Scottish charity that promotes multi-culturalism, and improves intercultural relations in the community.

Doesn't CVP apply equally to Bala Vihar children or Yuva Kendra members?

True. This is a vision that benefits all, young and old. Living its four aspects could transform anyone and everyone.

CVP integrates all within the institution, unifies all CEIs, and creates a link with all other activities and projects of CM, as well as a bond with the Global Chinmaya Family. Mission activities are held regularly in CVs. Parents, teachers, and students participate in the Mission activities, and Yuva Veers conduct value-education classes in Vidyalayas.

Chinmaya Vidyalaya (CV) and Chinmaya International Foundation (CIF)

Vedic Math workshop for CV students: Anzil of Grade IX, CV Kottayam, says, "After attending the course by Vinay Nair from CIF, math has become my favorite subject."

Sanskrit workshops for teachers: Many Vidyalayas conduct workshops for teachers on the Easy Sanskrit Course offered by CIF.

Vedānta course for teachers: Every CV teacher is expected to complete either the basic Vedānta or Gītā Course offered by CIF.

CVP IN ACTION **Samaṣṭi Sādhanā** — Pūjya Guruji gave all students and staff of the CVs a wonderful opportunity to pray to God, offer our bit for a divine cause, and bond with the Global Chinmaya Family. They wrote 'Om Gaṁ Gaṇapataye Namaḥ' twenty-one times each day for twenty-one weeks and offered a desired amount each week, for the construction of the Ganeśa Temple at Chinmaya Vibhooti, the Vision Centre of Chinmaya Mission. Books collected from around the world were placed under the sanctum sanctorum of the temple.

So did you have a CVP class or a CVP syllabus in your school?

That is a common misunderstanding. I will explain to you what CVP is not, in order for you to understand what it is.

What CVP Is Not

- It is not a specific activity, but a vision-inducing program.

CVP IN ACTION **Bitter Bite for the Better** — Traditionally children were asked to wash their mouths with soap water if they spoke foul words. CV Hyderabad included a healthy value-added step to this practice. Students who use abusive and foul language on the Vidyalaya premises were asked to chew neem leaves. This proved very effective in curbing such tendencies, besides literally cleaning up foul mouths.

- Schools and colleges have curricular, co-curricular, and extra-curricular activities. CVP is none of these, but forms the basis for all of them. It is the very spirit behind all activities.

CVP IN ACTION **Thanking for Thankless Jobs** — Gratitude is a great virtue. Students of CV Bengaluru presented the school āyās and sweepers with sweets and sarees on Gurudev's Jayanti day. CIRS annual day function starts with prayer by the school garden workers, fondly and respectfully called 'annās.' They also march with the rest of the students, eliciting the biggest applause, on the Annual Sports Day.

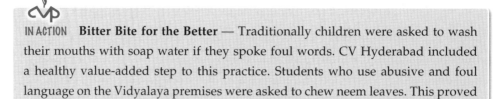

- CVP is not cosmetic, not just a value-add; it is the very culture of the institution.

CVP IN ACTION **Good News** — The values followed by students and teachers are also newsworthy. CV Kalladathur regularly acknowledges the good acts of its students as school news, during assembly. They even reported the honesty of one of their students, in returning a very valuable piece of jewelry to its owner to the local newspaper, which then published the story.

- CVP is not only value education, but also value-based education.

Value Education and Value-based Education — Value education is when values (different aspects of CVP) are inculcated at a specific time during school and college hours; for example, in the value-education class, celebration of festivals during assembly time. Value-education classes can be taught by a special value educator, spiritual guides (ācāryas), or regular teachers.

Value-based education inculcates values in and through the curricular, co-curricular, and extra-curricular classes, activities, and projects. Here each teacher in each class is a value-educator and each lesson or activity is a value-education lesson. For example, the value of truth and falsehood (Spiritual Development) is illustrated through lessons in math, and wildlife preservation (Universal Outlook) through lessons in zoology.

Sāttvic Rājasic Tāmasic

Sample Lesson Plan

Subject: Economics

Topic: Unemployment - Class XI CBSE

Management, CIRS (Teacher - Rajeshwari)

Unemployment

- **Integrated development - Mental development**: Mental state of unemployed person-strain, stress, addiction, suicide... giving them a few facts.
- **Indian Culture**: Touch on Varṇa system (temperament and profession) through example.
- **Patriotism**: Brain drain - few facts; discussion on: Is employment outside the country good for the Indian economy?
- **Universal Outlook**: Objectives and a little work of ILO (International Labour Organization).

- CVP is not a portion-based or a time-bound program. We cannot complete CVP as we do the curriculum of other subjects. It is an ongoing attitude-based program. In fact, it is impossible to give emphasis to all aspects of the program in a given academic year.

CVP IN ACTION **Popularizing the Motto and Pledge** — The CV motto is 'Keep Smiling.' To emphasize its importance and encourage all to smile, the Vidyalayas organize a Best Smile Prize for students, as well as teachers. Classrooms and staff rooms have collages displayed of smiling faces of students and teachers.

The Mission Pledge is also a tool for value education. It has been widely popularized in Vidyalayas through discussions, competitions, poster-making, skits, dramas, dance, and music.

It must take a lot of time and effort for a school that implements CVP to become a 'school with a difference.'

You are right, Amrita. We need to have 'Management, Principals, Teachers, and Parents with a Difference' to nurture 'Students with a Difference.' That is a tall order, and our greatest challenge.

- **Visionary and Supportive Management**

> The wise man should guide, encourage, and support others (joṣayet sarva karmāṇi vidvān yuktaḥ samācaran). — Gītā 3.36

The management provides strategic planning for growth and efficient management of resources. They support the entire institution, giving it a firm foundation in its noble vision.

Silent Support — Pūjya Gurudev's direction was, "No member of the Vidyalaya Managing Committee shall enter the school after classes commence." What he meant was, total academic freedom should be given to the academic team and the management should only be silent observers and supporters.

Śrī K.K. Rajan, who has been involved in the management of CEIs since 1975

- **An Inspired and Inspiring Principal**

The leader creates the destiny of the institution or country (rājā kālasya kāraṇam). — Mahābhārata

A principle-centered Principal, inspired by the lofty vision of education, makes a truly inspiring CEO, leading the school to great heights. He or she is the meeting point for the management, students, parents, and teachers.

Gurudev felt that the principal must 'be like the conductor of the orchestra, under whose guidance all perform their roles to produce an inspired performance.' On another occasion Gurudev gave more detailed instructions, "The Principal should be aware of all aspects of teaching and see that they are implemented. The Principal herself must be the first to enter, and the last to leave the school. Her presence is a must at assemblies; she must maintain punctuality. She should create the proper atmosphere to draw out the best from both, the teachers and the students."

- **Dedicated and Efficient Teachers**

The teacher is like a lamp that lights the path of the student (gurustu dīpavat-mārga-darśakaḥ). —Subhāṣita

Remember — the children who come to you are not 'parent sent,' but 'God sent.'

Swami Tejomayananda

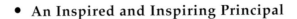

THE TEACHERS WHO ARE WORKING IN OUR INSTITUTIONS SHOULD NOT THINK THAT "I AM ONLY A SCHOOL TEACHER." YOU ARE SILENTLY CREATING TOMORROW'S HEROES — THE MIGHTY MEN OF ACTION, THE CREATIVE PEOPLE OF TOMORROW'S WORLD.

| SWAMI CHINMAYANANDA |

Teachers are made proficient with the latest teaching methodologies, and also have in-depth knowledge of teaching and children. Their critical role is to transmit values and culture along with knowledge and skills. A good teacher has love for knowledge, teaching, and children.

A teacher is like a gardener, who creates the right environment for learning and growth to happen. Thus the teacher's job is not to teach, but to facilitate learning. The teacher is like a potter, molding the minds of the students with the inner supporting hand of love, and the outer controlling hand of discipline. Teaching is the noblest of all professions — for it is a teacher who has trained and guided a doctor, and even a saint. In ancient India, teaching was a 24/7 profession. Even today, students spend long hours in schools and colleges — many more than the waking hours spent at home.

Grow and Glow

When we work with a noble attitude, we see spectacular results. It is not because of the cross-ventilation in the room or the type of textbooks that have been taken, that the student studies better; but the very ardor, inspiration, and purity of the mind of the teacher that brings the results.

Demonstrate your readiness to sacrifice for others. Let children see that you are anxious to help. Children are very observant. No action of the teacher is insignificant to the children. They watch and learn to imitate and reflect upon their teacher's actions and words. You must grow and glow as you teach the students.

Chinmayananda.

THE GĪTĀ AND UPANIṢADS ARE TO BE TAUGHT TO TEACHERS IN A WEEKLY CLASS. THEY WILL THEN BE ABLE TO BRING OUT THE BEAUTY THAT IS INHERENT IN THE STUDENT.

| SWAMI CHINMAYANANDA |

- **Sensitive and Co-operative Parents**

REMEMBER, ONE LITTLE CHILD CAN CHANGE THE HISTORY OF THE COUNTRY. FROM CHILDHOOD ONWARDS, NOBLE IDEAS WERE INCULCATED INTO ALL THE GREAT MEN OF THE PAST AND THEY INVARIABLY DECLARE THAT FOR THE GREATNESS THEY ACHIEVED, THEY ARE INDEBTED TO THEIR MOTHERS.

| SWAMI CHINMAYANANDA |

Parents should actively participate in the holistic education of the child. The parents' role is to provide a secure home environment, while raising children with love, care, and discipline, along with bestowing values and culture aligned to the vision of the school.

THE SCHOOL IS A BACKYARD, AN EXTENSION OF THE HOME.

| SWAMI CHINMAYANANDA |

Educating the Parents

These are strange days for educational institutions. They have a responsibility not only to the students but also to their parents. We have to educate the parents. They are under the impression that once they send out their children to schools, their entire responsibilities are over; this is especially true with rich people.

The rich generally demonstrate their utter ignorance by spending money ON their children. And, they are most unwilling to spend money IN the children.

All these need enormous funds—building of the school, giving better wages for teachers. For that, the parents hesitate ... The developed nations realize that the greatness of a nation lies in its growing generation. But alas, in our country!

Chinmayananda.

To Kalyani Nambiar, Principal, CV Pallavur on 10.2.1990

Guruji on CVP — Man identifies with the physical body most naturally, it being the closest to him. Then, he is willing to make sacrifices for his children. When he identifies with the nation, his selfishness drops even further. But if the mind realizes its oneness with the totality, the entire universe, his vision becomes all-inclusive and there is not a trace of selfishness left in such a person. It is this holistic concept that is translated into educational terms as the Chinmaya Vision Programme.

Let us put CVP to test with some benchmarks for evaluating a good philosophy:

Evaluation of a Philosophy:*

1. **Fundamentals**: It addresses issues at the most fundamental levels of existence, and motivates us to ask the most basic questions. *CVP addresses questions such as: what is true education, what is the purpose of life, and what is one's relationship to the world?*
2. **Understanding**: It should be based on understanding, rather than on mere beliefs. *CVP explains the what, why, and how of all aspects.*
3. **Communicability**: It should be easily communicable to everyone. *CVP is communicated to all the stakeholders — management, parents, teachers, and students.*
4. **Universality**: It should be of universal appeal and applicability, across cultures and civilizations. *A teacher who attended a CVP session in Tanzania said, "All we need to do is substitute the Indian Culture aspect with Tanzanian Culture and this program fits us perfectly."*

5. **Comprehensiveness**: It should be able to generate guiding principles for all spheres of life, especially contemporary life. *CVP integrates a person with the family, society, country, and the world.*
6. **Solutions**: It must lead to solutions. *CVP is practical and doable.*
7. **Empowerment**: It must empower and infuse hope and confidence in people. *CVP is enriching and ennobling.*
8. **Realizability**: It should clearly manifest in the lives of all individuals. *To the extent CVP is implemented, to that extent transformation is evident.*
9. **Feasibility**: It must be socially and logistically feasible and it must be demonstrably so. *CVP complements all curriculums, and is implementable in an educational institution of any background.*
10. **Open Source**: Like good software, it must be an open source, so that anyone can participate in the process of developing, creating documentation for, and applying that philosophy. *CVP is available to all educational institutions.*

* Vinish Gupta, Centre for Holistic Learning

Very few schools in India must have such an all-encompassing and clear vision. Has this program received any national or international recognition?

Yes. The Central Board of Secondary Education (CBSE) in India has recommended CVP to schools affiliated with it.

Feather in the Cap of CVP — The CBSE, which has the highest number of quality schools around the country, has recognized CVP as a worthy educational program and recommended it in its 'Value-Education Handbook for Teachers' (page 108). In fact, the recently introduced Continuous and Comprehensive Evaluation (CCE) covers most aspects of this program, except Spiritual Development and Indian Culture.

Swamini Vimalananda was invited as the keynote speaker to the International Baccalaureate Asia Pacific 21st Annual Regional Conference: 'Values and Internationalism,' in Hanoi, Vietnam, in 2006. It marked a milestone, as CVP was introduced for the first time in an international arena to a large gathering of educationists — and it received an overwhelming response!

That's really whetted my appetite ... now I am curious to know about all the Chinmaya Vidyalayas and Colleges that implement this vision.

Good timing! We have just landed.

I am going to my former school — Chinmaya Vidyalaya, Chennai, next week. Do come along and I shall show you around. Hari Om!

III

The Edifice of Education — Chinmaya Education Institutions

The unmanifest Lord first creates the entire subtle world. The potential to create becomes the dream of creation and, from there, to the vision of creation. The vision takes up form and color, roots and wings, walks and talks, feels and thinks, expands, and expresses as this perceivable and beautiful creation. He then infuses all with His life breath and enlivens it. (avyaktādvyaktayaḥ sarvāḥ prabhavantyaharāgame). (tatsṛṣṭvā tadevānuprāviśat tadanupraviśya sacca tyaccābhavat niruktaṁ cāniruktaṁ ca nilayanaṁ cānilayanaṁca ...).

— Gītā 8.18, Taittirīya Upaniṣad 2.6

Chinmaya Mission is Gurudev's love made visible, and Chinmaya Education Institutions (CEI) are the edifices enlivened with his holistic and grand vision.

WE MUST SUCCEED. THIS IS OUR EXPERIMENT. WE SHALL NOT FAIL THE NATION AND THE SILENT DEMAND OF THE INNOCENT CHILDREN GROWING UNDER OUR CARE TO MAKE A CULTURAL HISTORY OF THE MORROW.

| SWAMI CHINMAYANANDA |

Hari Om! Welcome to my school, my alma mater.

Hari Om! Nice meeting you again. This place definitely feels welcoming. The guards greeted me with a 'Hari Om' and folded hands; at least ten students called out "Hari Om, Didi!"

That is the school culture. Every one greets each other with Hari Om. It is quite contagious.

True, I too greeted them back with a Hari Om! I have been thinking; I can understand ashrams and gurukulas, and the vision behind them, but why did a Swami start educational institutions? That is the task of the government, businessmen, or philanthropists. Whatever the reason, I am glad he did.

Noble Saṅkalpa — Only strength can remove weakness. Chinmaya Vidyalayas (CVs) were started with the idea of giving youngsters the values of our Dharma and to mold them into a productive force in society. To open schools is the job of the government. But we do this with nobler motives in mind. We may not be applauded if we succeed, but we shall have the satisfaction of having done our duty. We may even be harassed, kicked around, and laughed at. But we should develop the inner strength to bear it all and carry on undaunted.

Swami Chinmayananda,
at the All India CV Teachers Camp, Sandeepany Sadhanalaya, Mumbai

anna-dānam mahaddānaṁ,
vidyā-dānam mahattaraḥ,
abhayam-dānam mahattamaḥ
— to give food is great, to give knowledge and education is greater but to give spiritual knowledge is the greatest, as spiritual knowledge alone makes you fearless.

Spiritual Education Institutions and Courses of Chinmaya Mission

Vedānta Courses: Two-year residential courses are conducted to train full-time seekers with comprehensive knowledge of Vedānta in different languages at Sandeepany gurukulas located in different places. The students (Ṛṣi-putras) who carry forward the teacher-taught lineage (Guru-śiṣya paramparā) are then initiated and designated as Ācāryas who later serve society with their knowledge.

Purohit Course: One-and-a-half-year residential course for training the priests who conduct rituals and all religious ceremonies.

▲ VEDAPUTRAS, STUDENTS OF PUROHIT COURSE

Dharma Sevak Course: An annual six-week residential course meant especially for students and householders, who later conduct various grass-root level activities in their home towns and serve as spiritual guides.

Youth Empowerment Program: An annual one-year course wherein youngsters between the ages of seventeen and thirty receive training for three months. These youngsters then serve the Mission full-time for nine months in various capacities at different centers of the Mission.

Jñāna Yajñas: Three-to seven-day public discourses are conducted by an Ācārya of the Mission. Yajña signifies the offering of one's ignorance in the fire of spiritual knowledge.

Spiritual Camps: These are week-long spiritual retreats for individuals and families in various places in India and around the world. Special camps are also held for children, youth, senior citizens, and professionals.

Grassroots Level Weekly Classes: Weekly classes are held by trained sevaks for children, youth, adults, and the elderly. Spiritual knowledge is disseminated in a way best suited for every age group.

Vedānta Home Study Courses: CIF conducts foundation and advanced Vedānta, Bhagavad-Gītā and Sanskrit postal and online courses. More than one lakh people throughout the world have benefited.

Research Center — Chinmaya International Foundation (CIF): This research center for advanced study in Indology and Sanskrit serves as a bridge between the East and the West, and between science and spirituality.

My aunt used to attend Swamiji's spiritual discourses, and she talks about how effective a teacher he was even in a 1:5000 ratio. Don't the Bala Vihars (BVs) of the Chinmaya Mission also impart values and culture? Then why Chinmaya Vidyalayas?

BVs and CVs

IT WAS FELT THAT THESE WEEKLY BALA VIHARS ALONE CANNOT REALLY BRING ABOUT THE FULL SPIRITUAL UNFOLDMENT AND MORAL BEAUTY IN A CHILD, UNLESS THERE IS CONTINUITY AND REGULARITY FOR A LONGER PERIOD OF TIME, IN A MORE SUSTAINED MANNER. THE SOLUTION FOR THIS WAS FOUND IN THE CONCEPT OF NURSERY SCHOOLS, LATER TO BECOME CHINMAYA VIDYALAYAS AND CHINMAYA COLLEGES.

| SWAMI CHINMAYANANDA |

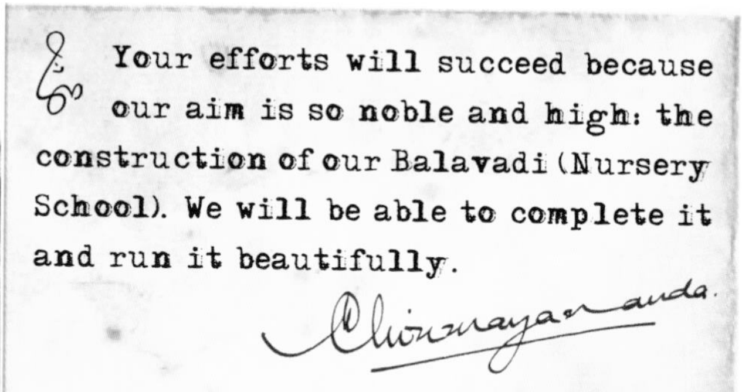

Your efforts will succeed because our aim is so noble and high: the construction of our Balavadi (Nursery School). We will be able to complete it and run it beautifully.

Chinmayananda

To Śrī K. K. Rajan, Kannur, Jan 1980

The Chinmaya Vidyalayas (CVs) and Chinmaya Colleges (CCs) are Gurudev's invaluable gift to society as they give both — secular and spiritual knowledge.

So tell me the story of the first school — when and where did it start?

It started like a fairy tale. A king met a queen or, rather, the queen met the Master with a royal offering.

The Royal Start — Chinmaya Vidyalaya, Kollengode

Gurudev was on his global tour. The queen of Vengunad, Radha Devi, was the president of the Kollengode Chinmaya Mission in Kerala.

◀ KOLLENGODE PALACE

There was a request to start a school — but where? A part of the palace was offered, and so the Chinmaya Education Movement (CEM) was flagged off with the inauguration of a nursery school on May 20, 1965, with royal patronage, by Śrī K. P. S. Menon — ex-Ambassador to Russia as well as a letter that Gurudev wrote from London.

> Children are the very cream of our generation and they are the rulers and makers of tomorrow. Upon them depends the future of the nation and the safety of our culture and tradition. Let us give them a healthy physical and mental atmosphere to grow, ingrain in them respect for life, love for living creatures, team spirit, national fervor, and pride in our hallowed, divine culture. I am sure such schools will grow everywhere through the country under the benign patronage and service of our Mission branches. They should never be run for profit at any time. We shall use all income to pay the teachers well, expand the infrastructure, and enrich education.
>
> Chinmayananda.

The Chinmaya nursery school, as expected, grew and Gurudev himself inaugurated the primary school on June 17, 1969, in a separate building near the palace. It has over time become a higher secondary school and is considered the best in Kollengode, with 555 students, a staff of thirty-seven, and a wonderful structure and infrastructure. Śrī Santosh Menon toiled hard as the secretary, and presently, Smt. Neema Nair, the Principal, is ably fulfilling her role. The school is shouldering well the special honor of being the 'first of its kind.'

IN ACTION **Braveheart and Little Master** — The school honored the brave act of Jaikishan Menon, a student of Grade VII who jumped into a lake and saved the neighbor's little daughter from drowning. He was given a hero's welcome and a trophy.

Visweshwar, specially trained by his teacher, passed the degree exam of Hindi Visharad of the Dakshina Bharat Hindi Prachar Sabha with flying colors. He was acknowledged as qualified by them for teaching Sanskrit; he was only twelve years old at the time!

> To Gurudev, education was neither a matter of academics, nor just information dissemination, nor a stepping-stone to a vocation, but a way of developing the student's potential to the fullest through a holistic approach. That is how value-based education has been an informal part of the CV curriculum since the first nursery school started in 1965.
>
> Swamini Samvidananda, formerly Executive Education, CCMT (1988–1998)

The sacred seed and royal sapling planted in Kollengode was to grow into a mighty tree of knowledge, with eighty-eight CVs and CCs across India and beyond.

A CV in every City?

To dream is one thing; to execute the dream, we need a different temper and quality of people. My experience is that advisors are many; but real men of action are few in almost all departments of activities in India. Let us start doing something that we can do instead of merely dreaming great and glorious schemes without qualified people to work at it.

Chinmayananda

Response to a proposal by a devotee to start CVs and CCs in every state capital and district HQ in India. 19.10.1989

So exactly how many CVs and CCs to date and where?

- 7 Chinmaya Colleges
- 81 Chinmaya Vidyalayas
- 5,000 teachers in CV campuses
- 85,000 students
- 850,000 ex-students

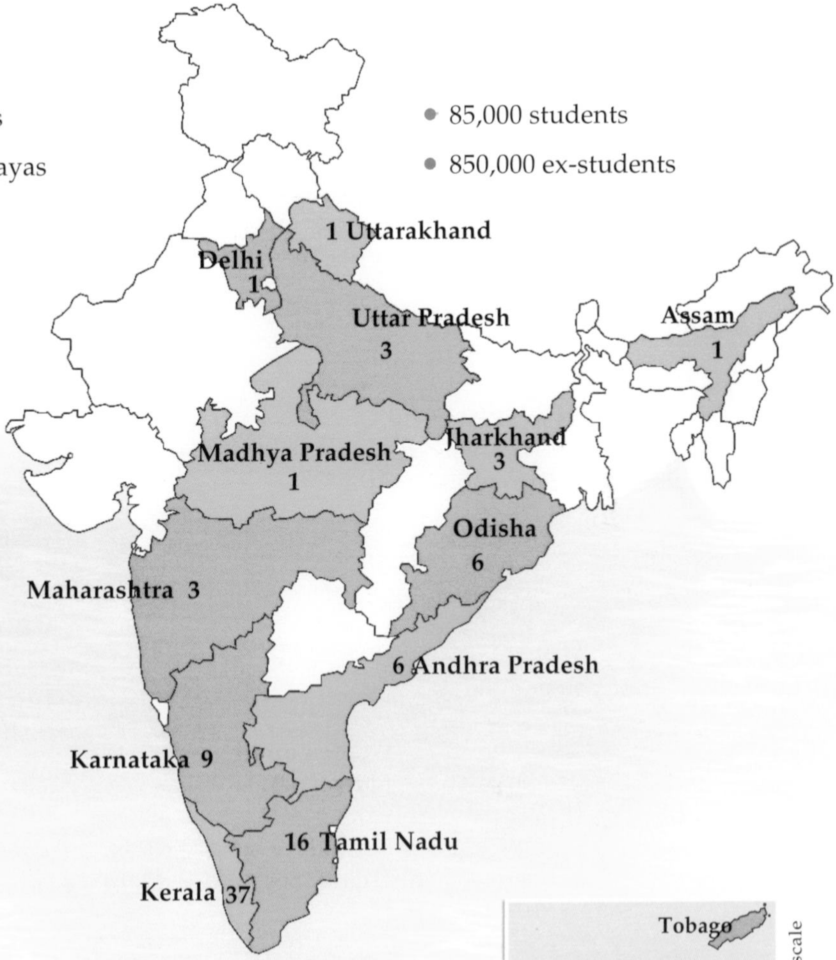

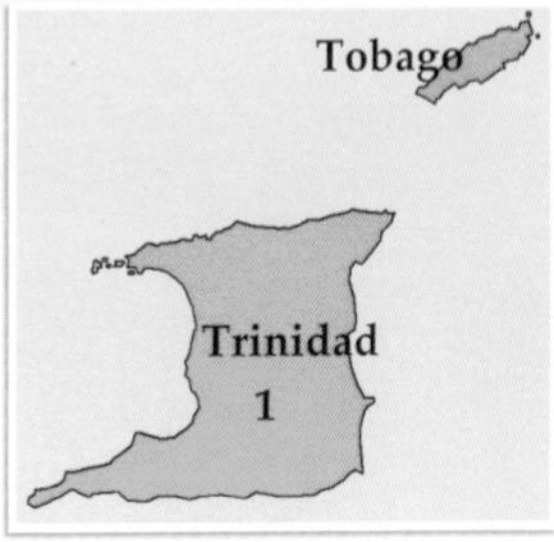

Maps not drawn to scale

Are all the Vidyalayas English medium, affiliated to the same board and run by local Chinmaya Mission centers?

No. They fall into various categories; some are in remote rural places and others in the hub of a metropolis.

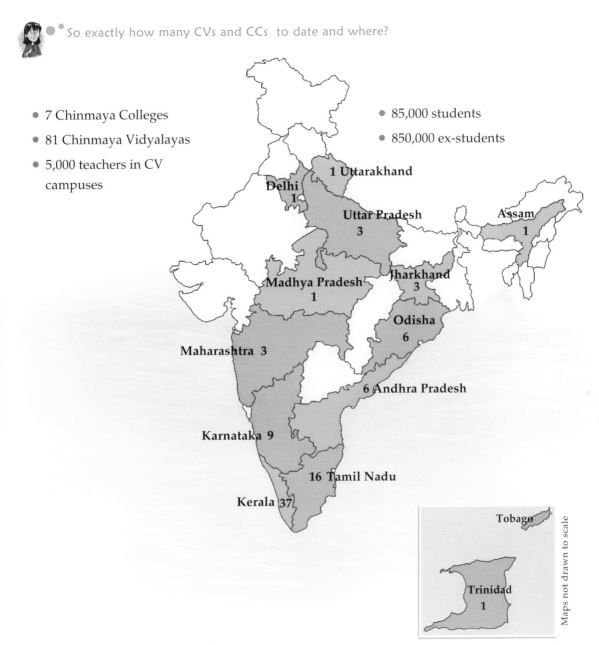

Categories of Vidyalayas

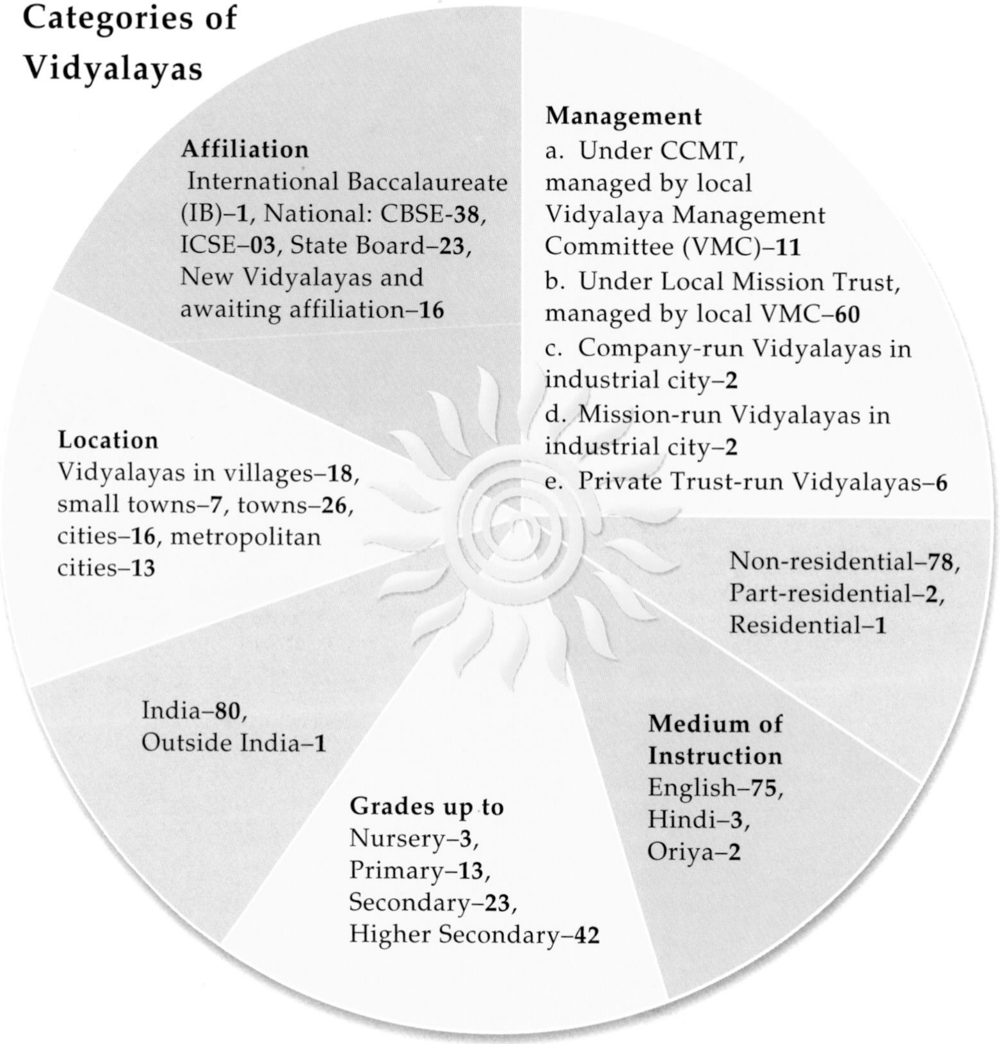

The starting of each CV and CC was like the rising sun which brought the light of knowledge and a vision into the lives of thousands in that place. Let me take you through the important events in the **timeline of the Chinmaya Education Movement** and also show you a **sample of the CVs and CCs** so you can get the 'Chinmaya SWAD' — its special flavor. Why not start from where we are — CV Chennai.

1916

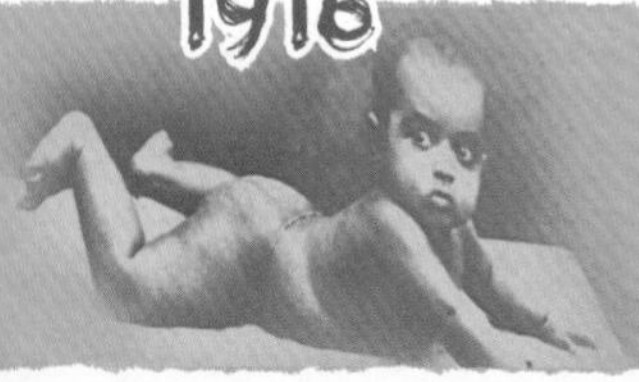

1. Gurudev's Birth

I saw a lovely collage of smiling faces of teachers in the entrance foyer. That is unusual.

'Keep Smiling' is the motto of all the Chinmaya Vidyalayas and 'You can, You must' is the motto of the Chinmaya Colleges. The Vidyalaya emblem and flag, too, bear the motto.

Keep Smiling — Inner equipoise expresses as a smile outside. The Chinmaya Vidyalaya prepares students with an inner equipoise to face all challenges of life with a smile.

You Can, You Must! — Gurudev's clarion call to all was, "We can, we must," so the Chinmaya College motto was adopted as 'You can, You must.'

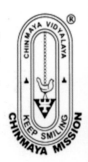

Significance of the Emblem — The lamp in India always represents Knowledge. The mythical swan is said to have the ability to separate milk from water. The swan in the emblem represents the ability to distinguish between right and wrong, matter and spirit. Knowledge helps us make the right choices and reach the highest.

Chinmaya Vidyalaya Flag

Yellow depicts a positive outlook or vision of life.

The hand gesture of jñāna mudrā represents knowledge of life and its purpose.

The Tricolor symbolizes love for and pride in our country and its culture.

The globe stands for a universal outlook.

'Keep Smiling' reminds us to face all challenges of life with a smile.

Gurudev's eternal presence and blessings are characterized by his signature of OM.

I am supposed to hoist the Vidyalaya flag. Thereafter, all will sing my favorite song and then I will address the special assembly. Come, let us go.

Chinmaya Vidyalaya Song

भारत माँ के लाल हम एक राग गायेंगे। तन अनेक प्राण एक भाव एक गायेंगे।
चिन्मय विद्यालय लायेगा नवीनता। चिन्मय विद्यालय लायेगा एकता।
कर्म धर्म प्रेम की ज्योत को जलायेंगे। विनम्रता मनुष्यता सहिष्णुता सिखायेंगे।
रूढी रीति-नीति और मूढता मिटायेंगे। सुमधुर स्वर्ग सी सभ्यता बनायेंगे। (चिन्मय विद्यालय ...)
भक्ति ज्ञान श्रद्धा के महत्व को बतायेंगे। विद्युत गति से हम परिवर्तन लायेंगे।
सर्वक्षेम के स्वर्ण बीज को हम बोयेंगे। वसुधैव कटुम्बकं की भावना फ़ैलायेंगे।
मुस्कुराते रहो सदा छंद को हम गायेंगे। भारतीय संस्कृति को खूब हम सजायेंगे। (चिन्मय विद्यालय ...)

We, the children of Bharat, sing together as one spirit in one voice, despite the differences in us. Chinmaya Vidyalaya will bring about a unique change and oneness. We will light the lamp of dedicated work, righteousness and love and will learn to be humble, humane and tolerant. We will root out all superstitions and false notions and will build a highly civilized society. We will propagate the great virtues of devotion, knowledge, and respect for all, and will transform within and bring about a rapid change in the world. We will sow the golden seed of universal welfare and will spread the noble thought that the whole world is one family. We will sing, follow the mantra 'Keep smiling,' and become luminaries of our sacred and ancient culture.

The CV song was written and composed by Smt. Vidya Mohanram, teacher of CV Chennai before Gurudev's Mahāsamādhi, but was adopted as the Vidyalaya song in 1998.

Respected Principal, teachers, parents, and dear students. Hari Om and Namaskāra! I have been asked to tell you in brief about the aims and objectives of our Vidyalaya and its influence on me.

The Vidyalaya aims to offer children a value-based and holistic education, which paves the way for the Integrated Development of the physical, mental, intellectual and spiritual aspects of the personality, enriched by knowledge of Indian Culture, a feeling of Patriotism and a Universal Outlook.

It aims to mold children into young men and women of moral strength who can face the challenges of modern life with a smile and make a difference in the world by their positive contribution.

It also aims to give a practical and judicious combination of academic excellence, extra-curricular pursuits, character building and personality development.

"There is no path; paths are made by walking," said Antonio Machado, a Spanish poet. It would be no exaggeration to say that all the paths that led to my success were paved by this school. My inspiration to make a difference I owe to Gurudev. May the magic of this school work for you also! Hari Om!

That was very inspiring indeed; can you tell me more about your school?

Divine Guidance — Chinmaya Vidyalayas, Chennai

The historical city of Chennai, where the British first established the East India Company, was formerly the capital of Madras Presidency. Now the capital of Tamil Nadu, Chennai is also called the Detroit of India and is the site of the famous Kapalishwar Temple. Every December, the city hosts a month-long bonanza of classical dance and music; also, it claims to have the largest IT park of Asia. Gurudev held his first Yajña here in 1953.

> Is this a sense of happiness - No! A sense of joy - No. It is indeed a sense of fulfillment! The opening of this CV in Madras is a definite milestone on the way to be walked by this Mission. Let God guide our way.
>
> Chinmayananda.

4. CV Kollengode, Kerala

In 1966, Gurudev first mentioned in a casual conversation that Chennai should have a CV, and through divine guidance, the first of the seven CVs was inaugurated in October 1968 by the famous Bharatanatyam dancer Rukmini Devi Arundale. The Vidyalayas are considered amongst the best in this metropolitan city and are managed under the Chinmaya Seva Trust, which also manages a CV in the holy city of Tirupati, in Andhra. The CM

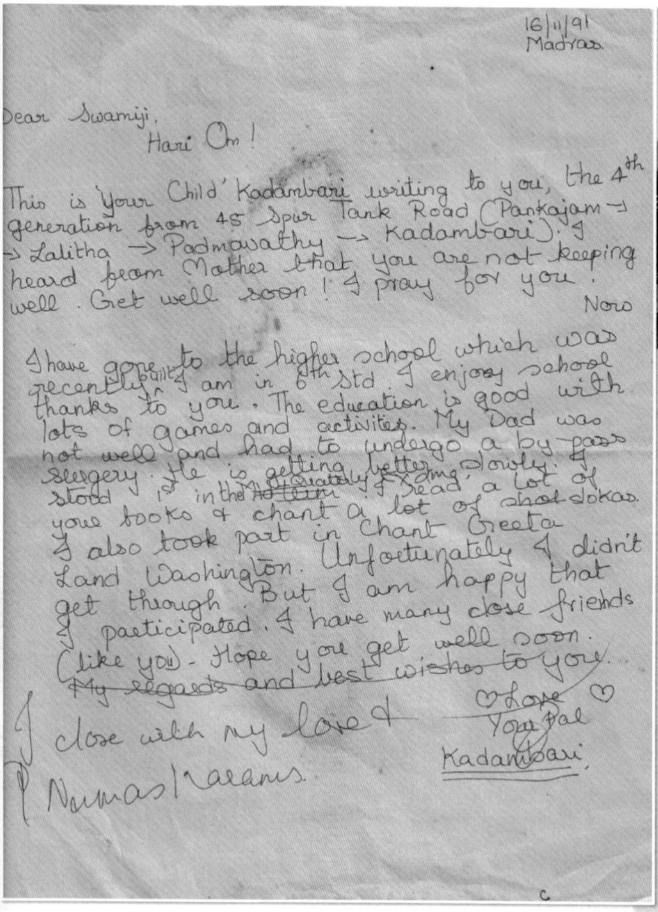

16/11/91
Madras.

Dear Swamiji,
Hari Om!

This is your Child 'Kadambari' writing to you, the 4th generation from 45 Spur Tank Road (Pankajam → Lalitha → Padmavathy → Kadambari). I heard from Mother that you are not keeping well. Get well soon! I pray for you.

Now I have gone to the higher school which was recently built. I am in 6th std. I enjoy school thanks to you. The education is good with lots of games and activities. My Dad was not well and had to undergo a by-pass surgery. He is getting better slowly. I stood 1st in the ~~1st term~~ quarterly exams. I read a lot of your books & chant a lot of shlokas. I also took part in Chant Geeta Land Washington. Unfortunately I didn't get through. But I am happy that I participated. I have many close friends (like you) - Hope you get well soon. ~~My regards and best wishes to you.~~

I close with my love & Namaskarams.

Love
Your Pal
Kadambari.

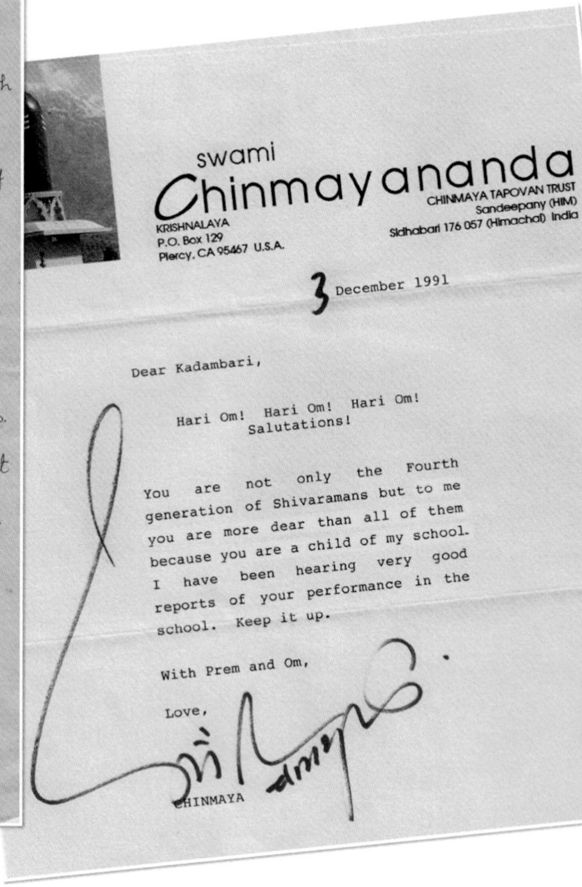

swami
Chinmayananda
KRISHNALAYA
P.O. Box 129
Piercy, CA 95467 U.S.A.
CHINMAYA TAPOVAN TRUST
Sandeepany (HIM)
Sidhabari 176 057 (Himachal) India

3 December 1991

Dear Kadambari,

Hari Om! Hari Om! Hari Om!
Salutations!

You are not only the Fourth generation of Shivaramans but to me you are more dear than all of them because you are a child of my school. I have been hearing very good reports of your performance in the school. Keep it up.

With Prem and Om,

Love,

CHINMAYA

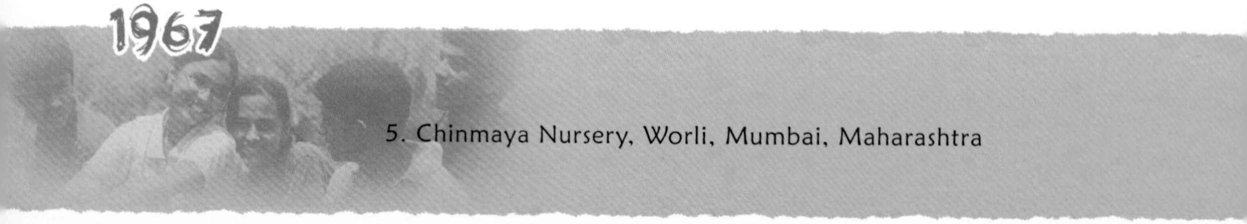

5. Chinmaya Nursery, Worli, Mumbai, Maharashtra

ashram at Tamaraipakkam in the rural outskirts of Chennai, undertakes various service projects. In 1990, it started the Hari Har Chinmaya Vidyalaya, offering free education with kindergarten classes. CV Anna Nagar adopted the school in 2010, added a new building, and has initiated plans to teach up to Grade X, as well as offer vocational training.

GROWTH OF CVs AT CHENNAI

NO.	CVs IN DIFFERENT AREAS	AFFILIATION	SCHOOL OPENS	STUDENTS IN YR. OF STARTING	STUDENTS IN 2012	GRADE UP TO
1.	Kilpauk	CBSE	1968	30	2125	Nursery to Higher Secondary
2.	Virugambakkam	CBSE	1970	50	1950	Nursery to Secondary
3.	Anna Nagar	CBSE	1989	11	2000	Nursery to Higher Secondary
4.	Virugambakkam	State Board	2002	20	175	Higher Secondary
5.	Tamaraipakkam (Hari Har CV)	—	2010	20	170	Nursery and Primary
6.	Sri City	—	2011	120	250	Nursery and Primary
7.	Avadi (VGN CV)	—	2011	30	350	Nursery and Primary

Indian Shenzen — Sri City, spread over 6,000 acres, is on the Tamil Nadu-Andhra border. "What Shenzen is to Hong Kong, Sri City will be to Chennai," said Ravindra Sannareddy, MD, who is on a mission to transform his native village, in this underdeveloped region. Sri City has adopted innovative green initiatives and is home to more than seventy companies from twenty-two countries.

6. CV Kilpauk, Chennai, Tamil Nadu

CV Sri City is the first CBSE school in this rural area. It caters to the children of farmers and employees of the local companies. There are also plans to start a Hari Har school.

The Guides ... In 2003, C. Sathiamoorthy, Principal, CV Kilpauk, received the National Award for Teachers instituted by the Human Resource Development Ministry, from the President of India. He was also the recipient of a Chinmaya Gaurav Award, presented by Guruji.

Gowri Ramakrishnan, Principal, CV Virugambakkam, received an award instituted by Gandhi Peace Foundation, for 'promoting peace, justice, love, and truth,' from Śrī R. Venkataraman, Vice President of India, in 2001.

CVP IN ACTION **Art in Her Heart** — M. S. Shwetha in IX Grade of CV, Kilpauk, has won numerous state and national awards for her unique artistic talents. Her achievements include first prize in the Young Artist Contest and competition organized by WHO, displaying fifty paintings at the prestigious Lalit Kala Academy, and having fifty of her paintings screened for the title song of the popular Tamil movie Ninaiyvil Ninḍraval. She says, "My teachers even in the initial years when I did not win prizes, had faith in my talent and encouraged me."

Blind (G)Love — Manoj Kumar, CV Virugambakkam, won an award from the National Innovation Foundation (NIF) for designing a glove which helps the visually challenged to detect obstacles.

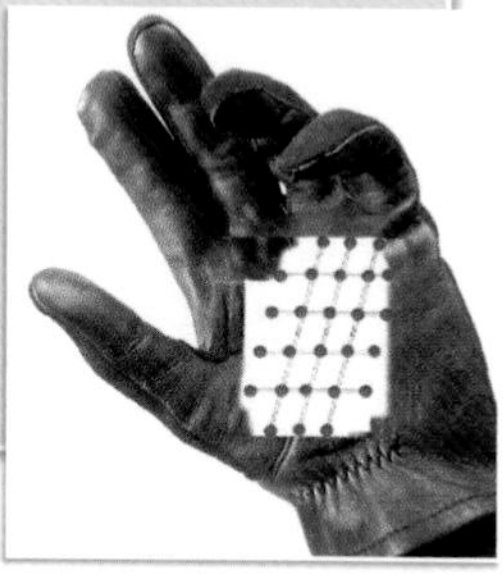

1969

7. CV Hindupur, Andhra Pradesh
8. Chinmaya Nursery, Kemp's Corner, Mumbai, Maharashtra
9. CV Kozhikode, Kerala
10. CV Vazhuthacaud, Trivandrum, Kerala

From Vidyalaya to Sadhanalaya

I studied till Grade III in CV Virugambakkam. When I was in twelfth Grade I went to Sidhbari to seek Gurudev's permission to join the Vedānta Course, even though I did not have a degree (the basic requirement for the course). Gurudev told me I could join the course only if I got a distinction in my twelfth grade exams. So I studied very hard and got it. He then asked me to meet him in Secunderabad. Gurudev looked me up and down and said, "You look so innocent; you need to learn something about the world before you join! Teach at the Chinmaya Vidyalaya here." So I taught English, Science, and Social Studies to fourth and fifth graders for ten months. That was when I experienced the joy of teaching. I loved the children and they loved me. They still keep in touch with me. The experience polished me. I learned the art of teaching and now I teach brahmacharis at Sandeepany Sadhanalaya.

Swami Advayananda describing his journey from a Vidyalaya student to Sadhanalaya student, and from Vidyalaya teacher to Sadhanalaya teacher

Divine guidance and divine protection is experienced in all CVs.

Protected by Grace — Nagapattinam in Tamil Nadu was the worst affected by the tsunami of December 2004, with hardly any building left intact and with heavy loss of life. The locals believe that CV Nagapattinam, which is right on the seashore, was not affected because of regular Gītā chanting.

▲ CV NAGAPATTINAM

I love traveling. You meet interesting people and new avenues open up. Come, let us go further South to a new experiment at Rajapalayam.

11. CV Rajapalayam, Tamil Nadu
12. CV Virugambakkam, Chennai, Tamil Nadu

Raja Vidya under the Baobab Tree — Chinmaya Vidyalaya, Rajapalayam

A few generations back, the Raju community from Andhra Pradesh settled in Rajapalayam, a small town in Tamil Nadu. Then came the boom. Spearheaded by Śrī Ramalinga Raja, the textile industry took root. At present, more than seventy percent of the forty textile mills and the famous Madras Cement are owned by his son Śrī Rama Subramania Raja of Ramco Industries. In addition to being a prosperous textile town, it is famous for Rajapalayam mangoes and Alsatian dogs.

The Life-transforming Journey — "I was traveling in the first-class compartment of a train from Chennai and was intrigued to see an ochre-robed Swami sitting opposite me, reading an English language newspaper, so I initiated a conversation with him. Swami Chinmayananda and I bonded instantly, and I was enthralled that he accepted my invitation to visit my home and we alighted the train at Rajapalayam! This chance encounter changed my life."

Śrī Rama Subramania Raja, M.D., Ramco Industries

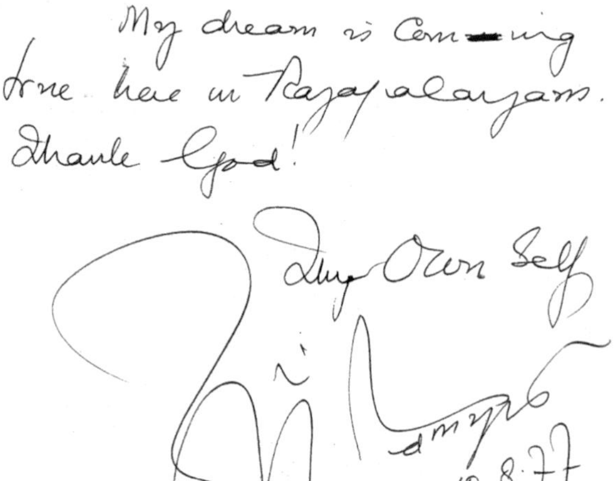
My dream is Coming
true here in Rajapalayam.
Thank God!
Thy Own Self
10.8.77

This train journey was to set the Raja family and many generations of children on a new track. Captivated by Gurudev, the entire Raja family basked in Gurudev's presence and satsaṅg, year after year, and on April 19, 1979, the foundation stone for the CV was laid in the lush green thirty-acres ground, resting amid mountain peaks.

1971

13. CV Pillikunnu, Kasaragod, Kerala
14. CV RS Puram, Coimbatore, Tamil Nadu
15. CV Vadavalli, Coimbatore, Tamil Nadu
16. CV Vaduthala, Kochi, Kerala

The school has more than 900 students and forty-eight teachers, and is considered the best in the town. The royal patronage of the Rajas has ensured that Gurudev's vision is coupled with the best in academic excellence, facilities, and training.

Special Features

- **The African Grandma** — The majestic Baobab tree famously called 'the tree of life' is one of the longest living and largest trees in the world. Native to the African soil and a rarity in India, it is nestled in the heart of the CV campus. It is the oldest life-form in the local area, with an estimated life of 2,000 years, out of a possible 5,000-year-long lifespan. The tree is fondly called the 'great grandma' of the campus and will see many generations of students graduating. It is the most revered member of the school's nature club.

- **Indian Pride** — Some forty-to-fifty peacocks and peahens move around — uninhibited, as the children pause when they cross their path. The children feel 'as proud as a peacock' about this unique feature of their Vidyalaya.

- **The Father's Prayer** — Mahatma Gandhi, the Father of the Nation, came to Rajapalayam on January 25, 1934. He conducted his evening prayer meeting under this baobab tree — a blessing indeed for the city and the school.

1974

17. CV Pallavur, Kerala
18. AUPET CV Tirunelveli, Tamil Nadu
19. CV Tripunithura, Kerala

• **The Mother's Canopy** — The mighty mountains and the hundreds of trees inspired the architect to design pyramid-roofed classrooms under the shadow of Mother Nature's lush green canopy, as he felt, 'No building should be taller than the trees.'

LET THE INNER NATURE IN CHILDREN BE NURTURED AND BROUGHT OUT IN A SERENE ENVIRONMENT.

| SWAMI CHINMAYANANDA |

CMP IN ACTION **On the Right Track** — Trekking in the local mountains is a favorite activity, and the Himalayan track is an annual calendared activity in which the principal, who has been around for three decades, often participates.

Amongst the many sayings I read in the Vidyalaya one was, 'Enter to learn and leave to serve.' That would be the result of a noble vision.

Let us now travel to the best Vidyalaya in the East.

The Ultimatum That Gave the Ultimate Result — Chinmaya Vidyalayas, Rourkela

Rourkela, with a population of five lakhs, is a township of Rourkela Steel — a Central Government and German collaboration run steel company, in the mineral-rich state of Odisha, the land of Lord Jagannath. The company that started in 1958 was one of several such large-scale public sector undertakings set up in post-independent India.

1975

20. Chinmaya Mission College, Palakkad, Kerala
21. Chinmaya Mission College, Talap, Kannur, Kerala
22. Chinmaya Mission College, Thrissur, Kerala

Gurudev created waves with his very first Jñāna Yajña in 1966. The local CM grass root level activities started thereafter. The company was running two Odiya and Hindi medium schools from Grades I to VII. The steel plant authorities approached the Mission to start an Odiya medium school — from the eighth grade — that, too, in three days! The urgency was due to certain statutory rules of the educational authorities of Odisha.

The ultimatum was accepted. The school started in a bungalow with fifteen students — mostly dropouts and low performers. Gurudev later chided Śrī K. C. Patnaik (CM Secretary, and currently General Manager, CCMT Publications) with the words, "Starting a school is not like going to the market to buy vegetables." He added, "Once a school is started, it is our committed responsibility to the community to run the school smoothly, even if the steel plant authorities withdraw their support." Later, it was shifted to its present premises in Sector 7, and the Vidyalaya flourished to become the best state-board-affiliated school of Odisha. The ultimatum yielded the ultimate result!

Besides various awards and recognition, the Vidyalaya also received the Chief Minister's Merit award in 2008, 2009, and 2011.

1977

23. CV Kolar, Karnataka
24. CV Bokaro, Jharkhand
25. CV Thattamangalam, Kerala

The Best Gives Chance to the Second Best — Each year the rolling award of the Dibakar Patnaik Memorial Shield from the Rotary Club for the best school of Rourkela went to CV. Finally the Rotary Club decided that instead of giving the award year after year to the CV, it should be given to the second best school — so the others, too, got a chance.

Narrated by Śrī K. C. Patnaik

Meanwhile the Mission bought about four acres of land in Chend Colony. Gurudev laid the foundation stone on November 23, 1990, and a CBSE-affiliated English medium CV is now flourishing there — again recognized as the best English medium school in Odisha. Śrī Kabisatpathy, a retired headmaster of the steel plant school, was the Secretary of the schools from their inception, and he continued to be the guiding force for the English medium school till he passed away. His daughter Sharmistha Kabisatpathy has been the principal of the school since April 1993. From thirty-two students in 1992, the Vidyalaya now has 2,500 students from nursery to Grade XII.

IMPACT **Bhakti se bhītī bhāgati** — The first batch of students of CV Chend Colony appeared for the ICSE exam in 2001 in a center that was not their own school. As is usual on the first day of any board exam, there was anxiety among parents and nervousness among the students. To everyone's astonishment, they heard the CV students diligently reciting the twelfth chapter of the Gītā, shooing away their fears (bhakti se bhītī bhāgati). The confidence and the calmness that was portrayed on their faces was the talk of the town.

That was interesting. I did my schooling in Delhi. I wish I could have gone to the CV in Delhi. I've heard it is a good school.

1978

26. CV Kanhangad, Kerala
27. CV Kannur, Kerala

Capital Education — Chinmaya Vidyalaya, Delhi

The ancient city of Hastināpur (of Mahābhārata fame) later became Delhi and retained its pivotal position, political nature, and capital status. This new Luyten-designed, colonial-style city and its charming old counterpart have some of the most beautiful, ancient, and modern landmarks. To this city of mean politicking and power-play came the healing words of the Master.

Gurudev conducted his third-ever Yajña lasting three months in 1953 for the first time in Delhi to an audience of thousands.

Capital Difference — One little child can change the entire history of the country. That is how all the great men of the past were made — a Shivaji, an Einstein, a Tagore, a Mahatma Gandhi. From childhood onward, noble ideas were inculcated into them. We must teach our children to have the courage and heroism to live up to their convictions. A real intellectual cannot keep quiet when he sees injustice, and he doesn't care what the consequences are.

Gurudev's address given at the Jamnabai Narsee School, Mumbai, 1987

Constructed in 1979, CV Delhi educated its first students in a small building, shifting later to its present site of nearly four acres in the sophisticated South Delhi suburb of Vasant Vihar. It was Swami Jyotirmayananda of CM Delhi, with his sweat and toil, that brought together man and material and forded through the political corridors of Delhi to give concrete shape to this CV. Gurudev himself attended numerous fundraisers for the school building. Smt. Indira Bhardwaj, the first

1979

28. Vidya Bharathi CV Telco, Jamshedpur, Jharkhand
29. CV New Delhi
30. CV Thrissur, Kerala
31. CV Mysore, Karnataka
32. CV Sector 7, Rourkela, Odisha

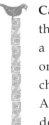

principal of the school, continued to lead it effectively until her retirement in December 2005. The school is presently guided by Swami Nikhilananda and a team of dedicated Mission members.

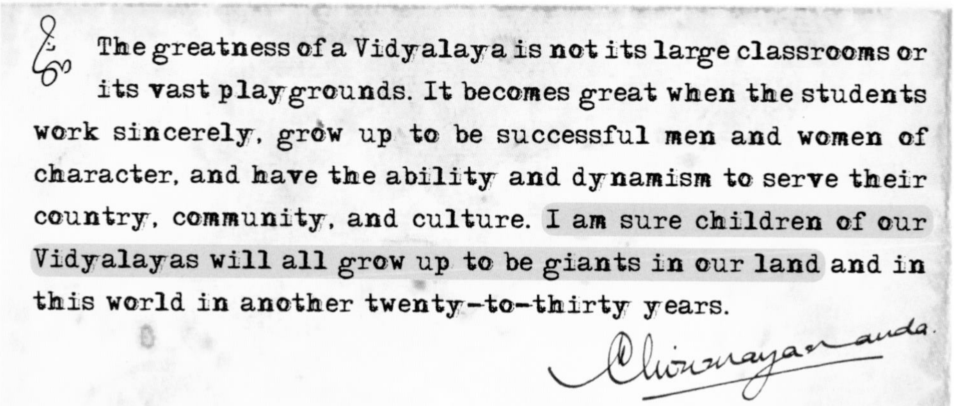

The greatness of a Vidyalaya is not its large classrooms or its vast playgrounds. It becomes great when the students work sincerely, grow up to be successful men and women of character, and have the ability and dynamism to serve their country, community, and culture. I am sure children of our Vidyalayas will all grow up to be giants in our land and in this world in another twenty-to-thirty years.

Chinmayananda.

Letter to a Grade IV student of CV Delhi when they moved into the new building

Bodha Under the Bodhi Tree — Once, on a visit to Delhi Vidyalaya, Gurudev said, "An educational institution is like a banyan tree supporting and nourishing all under its divine shade. The Vidyalaya should have a banyan tree."

Narrated by Bharati Sukhtankar

This Vidyalaya was patronized by Gurudev, and visited by many great souls.

High Capital Gain — Gurudev blessed the school with a visit when he came to Delhi each year for a Yajña and whenever he was in transit. He also had the first CM National Camp on the school campus in November 1985. Guruji, too, has held Yajñas on the Vidyalaya grounds. Other ācāryās of the Mission also visit and conduct sessions for teachers and students. Dignitaries, from government ministers and renowned educationists to the President, have visited, on hearing the name 'Swami Chinmayananda.'

1980

33. CV Chengannur, Kerala
34. CV Kunnumpuram, Thiruvananthapuram, Kerala
35. CV Therubali, Odisha

Capital Alumni

- Harshvardhan Nawathe — the first winner of the popular TV show Kaun Banega Crorepati (Indian equivalent of 'Who Wants to be a Millionaire')
- Sumesh Unini — received first prize in Chess Competition by INTEL in 2001
- G. Aparna — Gold Medalist, B.S. Zoology, 2001, Delhi University
- Arjun Punj — model, film, and TV actor
- Nidhi Agarwal — National basketball player
- Meenakshi Sheshadri — Bollywood actress (real name Shashikala Sheshadri) performed classical dance and sang with the guitar for Gurudev. Also, her mother was a music teacher of CV.

IN ACTION **Pitamaha devo bhava** — It was on one of Swami Chinmayananda's frequent stop-offs at the school in the early 1980s that he attended a Mother's Day event. He emphasized the importance of respecting the elders and the elderly, so the school started an annual Grandparents' Day. On the first such event, there were tears rolling down the cheeks of most of those worshipped grandparents (pitāmahas) in attendance.

Strengthening the Weak — CV Delhi provides free education to children from the Economically Weaker Section (EWS) at its remedial school named Jagriti. This afternoon school, started in 2008, supports first-generation learners from Grades I to V.

1981

36. CV Ulsoor, Bengaluru, Karnataka
37. CV Attukal, Thiruvananthapuram, Kerala

The children and teachers share a wholesome, simple meal before they start their classes in small groups in an informal atmosphere. Regular interactions with the parents and feedback are distinct features of Jagriti. This has improved the academic performance and has brought about positive behavioral changes in many children.

My brother studied at IIT Delhi. His roommate is brilliant and he is from Bokaro, I think it was a Chinmaya Vidyalaya.

I wouldn't be surprised. In 2011, twenty-eight students, and in 2012, forty-six students got into IIT from CV Bokaro! The principal Dr. Ashok Singh, who has authored many texts on mathematics, is one of the thirty-two recipients (selected from more than 12,500 CBSE affiliated schools) of the prestigious 'CBSE Awards to Teachers' for 2012 given by the HRD Department of Government of India.

I never knew the state of Jharkhand had such good schools. Any more such schools?

Company of True Education — Chinmaya Vidyalaya, Jamshedpur

> I do not want my country to become an economic superpower. I want my people to be happy.
>
> J. R. D. Tata, on being told that India would become an economic superpower in the 21st century

Founded by the great visionary industrialist Jamshedji Nusserwanji Tata, this steel township is the location of Telco, Tisco, and many big industries, and is called Jamshedpur or Tatanagar.

1982

38. CV Vidya Nagar, Kasaragod, Kerala
39. CV Tiruchi, Tamil Nadu
40. CV Guntur, Andhra Pradesh

Gurudev first held a Yajña at Jamshedpur in 1970. Śrī S. M. Khorana, the then G. M. of Telco, was largely responsible for setting up the first company-sponsored and run 'Vidya Bharati Chinmaya Vidyalaya' under Gurudev's direct guidance. Guruji inaugurated the Vidyalaya on February 1, 1979, as the thirtieth Chinmaya Vidyalaya.

Unusually, the school started with Grades I and V, and every year two grades were added — two and six, three and seven, and so on until it became a full-fledged higher secondary school. CV is the first school in Jamshedpur to get CBSE affiliation in 1988-89. The Ādivāsīs (tribals) offered their land to the school, and so till date, the school gives free education to Ādivāsī students.

A Tribal Story — When Col. Datta, security-in-charge of Telco, went to access the feasibility of getting land for starting a CV, he was faced with armed tribals who told him that they have always been uneducated and were quite happy about it! The most educated among them was persuaded, and he negotiated on behalf of the clan for free education for five tribal students per class.

However, since all the students were to be taken on merit, the education wing, Shiksha Prasar Kendra of Telco, hired a teacher to teach them basics so that the little tribal children would qualify in the entrance interview. This went on for many years. Now the parents are educated and their children qualify against the best without coaching!

1983

41. CBB Primary School, Sector 7, Rourkela, Odisha
42. CV Kattakada, Thiruvananthapuram, Kerala
43. CV Naruvamoodu, Thiruvananthapuram, Kerala
44. CV Nileshwar, Kerala

The Dynamic Paramparā of Excellence

- Śrī Govardhan Gupta, Principal (1980-1996), was specially sent by Gurudev to inspect and report on all the schools in Kerala.
- Smt. Shanti Krishnamurthy, Principal (1996-2002), was highly inspired by CVP, and with a team of teachers introduced it in many reputed schools of Jamshedpur. The school came to be recognized as a 'school with a difference' and is among the best in the township. She is presently the principal of CIRS and a member of the CCMT Education Cell.

Transforming Vision — Soon after CVP was launched, I took over as principal. There were major discipline issues at the time. I saw CVP as the answer. And it was; it completely transformed the Vidyalaya. We conducted sessions for parents and they felt connected to CVP and CM. They felt that they, too, were part of the molding of their children. We won the Vision Award that year (1996). It was a big boost to the school, and made a big difference.

Smt. Shanti Krishnamurthy

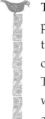

- Under the principalship of Smt. Vipin Sharma (from 2002), the Vidyalaya has received the prestigious Dr. J. J. Irani Education in Excellence Award constituted by Tata Steel. Dr. A. P. J. Abdul Kalam presented the award for the Vidyalaya's 'strong commitment to educational excellence' in February 2012.

Many of the teachers have won awards for the consistently outstanding standards they display, and many of them are now heading schools located all over the country.

1984

45. AAAM CV, Punithura, Kerala

IMPACT **Illumined Alumni** — Shibani Khorana, an alumnus of the school, graduated with a B.Com. and M.B.A., worked in the HR dept of IT firms, and later worked in developing experiential learning techniques with iDiscoveri. Inspired by the cause of CM right from her schooldays, she first joined the Chinmaya Youth Empowerment Program and later the two-year Vedānta Course at Sandeepany Sadhanalaya, Mumbai. She presently serves as an invaluable full-time sevikā in CM. She says, "I felt very much at home and loved studying at my Vidyalaya. The school instilled a sense of respect, rather a reverence for Indian culture and tradition."

The Offshoot

Unable to manage the schools mushrooming under their wings, Tata Steel decided to give them away to private trusts. The local CM leased one of these schools and has been running a CV at Bistupur since 2001 under the able guidance of the Secretary, Śrī Surendranath.

Now I'll take you through a whole range of different schools we run.

Nourishing Nursery — AAAM Chinmaya Vidyalaya, Punithura

Pamper the child for the first five years of his/her life (pañca varṣāṇi lālayet).
— Subhāṣita

"All I really needed to know about life I learned in kindergarten."
Robert Fulghum

1986

46. Chinmaya Hari Har Vidyalaya, Ellayapalle, Andhra Pradesh

Tripunithura, or Punithura, is a small town near Kochi, well known for its ancient Sri Purnathrayesa (the Infinite Lord of the Three Vedas) temple established by Arjuna of Mahābhārata fame on the fifth day of Kali Yuga. It also is home to Kochi's Royal Family Hill Palace that was built in 1865 on fifty-four acres of land; it has the largest Archaeological Museum in Kerala.

Tripunithura hosted Gurudev's fiftieth Yajña during his first visit in 1958. CV Tripunithura started in 1974 and now has classes from Grades I to XII.

Mother's Last Wish Resulted in a Century-old Relationship — Despite having to bring up eleven children on her own, my mother would educate one needy child every year. Before she passed away, she told me that she wanted me to continue doing this service in her name.

Śrī C. G. Menon, Secretary CV Tripunithura, requested my husband to build a nursery section for the school. This, my husband and I felt, was a God-sent opportunity to fulfill my mother's noble wish. Gurudev gave us his wholehearted approval, and thus commenced the building work.

On September 20, 1985, Gurudev formally inaugurated the school with ninety children and four teachers. It came to be called Ambady Ammu Amma Memorial Chinmaya Vidyalaya (AAAM-CV). We became affiliated to the Chinmaya Seva Trust, Kerala, and from then on this school became the kindergarten campus for the main school.

I am seventy-five this year and this school is twenty-five years old today. Together we have hit a century. I never thought we would reach a milestone like this. But again, I feel it is all Gurudev's blessings.

Smt. Shanta Balakrishnan, Managing Trustee, September 2010. (She passed away peacefully within a year of her century-long run with the school.)

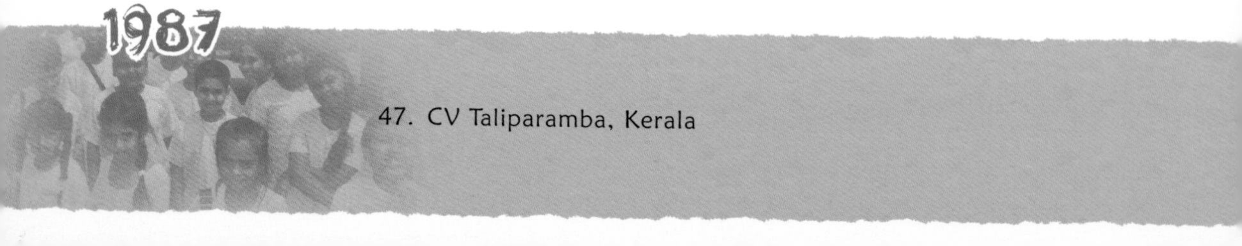

1987

47. CV Taliparamba, Kerala

IMPACT **Mother to Daughter** — On the auspicious day of Vijaya Daśamī in 1985, this school came into existence. It was a simple ceremony and we started writing the first words in our lives for the first time on this campus. Later, Pūjya Gurudev did the formal inauguration. Now I am waiting to enroll my daughter in the Kindergarten of AAAM-CV, as I wish to give her the same education that I had the privilege to receive.

Smitha S. Menon, first student enrolled in the school

The first principal, Dr. (Smt.) Leela Ramamurthy, later became the principal of CV Anna Nagar, Chennai. The nursery also adopts some Montessori techniques. The teachers are well-trained in teaching methodology as well as values and culture. In 2003, a full-fledged activity center was established to develop the motor skills and improve the concentration of the children. "The foundation (core values) of this school is strong," says Śrī Pramod Balakrishnan (architect of the school, trustee, and son of the founder).

There is a joy when I enter the school, and as long as this excitement remains, I will stay young like my little ones. Today after ten years, this nursery school is my life, and I would not change a single thing about the path my life has taken. I believe it is destiny, and Gurudev must have had a plan for me all along. Thanks to him and my parents, today I have a purpose in life and am doing something worthwhile ...

Smt. Indu Ajay Kumar, Trustee, AAAM CV and Correspondent, CV Tripunithura

IN ACTION **Three Tiny Steps in Service** — Since 2008, the Vidyalaya has introduced three projects to help the little ones understand the value of caring

1989

48. Chinmaya Degree College, Haridwar, Uttarakhand
49. CV Badiadka, Kerala
50. CV Anna Nagar, Chennai, Tamil Nadu

and sharing. Oru pidi ari — a fistful of rice: Children keep aside a fistful of rice at home daily. They bring this to school, and it is then used for midday meals of poor children in the locality. Kili ootu — bird feeding: Children are encouraged to bring small amounts of grains, and they feed the birds in their school every morning after assembly. The third project is easing the disease: On important days like birthdays or parents' anniversaries, the parents voluntarily donate a sum of money. At the end of the year, this money is used to buy medicines and the like for patients in the local government hospital.

▲ STUDENTS SHARING A FISTFUL OF RICE

The Path-breaker into Rural India — Hari Har Chinmaya Vidyalaya, Ellayapalle

Ellayapalle. The last place anyone would think of settling in — dry, hot, barren, no water, and no electricity with the majority of the population of around 300, existing below the poverty line.

Swamini Saradapriyananda. A dynamic lawyer, Gandhian and freedom-fighter turned sannyāsinī — one of the senior-most disciples of Gurudev. Her passion to serve the poorest of poor, give them not only material succor but also spiritual solace, brought into existence, Chinmayaranyam — the ashram — in 1982 and consequently the Hari Har Chinmaya Vidyalaya and many more projects, Mission Centers, and ashrams in the rural heartland and the smaller towns of Andhra Pradesh.

1990

51. CV Allahabad, Uttar Pradesh
52. CV Vivekanand Colony, Hubli, Karnataka
53. CV Payyannur, Kerala

▲ GURUDEV, SWAMINI SARADAPRIYANANDA AND PATHSHALA STUDENTS

Mahatma Gandhi. His vision of a free India was not of an urban-job-dependent nation, but a confederation of self-governing, self-reliant, self-employed people living in rural communities. He believed every village of independent India should have its own carpenters, shoemakers, potters, builders, mechanics, farmers, engineers, weavers, teachers, bankers, merchants, traders, musicians, artists, and priests.

Gandhiji believed that education must cater to the learner's need and inherent aptitudes. White-collar jobs, city life, and the lure of quick money attract millions from the villages who become the uneducated urban slum dwellers struggling to make ends meet and losing both their identity and dignity.

Swami Chinmayananda. He knew that a strong village-rooted project alone will stop this mad rush into cities. He also realized that rural India did not need the urban-oriented education. He envisioned that the Hari Har schools would provide this strong base for the rural poor through rural-oriented education.

Hari Har Schools

We propose to launch many Hari Har Schools within the next five years. The students, Harijans (children of God) will be given vocational training in their traditional

1991

54. Gurudev's 75th Birthday/Suvarṇa Tulābhāram
55. CV Kannamally, Kochi, Kerala
56. CV Manjeri, Kerala
57. CV Samesi, Uttar Pradesh
58. CV Salem, Tamil Nadu

arts and crafts besides the basic literacy and skills needed to manage their trade profitably. Each school will have a workshop, a common prayer hall, and other required facilities. The vocational teachers will be experienced craftsmen of the locality. The students would also be given leadership skills and a strong base of culture and values, and become independent and self-employed, proud of their culture and confident of their own ability to contribute to the community. They would become the future leaders of their village and guide their entire community towards progress and prosperity.

Chinmayananda.

> The purpose of education is to make man civilized and cultured, while the purpose of a profession is to provide a means for earning one's livelihood.
>
> Swamini Saradapriyananda

The Chinmaya Gurukula Pathashala started in 1983 with informal education and a strong spiritual and cultural background given on the āśrama premises to poor children, mostly orphans. Thereafter, in 1986, the Telugu medium Hari Har Chinmaya Vidyalaya was started next to

the āśrama. Both schools continued until they were merged, and finally, in 2011, with the graduation of the last Telugu medium students, the school became an only English-medium school. Through years of effort and donations, the building, with all the necessary infrastructure, was completed. Today, more than 700 pupils are studying in the school from Grades I to X.

1992

59. CV Alakkode, Kerala
60. CV Alappuzha, Kerala
61. CV Chhend Colony, Rourkela, Odisha

Special Features:

▲ FREE AFTERNOON MEAL

- 130 students of the school (mostly orphans or abandoned children), stay in the aśrama and receive free food, clothing, and health care.
- 300 village children receive free education or concessional education, and also a free afternoon meal. Thirty villages are covered by the school bus transport system.
- Children have access to the thousands of fruit trees that have been planted in and around the Vidyalaya, a project inspired by Swamini Saradapriyananda.

> Nature is inherently pure. But when man pollutes her, she requires a long time to get purged of all impurities. So education must develop in man a healthy respect towards bountiful nature and be cautioned not to take undue advantage of her wealth and generosity.
>
> Swamini Saradapriyananda

▲ STUDENTS PERFORMING HOMA

- Merit scholarships are given from first-to-the-tenth grade, and students are also granted free education, as well as loans, until graduation.
- The teachers participate daily in the spiritual activities of the āśrama, and study one chapter of the Gītā each year in the Gītā Sadas.
- Sarada Vocational Training Centre, inaugurated in 2008, trains women in tailoring, embroidery, and handicrafts. Free sewing machines are distributed to many villagers.

1993

62. Gurudev's Mahāsamādhi
63. CV Hyderabad, Andhra Pradesh
64. CV Kalladathur, Kerala

> I am introduced to the bright-eyed children of Hari Har school, who sing a ballad in Telugu for me. They all seem to be vying to sing the loudest and best. I have visited many such schools, throughout India, and I have never noticed a single, bashful child. In the evening, just before sunset, all the children gather to chant verses from the scriptures for Swamini Saradapriyananda. I wish I could describe the joy I feel in listening to these innocent voices chanting Vedic hymns. I am transported to a time when life was true, open, flexible, and sacred. I breathe in these whispers of our ancient roots and feel whole.
>
> Extracted from Journey through Timeless India (1999) by Nancy Patchen, a long-standing devotee of Chinmaya Mission

Empowered Education — Chinmaya Vidyalaya, Tarapur

Located one hundred kilometers away from Mumbai, Tarapur is empowered by India's first Atomic Power Station and the famous Bhabha Atomic Research Centre, and it is enriched by a huge and thriving industrial estate. Tarapur became spiritually empowered in 1983 with Gurudev's first Jñāna Yajña, at which time the grassroots activities of the Chinmaya Mission began.

A great saint's blessings never go in vain. In 1993, Gurudev blessed the saṅkalpa of the Tarapur Mission members to start a school, and the groundbreaking ceremony (bhūmi pūjā) was performed in 1994 by Guruji. Swami Purushottamananda inaugurated the first phase of the Vidyalaya in June 1995 with a generous monetary contribution from Śrī K. B. Shroff.

▲ CHINMAYA GAURAV AWARD TO SRI K. B. SHROFF

1994

65. GNT CV Guwahati, Assam
66. CV Kurumathoor, Kerala

The Vidyalaya, which started with seventy-two students and four teachers, presently has 1,700 students and seventy-five teaching and non-teaching staff and is considered one of the best schools in the Thane District. Principal Śrī Anil Kumar, a recipient of the Rajiv Gandhi Siromani National Award (2007), says, "The Vidyalaya is recognized as a school with a difference because of the complete cooperation of the Managing Committee headed by Śrī T. B. Thakur and the hard work and teamwork of the teaching and non-teaching staff." The Vidyalaya has secured 100% first class from the time the first batch gave the CBSE 10th Board exams (2004), and students have won many state and national awards in various fields.

▲ ANIL KUMAR RECEIVING AWARD

The Club activities of the Vidyalaya are unique and include the Ramanujam Mathematics Club, Tagore Language Club, C. V. Raman Science Club, and even a Disaster Management Cell.

The Vidyalaya received the Chinmaya Vision Certificate in 1999 and the Chinmaya Vision Award in 2002 for effective implementation of CVP.

The Vidyalaya also arranges workshops and orientation programs for parents by eminent personalities in various fields and enables them to deal with problems relating to their children. It organizes monthly sessions of School Teachers In-service Training (STIT) for teachers to improve their professional knowledge.

1995

67. Chinmaya Vidyapeeth Kochi, Kerala
68. CV Koramangala, Bengaluru, Karnataka
69. CV Tarapur, Maharashtra
70. CV Unchahar, Uttar Pradesh

CVP IN ACTION **Satyam eva jayate** — The Value Education Cell has set up a shop without a vendor in the Vidyalaya. Articles like pencils, pens, notebooks, and compass boxes are kept for sale along with the price tag. The students buy what they need and drop the money in the box. It is indeed heartening that the office staff gets the exact amount after each day's sale from the box. The children have realized that truth alone wins in life (satyam eva jayate).

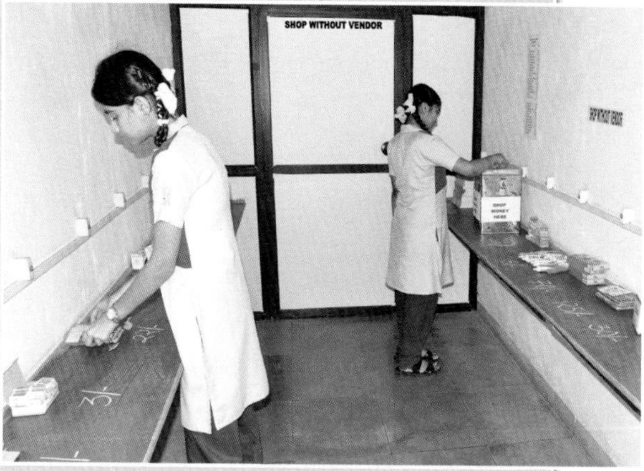

The Vidyalaya conducts tests without any invigilators, which has proved very successful in promoting honesty and trust.

India has gone global, not just in business, but also in education. It has the highest rate of growth of International Baccalaureate (IB) schools in the world. Gurudev's universal vision fits beautifully with this international school diploma course, well-recognized the world over.

Internationally Yours — Chinmaya International Residential School (CIRS), Coimbatore

> The forest [men] entered into a close living relationship with their work and leisure, with their daily necessities and contemplations. They could not think of the surroundings as separate or inimical. So the view of Truth, which these men found, was not of differences, but rather the unity of all things.
>
> Rabindranath Tagore

1996

71. Chinmaya Institute of Management, Bengaluru, Karnataka
72. Education Cell, Coimbatore, Tamil Nadu
73. CIRS Coimbatore, Tamil Nadu
74. CV Kollam, Kerala

Coimbatore, formerly called the Manchester of the South and the poor man's Ooty, is surrounded by the Nilgiri Mountains. The city is famous for textile looms, textile machinery, the ancient temples of Perur and Maruthamalai, and its water supplied by the Siruvani River, claimed to be the second tastiest water in the world after the Nile.

Thirty-five kilometers from the city, five kilometers from the Siruvani Falls and within sight of the famous Vellangiri hills is nestled CIRS, among forest-laden foothills, in one of the seven largest biospheres in the world. CIRS replicates the ancient gurukula experience in a contemporary context. Adjoining Chinmaya Gardens, the āśrama of Chinmaya Mission, CIRS is a place where elephants, deer, wild boar, peacocks, and monkeys live as neighbors to the school in their natural habitat. The earth, mountains, and sky elevate creative thinking to greater heights, and all who visit CIRS speak of the beauty and tranquility that the environment generates. Gurudev called it the Sidhbari of the South — where instead of snow-capped Himalayas, there are perennially verdant mountains. Guruji jokingly says that it is the only place that inspires a lazy person like him to walk!

Here our children with a Western education but steeped in Indian culture can grow as ideal men and women — materially successful outside and spiritually peaceful within.

Chinmayananda.

To Śrī Rajendra Prasad, U.S.A.

1997

75. CV Kottayam, Kerala
76. CV Nagapattinam, Tamil Nadu
77. CV Satna, Madhya Pradesh

For all the material prosperity that Indians in foreign lands have worked hard to gain, Gurudev was concerned for the spiritual loss that would naturally occur as ties with the Motherland were severed over the generations. "We have gained a lot, but at what cost?" lamented one NRI (Non-Resident Indian) parent. She describes her children as 'typical ABCDs' — American Born Confused Desis, having lost completely their Indian identity and values.

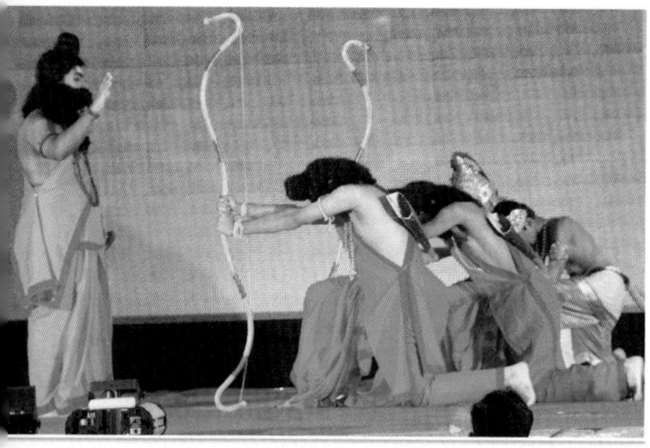
▲ CULTURAL PROGRAM AT CIRS

For these and many more Indians settled all around the world, Gurudev envisioned an International Residential School, which would 'integrate the best of the East and West, a cultural home away from home to unearth the beauty and hidden potential of tomorrow's leaders.'

Gurudev's Invitation to Young Parents Abroad

> Those who have gone abroad with their families try to integrate the lifestyle of the adopted country with their Indian ways. At times, such attempts create pressures and conflicts over moral values and cultural patterns. Children see one thing at home and meet contradictory situations outside. Because of this bicultural experience, they run the risk of picking up attitudes potentially dangerous and sometimes suicidal to their happiness and success.
>
> CIRS will provide an environment that will help integrate the best of each culture. Send us your children. Let them

1998

78. Chinmaya Chetana, Hubli, Karnataka

Gurudev's vision of education. It boasts state-of-the-art structure and infrastructure facilities. CIRS is headed by Swami Swaroopananda (Director-in-Charge), Smt. Shanti Krishnamurthy (Principal), Smt. Jaya Ravishankar (Headmistress), and Br. Rishi Chaitanya (spiritual guide). In 2011, it won the British Council International School Award. It also won the Chinmaya Vision Award for excellent implementation of CVP, and was ranked as one of the top ten boarding schools of India by Education World Magazine in 2012.

Śrī Pramod Balakrishnan, with conceptual inputs from Swamini Vimalananda (an architect in pūrvāśrama), designed each block around courtyards to create a space to share and bond in smaller and larger groups. The school, which is in synchrony with nature, has a breathtaking backdrop of the Nilgiri Mountains.

The USP of CIRS

The core task at CIRS is to inculcate values. The creativity of children is incredible here. Because the school is residential more energy is invested in creative activity like learning about, and participating in, Indian classical and Western music, dance, and drama. Children are encouraged to become independent and are well-equipped to face life after school. Our spiritual department is something they will not get anywhere else. Children run to our Ācāryās — Swamis and Brahmacharis, who are loved and admired by all the children.

Smt. Shanti Krishnamurthy, Principal, CIRS

2002

83. Chinmaya Institute of Technology, Chala, Kannur, Kerala

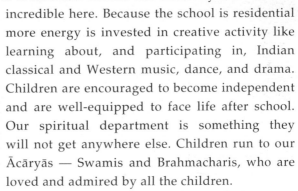

Close Spiritual Touch — When you teach children, their innocence affects you. Once during Janmāṣṭamī, I told the fifth graders, "Kṛṣṇa is with you all the time. When you drink your milk, see that He, too, drinks; otherwise, He will go hungry." The children fully accepted this. Later when I went to sit on an empty chair in the dining hall next to little Meera, she said with total belief, "Don't sit here Bhaiyā, Kṛṣṇa is already sitting here."

Swami Advayananda, spiritual guide, CIRS (1996–2000)

"Students here handle failure better, and use it as a springboard to success. This comes with a spiritual and cultural upbringing," says Swami Swaroopananda.

IMPACT **The Click That Clicked** — The beautiful surroundings at CIRS prompted me to take up photography in the ninth grade. We had a photography club and, seeing my growing interest, our Principal encouraged me to participate in regional and national competitions and exhibitions. One of my best memories is the Photo-Booth we set up to raise funds for differently-abled children. Our teachers encouraged our passions with the underlying motive of serving society. That is great. Without them, I would have never been initiated into this creative arena.

Akash Ghai,
who just graduated from CIRS, has won many international awards, including two Bronzes at the Epson International Photographic Pano Awards in 2011; his photographs are permanently displayed at the United Nations in New York.

Does the Chinmaya Vidyalaya concept work outside India?

Yes, not only do our cricketers go to the West Indies but so do our Swamis and their vision.

2003

84. Chinmaya Arts and Science College, Chala, Kannur, Kerala
85. CV HS, Virugambakkam, Chennai, Tamil Nadu
86. CV Deogarh, Odisha
87. CV Trinidad

Care in the Caribbean — Chinmaya Vidyalaya, Trinidad

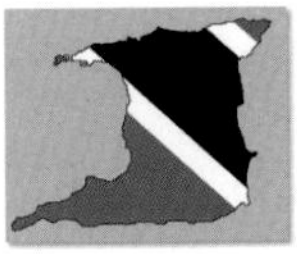

One-way Ticket from East to West — A genocide ordered by Spanish colonizers largely wiped out the native Amerindian population on the Caribbean islands, including Trinidad and Tobago. So, British colonizers later brought in African slaves to supply labor on sugar plantations. After the abolition of slavery in 1838, ex-slaves refused to work on plantations, even for wages. As many as 139,000 Indians, mostly from the states of Bihar and Uttar Pradesh, left the shores of India between 1895 and 1917, to become indentured immigrants in the distant land of Trinidad.

After many generations, Indians in Trinidad have fully integrated into life in the West Indies. They make up just under half of the population and have attained great success. Rudranath Capildeo, the child of an indentured laborer, was the first and only Nobel laureate (Mathematics) of Trinidad. The very first President and two Prime Ministers, including the present, are also of Indian descent.

Religion, culture, and traditions were maintained even though colonial masters ordered religious practices to be restricted to the home. But Indian culture has not survived without great threats posed by religious conversion in Trinidad. In response to this cultural threat, Badhase Sagan Maharaj, a local Hindu leader, began building schools to meet the educational needs of Hindus.

Swami Chinmayananda first visited Trinidad in May 1965. A Chinmaya Mission center was established by Swami Prakashananda (a native of Trinidad) in 1997. He realized that the local education completely lacked spiritual and cultural values and decided to do something about it. The first Chinmaya Vidyalaya outside of India was inaugurated in 2003.

▲STUDENTS WITH SWAMI PRAKASHANANDA

2004

88. Chinmaya Primary School, Hubli, Karnataka
89. CV Lathikata, Odisha

The Director of Studies, Śrī Ananda R. Ramkhạlawan, an eminent educationist, has played a key role in the school, achieving 100 percent passing grades in the national exams each year. The school also offers scholarships to meritorious students.

Growth CVs in Trinidad				
S. NO.	TOWN	YEAR OF STARTING	PRESENT STRENGTH	GRADES UP TO
1.	Couva	2003	210	Pre, Primary and High School
2.	Gasparillo	2005	80	Pre and Primary School
3.	Debe	2009	51	Pre and Primary School
4.	Penal	2011	3	Preschool
5.	Barrackpore	2011	13	Preschool
6.	Cunupia	2011	23	Preschool

Amazing Growth — Someone who had heard Swami Prakashanandaji's discourses on TV telephoned and offered land to open a new school. On another occasion, we were in Tobago and someone at the gas station who had never met Swamiji approached him and asked if we could open a Vidyalaya on his land. This is how our schools have been growing!

Children from different backgrounds (including African and Chinese) study at our Chinmaya Vidyalaya. We also have students from the U.S.A., Guyana, and one from India — most of them are children of parents who have been inspired by Swami Prakashanandaji who is also the Principal of the Vidyalayas. He received the 2012 Chaconia Gold Medal, the second highest award of the country, in recognition of his meritorious service to the people.

Śrī Rama Heeralal, Vice Principal, CV Trinidad

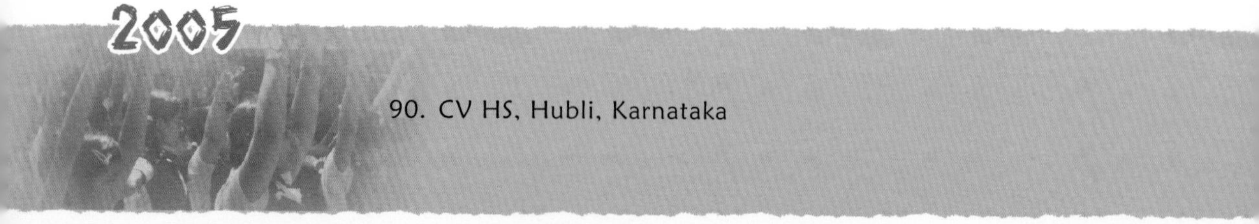

2005

90. CV HS, Hubli, Karnataka

Chinmaya Gaurav — The Pride of Chinmaya

In February 2012, two students of Chinmaya Vidyalaya Trinidad were presented with the prestigious Chinmaya Gaurav Award by Swamini Vimalananda. Former student Shivanand Seenarine received an award from the Ministry of Affairs National Youth Award for Excellence in Education and Darrien Da Silva, an eighth grade student, was awarded by the Ministry for Excellence in Sport.

CVP IN ACTION **A Rarity in Trinidad** — Students perform Sarasvati Pūjā at the beginning of each academic year. Hindu festivals are celebrated throughout the year. Vedic chanting, yoga, tasa (local traditional drums), music, and dance are also taught at the Vidyalaya. A Jñāna Yajña is conducted each year for the Vidyalaya teachers and parents by Swami Prakashananda. Sanskrit is compulsory from pre-primary grades. An annual Shanti Yatra and Memorial Lecture take place in remembrance of Mahatma Gandhi.

The Chinmaya Education Institutions seem to be treading on an ever-increasing demography.

Yes, but we also have had our ups and downs in numbers.

And Departing, Leave Behind Us ...

> Countless cosmoses come into existence and disappear like bubbles in the ocean (sarga-sthiti-layān yānti budbudānīva vāriṇi).
>
> — Ātma Bodha 8

Some of the experiments started as CVs, after having served society well, ended in time. They enriched the lives of the students who studied the 'Chinmaya way' and everyone associated with them.

2008

91. CV Mandya, Karnataka
92. GMR CV, Shamshabad, Hyderabad, Andhra Pradesh

S. No.	Place of CV	Year of Starting	Served Until
1.	Kurnool, Andhra Pradesh	Nov 1966	Mar 1986
2.	Secunderabad, Andhra Pradesh	Mar 1968	Dec 2011
3.	Adoni, Andhra Pradesh	Mar 1969	Mar 2005
4.	Palakkad, Kerala	June 1974	Mar 1999
5.	Puthenengady, Kottayam, Kerala	June 1978	Mar 2006
6.	Ayyappan Nagar, Trichy, Tamil Nadu	June 1982	Mar 2005
7.	Moolavattam, Kottayam, Kerala	Oct 1983	Mar 2009
8.	Coyalmannam, Palakkad district, Kerala	June 1983	Mar 2009
9.	Nalco, Angul, Odisha	July 1984	Aug 1995
10.	Damanjodi, Koraput, Odisha	July 1984	May 1985
11.	Fertiliser Corporation of India (FCI) Colony, Ramagundam, Andhra Pradesh	Aug 1985	Mar 1996
12.	Hari Har School, Sidhbari	Mar 1989	1998
13.	Nauni Solan, Himachal Pradesh	Mar 1992	Mar 2006
14.	Akola, Maharashtra	July 1994	Mar 2004
15.	NTPC Colony, Ramagundam, Andhra Pradesh	June 1994	May 2006
16.	Pallasena, Palakkad district, Kerala	June 1994	Mar 2009
17.	Karimnagar, Andhra Pradesh	June 1994	May 2006
18.	Deepshika, Odisha	Oct 1995	Mar 2011
19.	Gaya, Bihar	July 1999	Mar 2003

IMPACT The school made a big impact on me. My school's spiritual guide (Ācārya Vivek) was very similar to Gurudev. So we always felt as if Gurudev was around...

Ravi Chandra, Algorithmic Trader at Hedge Fund in New York City, alumni of FCI Colony, CV Ramagundam and frequent winner of the Gītā Chanting competition in school

2009

93. Chinmaya Naada Bindu
94. Chinmaya Community College, Chala, Kannur, Kerala

Mini to Maxi — As Director of CVs of Trivandrum, Śrī A. S. Menon witnessed a spurt of nursery and primary CVs started at different locations in rented premises in and around Trivandrum. Managing the twelve schools became difficult and the rented premises did not suffice for the growing number of students. The 'mini schools' were merged with the bigger ones at Vazhuthacad and Manacaud, and the newly started CVs at Naruvamood, Kattakada, and Kunnumpuram were used to absorb the teachers and students.

Narrated by Śrī Suresh Mohan, Chief Sevak, Thrissur Trust

School education in India is still better, but college education, especially in non-professional colleges, leaves a lot to be desired.

I'll show you a couple of Chinmaya Colleges. You will see the difference.

Parallel Education — Chinmaya Mission College, Thrissur

The city of Thrissur, centered around the ancient and huge Vadakkanath Śivā Temple, is famous for its Elephant Festival and popular medical entrance exam coaching classes.

Gurudev first visited Thrissur for a Jñāna Yajña in 1957. Both the Chinmaya Mission and the Chinmaya Vidyalaya were started in 1979.

Later, an inspired group of retired professors approached Gurudev expressing their wish to serve the Mission. To them he said, "Do something to activate the youngsters through education, so that their energy will be utilized and focused for the benefit of society." Once when Pūjya Gurudev visited a college in Kerala, he noticed that all the windows of the classroom were broken. Upon seeing this, he said: "I am happy to see this. It shows you have energy. My job is to channelize it."

95. CV, Vadavalli, Coimbatore, Tamil Nadu

A Chinmaya College for Girls? — At the time of setting up the college, many co-educational colleges changed to women-only institutions. The management voted for making the Chinmaya College a ladies college. But when Gurudev was approached, he said, "Let me ask all the mothers to give birth only to daughters from now onward; then we will go for the change!" And there ended the matter.

Śrī C. Raveendranathan, Principal, CC Thrissur

Chinmaya Mission College, Thrissur, was born in August 1975. It was affiliated with the University of Calicut, and by 1997 it was deemed to be the most reputed college of Thrissur, imparting computer education as a value-added course. Today the college hosts over 2,000 students and conducts courses for B.C.A., M.B.A., and M.C.A. under School of Distance Education, Bharathiar University; eleventh and twelfth grades under the Kerala State Education Board; and B.Com, B.B.A., and M.Com under Calicut University.

The Chinmaya School of Advanced Studies was started in 2000; it then became the Chinmaya Institute of Management and Technology in 2010. As a Partner Institution of Bharathiar University, it accommodates 900 students enrolled in professional courses. The college is judged as one of the best study centers of Bharathiar University.

The college inculcates the spirit of service through its extracurricular activities. In celebration of its silver jubilee in the year 2000, a free medical eye camp was organized in which 5,000 people were given free medical check-ups and 240 poor people had cataract surgery.

2011

96. MARG CV Tirupati, Andhra Pradesh
97. VGN CV, Avadi, Chennai, Tamil Nadu
98. CV Sri City, Andhra Pradesh
99. Hari Har Chinmaya Vidyalaya, Tamaraipakkam, Chennai

IN ACTION **Hub of Herbs** — The Herbal Garden within the campus is shared by CV and CC and has more than 800 herbal plants, shrubs, and trees. Each day the students are encouraged to see the plants corresponding to their birth stars in Nakshatravan. The garden is also home to rare varieties of herbs like somalatā and brāhmi, besides plants like dasapuśpaṅgal and dasamūlangal (ten basic flowering plants and roots used in āyurvedic medicine).

Launched in 2006, this project is supported by the International Organization for Industrial, Spiritual, and Cultural Advancement (OISCA) and the Government of Kerala. Students donate a herbal plant on their birthdays and cure themselves with the herbal medicines on their weak days!

High Tech, ChinTech — Chinmaya Institute of Technology, Kannur

Kannur in North Kerala is a place of sea and sand, and looms and lore. Gurudev's first Yajña in Kannur was way back in 1959.

High on a hillock, commanding a beautiful view of the Arabian Sea, is the 17.5 acre Chala Chinmaya Educational Campus housing the Kannur 'Best of Three': Chinmaya Vidyalaya, Chinmaya College of Arts and Science, and Chinmaya Institute of Technology (ChinTech).

Water Water Everywhere — When my father, Śrī Makhecha, and Dr. Shenoy first visited the Chala site, they were faced with a dilemma — even as they stood drenched by the monsoon rains — there was not a drop of water to drink. The members of the management invoked Gurudev's grace and struck a perennial water line — and now there is water everywhere — from the heavens and the earth!

Narrated by Manisha Makhecha, CV and CC Kannur alumni

The Morning Ritual — On many occasions, the morning assembly at the CV witnesses two birds circling the school and flying away. Everyone believes that these Garuḍa birds (the vehicle of Lord Viṣṇu) are circumambulating the sacred temple of learning — the Chinmaya Vidyalaya.

ChinTech opened its doors in 2002 as a high tech golden memoir for the Golden Jubilee (2001) of Chinmaya Mission. The institute offers postgraduate courses in Business Administration (M.B.A.) and Computer Applications (M.C.A.). The institute is affiliated with Kannur University and approved by the All India Council for Technical Education (AICTE), New Delhi.

Equipped with a state-of-the-art infrastructure and well-qualified faculty, the Institute has distinguished itself in the higher education arena of Kerala. ChinTech alumni are employed at globally reputed companies such as IBM, Wipro, Accenture, Infosys, and Citibank.

Its vision is to create 'spiritually elevated techno-managers.' They achieve this through a skilled faculty and special Student Empowerment Programs, Leadership Programs, Seminars, and Conferences.

IMPACT The teaching style at ChinTech is really futuristic and gives a spiritual and industrial exposure to the students.

— Alumni Shabeer, M.K.P., Executive, SIT Mobile Services, Kochi

Facilities at ChinTech are at par with premier institutions, but what makes it different is the attitude toward the students. Here the student's growth comes first.

— Alumni Jose Mathew, Senior Engineer, Symphony Services, Bengaluru

The Best Care for the Least Fare — Chinmaya Chetana

Chinmaya Chetana, Rugna Sevika Course under the Chinmaya Seva Trust, Hubli, is a vision of the late Dr. S. S. Gore. It is a high-quality, eight-month-long, low-cost course predominantly for disadvantaged ladies between seventeen and thirty-five. The courses started in November 1998, and so far has trained 812 boys and girls in 23 batches. Chetana imparts quality spiritual and professional education and provides responsible and qualified homecare nurses to society. Most of the students find employment before the training period is over.

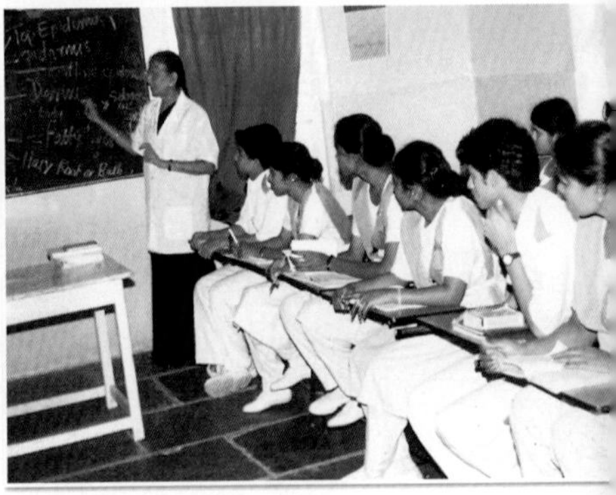

Selfless Seva — We are thankful to Chinmaya Chetana for valuable services provided to my mother Smt. Puribai by the nurse Ms. Basamma. During the period of her stay with us, she has provided utmost care and attention, and has selflessly served my mother. Without her support, my mother wouldn't have recovered so fast. We thank you once more and wish her a great future. Sd/- Mahaveer. B. Shah, January 5, 2012

CVP was given to many schools and colleges besides Chinmaya Institutions, across the country, and outside India. Did some of them adopt it? Is it a copyrighted program?

Good education is the right of all. Our ancient sages taught all knowledge for free. The CVP logo is copyrighted but not the program. Some schools that were serious in running their schools the Chinmaya way are affiliated with the CCMT Education Cell and have become Vision Schools.

Vision School Concept — The overwhelming success and widespread interest in CVP has led to the creation of Vision Schools. These are independently or privately administered schools that recognize and implement CVP as the vision of their school.

No.	Vision Schools	Yr. of Affiliation to CCMTEC
1.	Arya Gurukula, Kalyan, Maharashtra	2006
2.	St. Mary's High School, Kalyan, Maharashtra	2006
3.	Bhavans SL Public School, Amritsar, Punjab	2008
4.	Trinity Academy, Tiruvarur, Tamil Nadu	2009
5.	RISE School, Samayandipuram, Pollachi district, Tamil Nadu	2011
6.	Pushpalatha Educational Centre, Tirunelveli, Tamil Nadu	2012

The Noble Venture — Arya Gurukula, Kalyan

Kalyan, in Thane District, has big industries such as the Century Mills. It is famous for the historic Durgadi Fort, where the wife of the Muslim Sardār, whom Chhatrapati Shivaji had conquered in battle, tied a rākhī to Shivaji.

A patriotic entrepreneur (Bharat Mallik) married a gem (Neelam) of a person. He loved Gurudev right from his childhood (attending Yajñas with his father) and throughout his youth (as an active Chinmaya Yuva Kendra member). Later, as a father, he realized that he needed to give his only pampered son the 'Chinmaya' exposure, so admitted him into CIRS. During the orientation for new parents they were introduced to CVP, which sowed the seed of a noble (ārya) school based on Indian culture (gurukula).

Bharat built a building and Neelam got a school with a vision. The Arya Gurukula was inaugurated by Guruji in June 2006, and it went on to become the first Vision School affiliated with the CCMT Education Cell. Later, St. Mary's (their already functioning school) also became a Vision School.

Bharat, the President, and Neelam, the Principal, are both personally involved with the schools and with CM Thane, keeping the vision alive. With constant inspiration from the Mission's Ācāryās, including Swamini Vimalananda and especially Swamini Ujjwalananda, this is a Vision School with a difference.

IN ACTION **Back to School** — The teachers had a heart-to-heart sharing of their student life experiences and good practices followed in their schools. This formal trip-down-memory-lane session called 'kyun ki teacher bhi kabhi student thi' proved effective in making them sensitive to students and creating a bond, while giving them new ideas for learning and teaching.

Any future plans?

In India, it is most difficult to get a good teacher and even more difficult to get a good principal. With so many institutions, we are constantly in search of them. Moreover, we then have to train them to become 'Chinmaya' teachers. So in the future we will have our own Training Center.

A College for the Vidyalayas — Chinmaya Institute for Excellence in Education (CIEE)

Catering to the future need to supply this vast network of Chinmaya Vidyalayas and Colleges with dedicated 'Chinmaya' teachers, CCMTEC proposes to start CIEE to mark the Birth Centenary of the great educational visionary — Gurudev. A site of five-and-a-half acres has been designated in Coimbatore for the institution that will be administered by CCMTEC.

CIEE will offer 'vision orientation' and academic refresher courses for new and existing CV and CC teachers. It will also offer professional educational courses, including B.Ed, M.Ed., and Ph.D. in Education, and also act as an Education Research Center.

Future teachers will be given the opportunity to complete a degree in education that encompasses CVP. Also, short courses will be offered on the subtle art of teaching values through the curriculum.

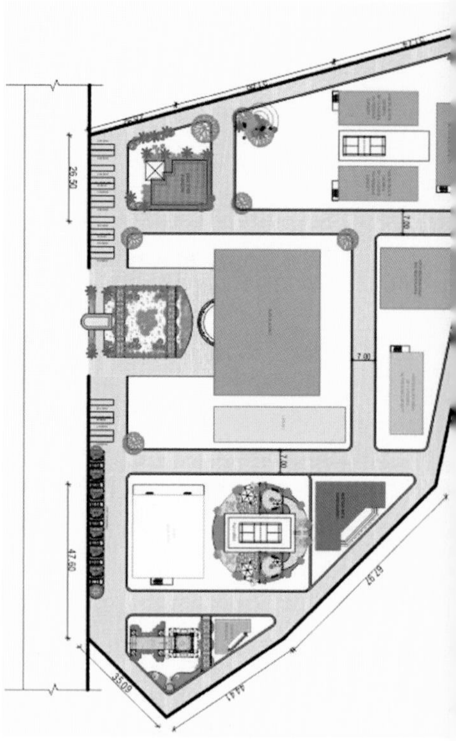

▲ PROPOSED MASTER PLAN OF CIEE

That is good planning — and what a diverse range of Education Institutions! I now see how CVP and its implementation is the common thread that makes all of them a beautiful garland offered as worship to Mother India and Indian Culture.

That's a good analogy! The CCMT Education Cell strengthens this thread and further beautifies the flowers that constitute the garland. It's role is pivotal in keeping the offering ever fresh and fragrant.

Could I attend one of the training seminars conducted by the Cell?

Sure. You will love to attend the next one as it is on dance. It is called Nritya Sangam and is in CIRS. I am invited to inaugurate it. So we will meet again. Don't forget to get your ghuṇgrūs. Hari Om!

IV

The Unifying Link — CCMT Education Cell

In me is everything strung like the thread in a necklace of beads or a garland of flowers (mayi sarvam idam protaṁ sūtre maṇigaṇā iva).

— Gītā 7.7

An organization is only as strong as its weakest link — where it is most likely to break. The skill of a multi-institutional organization lies in its ability to bring out the beauty and uniqueness of each institution and yet hold them together with a common bond and make them a part of the whole, much like the flowers in a garland.

Hari Om! Welcome to CIRS.

Hari Om! This place is truly beautiful. As we journeyed toward this place, I felt the silent pull of the mighty mountain beckoning me onto its green lap.

I saw the sign of CCMT Education Cell just before the CIRS gates. Is that not the body that links all the Chinmaya Education Institutions? Tell me more about it.

Solid Link

During the life of every organization, there comes a stage when some consolidation becomes necessary. Necessary, because we may otherwise forget our goals and pursue narrow, parochial interests.

Chinmayananda.

To the management and principals of all Chinmaya Vidyalayas, 2.1.1985

As Gurudev traversed the country, more and more Chinmaya Mission (CM) Centers and philanthropic individuals were inspired to start Chinmaya Vidyalayas (CVs) and Chinmaya Colleges (CCs). A need was felt to centralize and coordinate the management of these institutions. Thus spawned the creation of an Executive Education Office, which was managed in its formative years (1988-1998) by Dr. Shakuntala Varma (retired Principal, Women's College, Gwalior, who later became Swamini Samvidananda).

One Too Many — Ultimately I left my government job in September 1988 and proceeded to Sidhbari. While I was prostrating, Gurudev asked me whether I had come to him finally. As soon as I said 'yes,' he announced, "Good. You have left one college, now I am giving you fifty-six schools!"

Swamini Samvidananda, Advisor to EC

Remembering with Gratitude ... Some of the devotees who centrally managed the Vidyalayas in the early years as Directors or Administrators were Śrī K. N. P. Nair, Dr. Vajreshwari, Śrī R. V. Thampi, Śrī A. S. Menon, and Smt. Sanku.

Swamini Samvidananda headed the Executive Education Office in Mumbai, providing an essential link between the Mission and the CEIs.

The First Inspection — At Mumbai, Gurudev explained in detail his vision of education, the malady our schools were suffering from, and the remedy to make them self-supporting. He then asked me to inspect the schools. I sent my first inspection report to him in April 1989. He wrote back to me promptly, "Just now finished reading your report, which is exhaustive and to the point. I liked your precise evaluation ..."

Swamini Samvidananda

In 1994, the Executive Education Office at Central Chinmaya Mission Trust in Mumbai was closed down and reconstituted as CCMT Education Cell in January 1996 as the governing body of the Chinmaya Education Movement (CEM).

From January 1996 to August 2010, Prof. P. Shivram Iyer (ex-Principal Victoria College, Palakkad, and CV Pallavur), with the guidance of Swamini Vimalananda, efficiently managed all the Cell activities as the Administrator-Academics.

Taking the baton from Prof. Iyer, Smt. Ramani Thyagarajan, a very able administrator and academician, presently manages the ever-growing role of the Education Cell, with the guidance of Swamini Vimalananda.

The seeds sown in me by my father were nourished and nurtured by Gurudev, his teachings, and his Mission. I now have an opportunity to serve Gurudev and evolve as a person. I feel blessed that I am contributing to the CEM in my own small way.

Smt. Ramani Thyagarajan

The CCMT Education Cell was created to monitor, integrate, streamline, upgrade, standardize, and facilitate the efficient and effective maintenance and growth of all CEIs.

You mean just two ladies do the entire job of governing all the CEIs?

Do you doubt woman power? There is also a team with other members that accomplishes this.

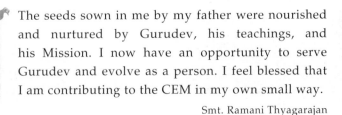

CCMT Education Cell Team

From teamwork and organization are born efficiency, capability, and lasting progress (saṅgho dadāti sāmarthyaṁ, samarthyāt sarva-yogyatā, yogyatvād yaḥ samutkarṣo, nirapayaḥ sa sarvathā).

— Saṅgha Gītā 32

▲ EDUCATION CELL MEMBERS, 2012

Swami Tejomayananda, as the Head of Chinmaya Mission, is Chairman of EC. The overall management is handled by the Administrator-Education, guided by Swamini Vimalananda. The other members are a competent, committed group from across the country, including Ācāryas and Mission members, from the academic and corporate world. Prominent members, such as Dr. Chhaya, Director (founder of National Navodaya School Scheme), have been involved since its inception; and others like Dr. Geervani, Executive Director (former Vice Chancellor, Tirupati Women's University), and Smt. Shanti Krishnamurthy (Principal, CIRS) play an active role in the Cell's multifarious activities.

CCMTEC

विद्या फलं स्यात् असतो निवृत्तिः

True Knowledge removes all that is false in our life

Education Cell Logo: It signifies that under the Cell's guidance and care, all CEIs are nourished by CVP and develop into schools with a difference.

Education Cell Motto: vidyā phalam syāt asato nivṛttiḥ

It means 'True knowledge removes all that is false in our lives.'

Good education gives a noble vision and strong character, which leave no room for false notions and immoral conduct.

Guruji, the head and the heart of the Education Cell, is also a great visionary, completely in tune with Gurudev's vision.

Chinmaya śikṣā darśaṇam — Chinmaya Vision of Education

जीविकामात्रमेतद्वै नास्ति विद्या-प्रयोजनम् ।सर्वाङ्गीणविकासो हि विद्ययाऽपेक्ष्यते बुधैः ॥ १ ॥
काले त्वाधुनिके दृष्टा विद्या मुख्या हि वृत्तिदा। लौकिकं बुद्धिचातुर्यं केवलं बहुमन्यते ॥ २ ॥
यया भवेन्न संस्कारश्छात्राणां शिक्षया शुभः ।निष्फला खलु सा शिक्षा श्रम एव हि केवलम् ॥ ३ ॥
उपाधिभिर्युताश्छात्रा विश्वविद्यालयस्य हि ।परिभ्रमन्तो दृश्यन्ते जीविकार्थमितस्ततः ॥ ४ ॥
साहसं न च सामर्थ्यं स्वातन्त्र्यं स्वावलम्बनम् ।निर्माणाय भविष्यस्य दूरदृष्टिर्न विद्यते ॥ ५ ॥
विना जीवनदृष्टिं हि विना सेवाव्रतं तथा ।विद्याऽपूर्णा भवेत्कर्म विना ब्रह्मार्पणं यथा ॥ ६ ॥
कटिबध्दा वयं चात्र लक्ष्यं साधयितुं वरम् ।शिक्षायास्त्रिविधं यद्वै ज्ञानं सेवा च कौशलम् ॥ ७ ॥

Merely earning one's livelihood is not the purpose of education. Wise men seek all-round education.

In modern times, education is mainly employment-oriented, and worldly smartness alone is given importance.

That education is indeed fruitless and a mere labor which does not inculcate noble virtues in students.

Equipped with university degrees, young people are seen wandering here and there seeking employment.

They lack virtues like courage, efficiency, independence, self-reliance and foresight that are necessary for making their future.

Without a vision of life and a spirit of service, education is incomplete, like work that is not dedicated to God.

We are determined to achieve the threefold noble goal of education, namely: vision, spirit of service, and efficiency.

— Swami Tejomayananda

Very inspiring. Your Vidyalaya is a CBSE affiliated school; CIRS is an IB school. What about others?

Accreditation and Affiliations

CBSE LOGO

BHARTIYAR UNIVERSITY

IB LOGO

SSLC LOGO TAMIL NADU

MG UNIVERSITY

SSLC LOGO KARNATAKA

Let me take you to Chinmaya Gardens. It has a very restful old-time gurukula look and a beautiful Gaṇeśa Temple. You can then see firsthand what the Education Cell does from its headquarters at the ashram.

What does the CCMT Education Cell do?

- **Common Policy**: Makes common and sound policy decisions for the benefit of all the Vidyalayas and Colleges.
- **Produces Resource Material on CVP** like manuals and newsletters sharing best practices.
- **Assessment and Guidance** of Academic, Vision, and Administration aspects for all Chinmaya Education Institutions.
- **Training**: Provides timely and regular training on all aspects of holistic education for the efficient running of the Vidyalayas and Colleges, to the top management, principals, teachers, and the administrative staff.
- **Scholarships**: Offers scholarships and education materials to needy students and schools.
- **Awards**: Recognizes and encourages excellence in management, principals, staff, and students through awards.
- **Student Meets/Camps**: Forges a close Chinmaya family bond through organizing of camps and All Chinmaya Vidyalaya events.
- **Unifying Link**: The most important role is that of a unifying link. It unites all as one whole, and integrates all the institutions with the Chinmaya Mission. It forges effective communication, interaction, and resource sharing among all the institutions under its umbrella, thereby fostering a stronger, cohesive Chinmaya Family spirit.

These days in India a school is judged not so much because of its management or systems it follows, as much as the results it produces. The Vidyalayas and Colleges do get brilliant academic results.

Success is not final. Failure is not fatal. It is the courage to continue that counts. Winston Churchill

CHINMAYA VIDYALAYAS

A Comparative Statement of the Public Exam Results of Class X — 2012 (CBSE)

Schools	ALAPPUZHA	BOKARO	CHENGANNUR	CHENNAI ANNA NAGAR	CHENNAI TAYLORS ROAD	CHENNAI VIRUGAMBAKKAM	COCHIN VADUTHALA	COIMBATORE CIRS	HUBLI (MAYURI ESTATE)	HYDERABAD	JAMSHEDPUR (TELCO)	JAMSHEDPUR (BISTUPUR)	KALLADATHUR	KANHANGAD	KANNAMALLY	KANNUR	KASARAGOD
	(1)	(2)	(3)	(4)	(5)	(6)	(7)	(8)	(9)	(10)	(11)	(12)	(13)	(14)	(15)	(16)	(17)
No. of students appeared and pass %	53/53 100	163/163 100	42/42 100	150/150 100	150/150 100	182/182 100	142/142 100	73/73 100	37/37 100	136/136 100	117/117 100	89/90 100	22/22 100	63/63 100	47/47 100	208/208 100	121/121 100

Schools	KOLLAM	KOLLENGODE	KOTTAYAM THAZHETHANGADI	MANJERI	NAGAPATTINAM	NEW DELHI	PALLAVUR	PAYYANUR	TALIPARAMBA	TARAPUR	TATTAMANGALAM	THERUBALI	TRIPUNITHURA	THRISSUR	THRISSUR	TRIVANDRUM ATTUKAL	TRIVANDRUM NARUVAMOOD	UNCHAHAR
	(18)	(19)	(20)	(21)	(22)	(23)	(24)	(25)	(26)	(27)	(28)	(29)	(30)	(31)	(32)	(33)	(34)	(35)
No. of students appeared and pass %	52/52 100	50/50 100	60/60 100	15/15 100	50/50 100	92/92 100	40/40 100	75/75 100	59/59 100	76/76 100	111/111 100	76/76 100	18/18 100	137/137 100	149/149 100	125/125 100	53/53 100	83/83 100

Very impressive results. So tell me more about the work of the Cell.

Common Policy

In taking some strict steps, our aim is to instill some degree of discipline. I have instructed CCMT to enforce discipline with restraint and without hurting my devotees. I am sure you will comply with the above requirements happily and promptly, in the interests of the Great Family to which we all belong.

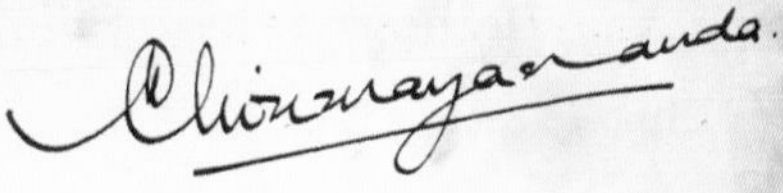

To the management of Vidyalayaș on February 1, 1985

The Education Cell formulates policies on common concerns, and for specific cases, gives instructions and guidance to all the institutions. It collates information and dispenses it to concerned parties, grants permission for starting new schools, and makes decisions on management issues.

The Education Cell also publishes resource material for disseminating its policies and effective communicate of CVP. Look at this book. It explains why we do pradakṣiṇā and namaskāra. Most Indians do these without understanding.

CCMT Education Cell Resource Material

> Inconceivable is the power of words (śabda śakter-acintyatvāt). The written and spoken words make us understand everything. Therefore, worship speech (vāgevaitat sarvaṁ vijñāpayati, vācam upāsva iti).
>
> — Sadācāra 18, Chāndogya Upaniṣad 7.2.1

Right from its inception, the Cell developed a wide range of resource material to inspire and guide the management and the staff on the implementation of CVP and running of the CEIs. Noteworthy among them are the *CVP Manual*, *SWAD* (School With A Difference), *Chinmaya Drishti* a biannual newsletter which shares the best practices of the CEIs, *Garden of Life* (the Value Education series with the highest sales in India for the past fifteen years), and *In Indian Culture — Why do we...* (the publication of Chinmaya Mission with the highest sales, which has sold over half a million copies).

Source the Resource
Administrator Education, CCMT Education Cell,
Nallurvayal (PO), Siruvani Road, Coimbatore 641114
Tel: 0422-2615663/ 04222613495
Email: ccmtec@gmail.com
Website: www.ccmtec.chinmayamission.com

Since the Vidyalayas and Colleges are all over India, how does the Cell keep track of what is happening?

The CEIs send regular annual consolidated reports and biennial CVP implementation reports. Also, a special team of trained experts assesses and guides the working of these institutions.

Assessment and Guidance

> A good teacher costs a lot. A bad teacher costs a lot more.
>
> Swamini Vimalananda

Defective products can be removed from the market; poorly educated people cannot. A faulty manufacturing unit gets closed, but an inadequate school does not; it keeps on producing poorly educated people.

The Cell conducts academic, administration, and vision assessment of each Vidyalaya on a regular basis. The purpose is to:

1. Provide critical assessment and guidance to the Vidyalaya.
2. Evaluate the standards, progress, and potential of the Vidyalaya.
3. Identify the weakest link and suggest ways of strengthening it.
4. Evaluate the position of the Vidyalaya with respect to other Vidyalayas.

The Vidyalayas are encouraged to do a self-assessment each year as per the guidance given. Assessors guide Vidyalayas to take up 360-degree feedback. Vidyalayas are also encouraged to do an external assessment from time to time. Some Vidyalayas get accreditation of associations like the International Organization for Standardization (ISO).

Glow and Grow in the Light of CVP — The light of Pūjya Gurudev's vision on education has been lit in most CEIs. The initial euphoria is over. Now, to keep it glowing brightly, it will need the fuel of consistent effort by the management, principal, and staff; innovations in implementation; transformations in thinking; and continuous inspiration and alertness to avoid complacency, name-sake efforts, and lethargy. Let not the light die away lest it needs to be lit every time. Let the vision not be laminated, but lived. Let our staff shine and students outshine in its glow.

Swamini Vimalananda, Director–CVP; addressing a CV teachers seminar

Gurudev believed that proficiency must get translated into efficiency, for which regular training is a must.

This ongoing seminar is really exciting. Do such events happen often?

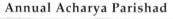

CCMT Education Cell — Workshops and Seminars

The most challenging task as the head of the Chinmaya Mission is to communicate the vision of Gurudev and the Chinmaya Mission to all the devotees and disciples working in the field. Swami Tejomayananda

Annual Acharya Parishad

For the last two weeks, I've been planning an All-India Chinmaya Vidyalaya Teachers Orientation Course for five or ten days at Bombay. Even if we expect (or accept) two or three teachers from every one of our schools, we will have in our hand about a hundred delegates.

I see it clearly—it will create a glorious tradition for the Vidyalayas. Please consult your executive committee and let me know your reaction to this suggestion of a summer Acharya Parishad yearly, once to be held either at Bombay or at Sidhbari or some other conducive location. Address your reaction to me c/o Education Cell, Sandeepany, Powai, Bombay 400 072.

Chinmayananda

To K. K. Rajan, March 14, 1983

The CCMT Education Cell conducts various workshops and seminars to:

- Communicate the Chinmaya Vision Programme to all
- Inspire all, so that they work with dedication and enthusiasm
- Train all, so that they are knowledgeable and efficient in what they do

Many of these are conducted at CIRS and Chinmaya Gardens at Coimbatore and more recently at Chinmaya Vibhooti near Pune.

Swamini Vimalananda, Director of CVP, has conducted more than 400 talks across the country on the various aspects of education to different schools and colleges. Vision-Inspiration-Training (VIT) is a continuous need that is satisfied through the Vidyalaya Improvement Programmes (VIP).

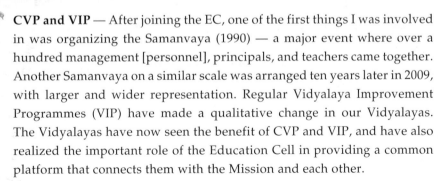

CVP and VIP — After joining the EC, one of the first things I was involved in was organizing the Samanvaya (1990) — a major event where over a hundred management [personnel], principals, and teachers came together. Another Samanvaya on a similar scale was arranged ten years later in 2009, with larger and wider representation. Regular Vidyalaya Improvement Programmes (VIP) have made a qualitative change in our Vidyalayas. The Vidyalayas have now seen the benefit of CVP and VIP, and have also realized the important role of the Education Cell in providing a common platform that connects them with the Mission and each other.

Prof. Sivaram Iyer

Training programs initiated and guided by Gurudev paved the way for all future programs.

A Reorientation Course for Teachers of Chinmaya Vidyalaya at Sidhbari, Himachal, March 15, 1983. Below is outlined the scope of the sessions:

1. Values and their role in Human Development: Theoretical input with examples of what values are, how they are defined, and how they affect human development their effects on thoughts, speech, and behavior.

2. Role of the teachers: Their contribution in imparting and inculcating social and human values as seen in a wider context.

3. Inculcating patriotism: The need for patriotism and national integration and what teachers can do to encourage patriotic thoughts in students.

4. Great men of India: Biographies of great men of India (drawn from various fields of activity, such as social reformers, religious leaders, statesmen, writers, and thinkers) to illustrate the process of inspired activity and leadership in any field.

5. Important festivals: Reinforcing human values through the correct understanding of the significance of festivals, with examples.

6. Stories and parables: Their use in imparting values. Stories from Hitopadesa, Panchatantra, Jataka series, Upaniṣads, the great epics, and the biographies of great souls such as Prophet Mohammed, Guru Nanak, Christ, Sri Ramakrishna, and Ramana Maharshi.

7. Our culture and heritage: An overview of Indian culture and heritage with emphasis on synthesis (unity in diversity), continuity and constant development and evolution (examples from Literature, Architecture, Music, and Dance).

8. Rituals: Reinforcing of human values through the correct understanding and significance of rituals, with examples.

9. Behavioral Science: Role of behavioral sciences in the process of education with reference to the relationship among students, teachers, and parents (expectations, stroking/encouragement, and ego states).

10. Techniques of teaching values: An overview of the various teaching techniques available and their correct use. Brief discussion with demonstrations and creative individual and group activities of storytelling, singing, social service, dramatization, projects, cultural programs, exhibitions, visits, pictures, slide shows, nature walks, etc.

Every day, delegates write notes on what has been discussed and submit them for review, failing which they will not enter the dining hall.

Chinmayananda

To Śrī S. M. Khorana, October 28, 1982

With such diligent reflection, I am sure none of the teachers ever forgot Gurudev's Seminar. I am unlikely to forget this one that I am attending.

There have been many such unforgettable and unique seminars.

Workshops/Seminars by CCMT-Education Cell for Chinmaya Education Institutions (CEI)

First All India Vidya Samanvaya — Seminar of the top Management of CEI	1990
ELP – Education Leadership Program-I	2000
ELP – Education Leadership Program–II	2001
Eureka: The Joy of Discovery — First All Chinmaya Vidyalaya Camp for students	2001
Vidya Vikas — Empowering the Principle-centered Principals	2002
Vidya Prathishta — Empowerment Seminar for Motivated Management	2003
Parivartan — Seminar for Initiating the Leaders of Change (Principals)	2004
Parivardhan — Seminar for Empowering Catalysts of Change (Teachers)	2004
Chinmaya Shubha Saahas — Adventure Camps for students of CVs	2005-2012
Chinmaya Parichaya — Orientation Programs for CV Teachers	2006-2007
Chinmaya Kaarya Kosha — Seminar for Office Procedures & Financial Management	2006
Kala Sangam — Seminar of Visual Art Education	2008
Swara Sangam — Seminar on Music Education	2008
Krida Sangam — Seminar on Physical Education	2009
Parivartan — Seminar for Initiating the Leaders of Change	2009
Chinmaya Khel Mela — First All CV Athletic Meet	2010
Seva Sangam — Seminar on the Role of Sevā in CEI	2010
Chinmaya Netritva — Workshop on Quality Leadership	2011-2012
Nritya Sangam — Seminar on Dance Education	2011
Amulya Shiksha — Seminar on Value Education	2011
Mano Dharma — Seminar on Behavioral and Career Counseling	2012

All India Vidya Samanvaya — Seminar of the Top Management Samanvaya means to join together, solve, resolve, and dissolve through introspecting, meeting, discussing, deliberating, planning, and committing. This goal was fully achieved at both the Chinmaya Vidya Samanvaya Seminars on Education Management.

The first seminar organized by the Education Cell was held at CIRS from December 10–12, 1999. It was attended by 101 principals and correspondents from fifty-three Chinmaya Vidyalayas and four Chinmaya Colleges.

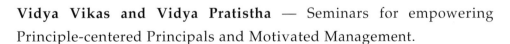

▲ FACULTY AND PARTICIPANTS OF CHINMAYA VIDYA SAMANVAYA, 1999

The Second Is the First — The second Samanvaya seminar held at Chinmaya Vibhooti from May 12–16, 2009, was the first training program held in Sudharma, the newly inaugurated state-of-the-art auditorium.

Vidya Vikas and Vidya Pratistha — Seminars for empowering Principle-centered Principals and Motivated Management.

Pratishtha means prestige, to be well-established and well-rooted. Vikas or growth is inevitable. It is desirable that growth periods are interspersed by periods of consolidation and fortification.

Parivartan and Parivardhan — Seminars for Initiating the Leaders of Change and Empowering the Catalysts of Change

Change is the very nature of the world. Change brings forth growth (as it happens in the case of population) or decay (as we see in values). Some changes occur without our awareness and yet others can be consciously brought about. Training and education are meant to bring about a meaningful, creative, and sensitive change, from within to without. A catalyst is a substance that triggers change without itself changing. Every institution needs a core group, which is deeply rooted in its vision and culture, and can inspire a change in others without changing its core values.

Chinmaya Parichaya — Becoming a 'Chinmaya Teacher'

Parichaya is to acquaint, familiarize oneself with, and become intimate with someone. 'Chinmaya Parichaya' is a seminar for the new teachers of

the Chinmaya Education Institutions to orient them as 'Chinmaya teachers.'

Kala Sangam — Seminar on Visual Art Education in CEIs

Kala Sangam (May 10–13, 2008) was a unique orientation seminar of Visual Art Education, which aimed at understanding the role of visual art in the overall development of a student, as well as the role of a visual arts department and education in schools.

The CCMT Education Cell provided the canvas; CIRS, Coimbatore, supplied the art material; the excellent resource team added creativity and beauty; the 150 principals, art teachers, and other teachers from Chinmaya Vidyalayas gave it color and form; the mountains framed the picture; Gurudev's vision enlivened and enlightened it; and God showered His grace on it, making the event a thundering (literally) success!

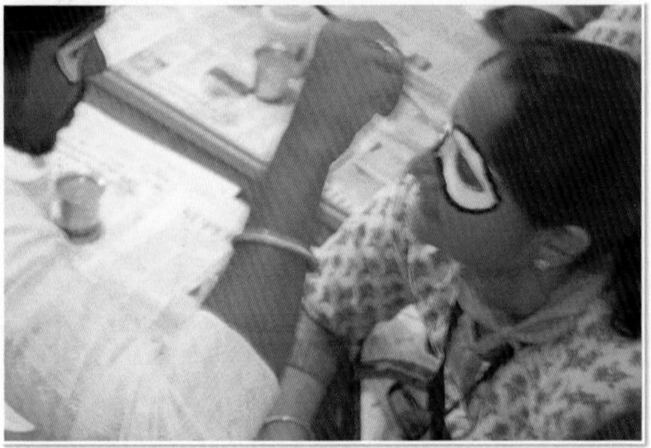

Swara Sangam — Seminar on Music Education

It is the first program that fulfills the very purpose for which Chinmaya Vibhooti was conceived.
Swami Tejomayananda

This 'svara saṁvāda' from December 18–21, 2008, explored the role of music in the overall development of the child and of music education in schools. Guruji was the unchanging divine presence, like the primal musical note 'ṣaḍaja–sā.' The 'vādi svaras' (dominant notes) were the ninety participants with a stalwart faculty that included Kala Ramnath (violin), Dr. Karaikudi Subramanian (vīṇā), Shubhendra Rao (sitar), Saskia Rao de Haas (cello), and Dr. Vikas Kashalkar (vocal). The 'saṁvādi and anuvādi svaras' (accompanying and supporting notes) were the CCMT Education Cell, who conceived and composed the melody, supported by volunteers. The 'mīṇḍa,' 'āndolan,' 'kheñca,' and 'gamaka' (nuances in music) were provided by the performances of the Ācāryas, participants, volunteers, faculty, and the Thane Chinmaya Swaranjali. The beauty of the melody was explored through topics that included Swara to Ishwara, Changing Definition of Music, Music Appreciation, Music Curriculum, Music Careers, and Universals in Music. Nature provided the rhythm with the mountains encoring Swara Sangam as a resounding success.

Seva Sangam — Seminar on the Role of Sevā in CEIs

Its aim was to inculcate the spirit of service (sevā) in students, to make it an integral part of the Vidyalaya and College culture, and to understand and appreciate the role of sevā in the overall development of students.

I have learned a lot about sevā at Seva Sangam and am too overwhelmed to express what I feel.

Padmashree Dr. Kshama Metre, National Director CORD,
Winner 2012, Guardian International Development Achievement Award

The Chinmaya **Bal/Yuva Sevak Certificate (CBSC) and Chinmaya Seva Award (CSA)** are meant to turn the theory of sevā and its benefits into the experience of thousands of students of CEIs.

The CBSE participating students complete a total of 120 hours of sevā over a two-year period by contributing in one or more of the following seven categories: sevā of the physically challenged, with a sevā organization, in society, for a universal cause, in cash/kind, at home, in the Vidyalaya.

Chinmaya Seva Award encourages teachers of Chinmaya Vidyalayas to nurture generations of young men and women who serve society and the nation.

Nritya Sangam — Seminar of Dance Education

Chinmaya Value Educators on the Role of Value Education (in Amulya Shiksha)

Transformation through values

Blossoming of personality

Confidence to face life

Moulds a child

Manifests talents and inner potential

Makes education holistic

Removes baser vasanas

Helps understand what is right and wrong

Imparts a vision of life

Person with values is respected and respects all

Teaches love of self and society

Complements and completes academic education

Makes life meaningful and purposeful and promotes man-making

Promotes thinking about man, nature, and God

Empowers (whereas academic education is only a tool of employment)

Teaches how to think and act

Adds fragrance, freshness, and new life to a person

Education without values is like a flower without fragrance, a ship without a navigator, a building without a foundation, and a body without a backbone.

AMULYA SHIKSHA FACULTY AND PARTICIPANTS ▼

Amulya Shiksha — Seminar on Value Education

This seminar was meant to understand the role of value education to explore the scope of value education, and to train value educators. All participants realized that the USP of the CVs is values and culture.

I have seen a school where the rich and the poor study together.

That is good. Gurudev once said, "Many will throw money over the wall for the poor but few will break the wall." The Vidyalayas and the Cell try to break this wall by the scholarships they offer.

Scholarships and Chinmaya Vidya Nidhi

> Give a man a fish and you keep him full for a few hours. Teach him how to fish and you keep him and his family full for a lifetime.
>
> Chinese Proverb

The CCMT Education Cell Scholarships (CECS) are awarded to students who are academically brilliant, strong in values, and gifted in various fields, but have financial constraints. Each Vidyalaya and College nominates two worthy students. Scholarships cover school fees, uniforms, books, stationery, and transport expenses. Their renewal is based on an annual review of student records. The scholarships are sponsored by generous donors and well-wishers of the cause of 'education for all.'

"Were it not for the scholarship which I've been receiving for the past four years, I and my two younger sisters would have to study in a Government School," says Divyalakshmi, the 2012 Grade X topper with 98 % aggregate and a centum in Math as well as Science, and 99 in Social Studies. She has studied in CV Coimbatore from kindergarten. "Gurudev is my inspiration. His words 'Work without sincerity and prayer without faith are like artificial flowers without fragrance,' have inspired me to study with sincerity and faith. I really want to become a surgeon," she adds, as she describes her school as the best thing that happened to her and her family.

"My father is a retired government servant and my mother a housewife. My education was most important to them. I have seen them struggling to make both ends meet. Then I was chosen for the Education Cell scholarship. It motivated me to study hard and I felt proud that I was sharing the responsibilities of my parents. When I become an earning member, I will surely contribute to my Chinmaya family."

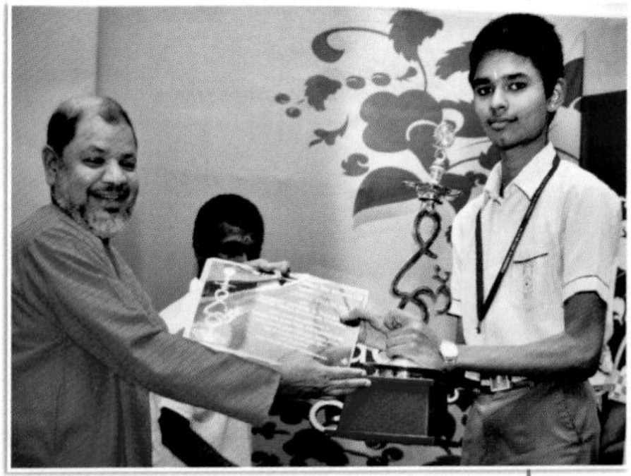

Madhav Shankar R Warrier, who studied in CV Kunnupuram, Kerala, has won the Balashree Award for Creative Arts; Vidyalaya topper in Grade XII, Chinmaya Gaurav Award winner 2012

Chinmaya Vidya Nidhi — The CCMT Education Cell accepts monetary and in-kind donations to provide educational infrastructure and learning aids to Vidyalayas and Colleges.

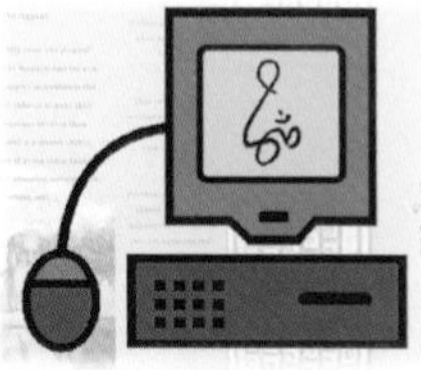

VIDYA NIDHI

What a beautiful trophy! It does not just sit in the principal's office but can also be lit!

Chinmaya Gaurav Award has the unique signature Om of Gurudev molded into a beautiful lamp. It signifies the grace of God (Om) and the effort of the awardee blessed by Gurudev, which lights the lamp of knowledge and brings glory in his or her life.

Chinmaya Education Awards

SUCCESS IS NOT IN THE TROPHY WON BUT IN THE RACE RUN.

| SWAMI CHINMAYANANDA |

The CCMT Education Cell instituted Chinmaya Education Awards to recognize all those who contribute to building schools with a difference. The awards encourage them to maintain and further their good work and inspire them to become role models.

The Chinmaya Vision Award is for the Vidyalayas that best implement CVP; the Chinmaya Gaurav Award is for students, teachers, and principals. Started in 2001 and presented by Guruji himself, the awards are a means to recognize schools, individuals, and their families, and encourage more stars to shine in the national and international space.

National Pride — The Annual National Balashree Awards for children are given for excellence in various fields by the National Bal Bhavan, Government of India, New Delhi. It is equivalent to the Padmashree Award and is presented by the President of India. Many Chinmaya Vidyalaya students have been recipients of this award.

GOPIKA OF CV VAZHUTHACAUD RECEIVING BALASHREE AWARD ▶

IMPACT **What Matters Most to the Chinmaya Gaurav Awardee**

A model student, Parvathy S., Chinmaya Gaurav Awardee in 2011, CV Thrissur, received the 'Gems of Seed Award' for her tireless enthusiasm, dedication, and hard work in planting hundreds of saplings on the grounds of an engineering college close to her Vidyalaya in Thrissur. She also made and distributed hundreds of paper bags made from waste paper.

She won the National Talent Search Examination Scholarship in 2010 and has won the Balashree Award for her creative scientific innovation. She hopes to forge a career as a scientist or a social activist. Parvathy says, "I am a shy person who likes to remain in the background, but doing something for the benefit of society really matters to me. So I will take the lead in time."

I see the teachers from different Vidyalayas really enjoying themselves and bonding at the seminar. Do students come together in the same way?

Yes. I remember the wonderful time I had when my school friends, and I attended the Eureka Camp, where more than 350 students from more than thirty-five Vidyalayas came together.

Student Meets and Camps

> A family that prays together and plays together stays together.
>
> Al Scalpone

The Education Cell creates opportunities for at least some of the 80,000 students studying in the Vidyalayas to come together, not just virtually (on Facebook), but actually in camps. Such camps provide learning with fun and fun with learning.

- Eureka: The Joy of Discovery — First All Chinmaya Vidyalaya Camp for students
- Chinmaya Shubha Saahas — Adventure Camps for students of Chinmaya Vidyalayas

'Dussāhasa' is to be foolhardy, rash, and impulsive. In Sanskrit, 'sāhasa' means to be adventurous, brave, and spontaneous. But 'shubha saahas' means to be adventurous, not for the thrill of it, but to face challenges bravely, to be fearless of the unknown, to walk the untrodden path with courage while remaining determined to overcome weaknesses.

Since 2005, the Education Cell organizes annual summer adventure camps for Chinmaya Vidyalaya students at Chinmaya Gardens, Coimbatore, or in the Himalayas to foster integrated development of body, mind, and spirit, equipping children

to face challenges in life. Professionals (ex-army officers and mountaineers) guide students in air, water, and ground sports, and in team games and adventure courses.

Chinmaya Khel Mela — The First All Chinmaya Vidyalaya Athletic Meet

Commonwealth Gold Medalist Shiny Wilson graced the scintillating opening ceremony. It was a treat to see 800 children marching with the Vidyalaya flags held high. All the three days were packed with sixty athletic, thirty-two aquatic, and eight gymnastic events. The CV Ernakulam was the overall champion and it will host the next Chinmaya Khel Mela in 2014. Pūjya Guruji graced the entire mega-event.

Chinmaya Khel Milan — Annual All Chinmaya Vidyalaya Tournaments

> In the game of life, everyone can be a winner, even as we compete with each other.
>
> Swami Tejomayananda

Hosted by different Chinmaya Vidyalayas under the guidance of the Cell, these tournaments are organized to strengthen the family bond and encourage excellence in sports. CV Kannur hosted the Tennis Tournament in November 2010; CV Chennai hosted the Basketball Tournament in November 2011, and CV Bokaro hosted the Volleyball tournament in November 2012.

Kargil to Kannur — In 2006 – 2007, CV Kannur adopted ten children to give them a safe haven and education away from the gunshots of the Kargil war. They blossomed into young achievers under the care of the teachers and love of fellow students. Jigmat and Gulam are Kannur District Tennis Champions in under-16 and under-19 categories respectively.

PRIZE WINNING TEAM (INCLUDING KARGIL CHILDREN), CV KANNUR

I really see the unifying link that the Education Cell provides. That is quite a task. Thank you for the wonderful time I had at the Seminar. What is inspiring is that the brilliant faculty members serve the cause of education and Chinmaya Mission free of charge!

The Chinmaya ripple-effect expands in ever-growing circles, touching the lives of millions. Such dynamic goodness cannot but influence all.

A brand name is not built in a short time. It takes decades to do so. But once it takes root a brand knows no borders. However, a fad comes into being overnight and disappears in no time. A leader in a category is most likely to become a brand name. The brand owns a word in the mind of the public, and the crucial ingredient in the success of a brand is its claim to authenticity.

Based on 22 Immutable Laws of Branding by Al Ries and Laura Ries

To be branded as good or the best feels great. To be branded with the best is indeed an honor. Branding helps us in setting a high standard which we have to live up to. It makes us responsible to strive and uphold the brand standard. It makes us identify with something much larger than our small self.

The word 'Chinmaya' is undoubtedly a brand name — more famous in India, but also known globally to those interested in Indian spirituality. Swami Chinmayananda was a leader and a pioneer, a Hindu missionary who propagated Vedānta in a modern context to the intellectual masses of India and the world over. He worked tirelessly for more than four decades and established the Chinmaya brand in the minds of the public through the Chinmaya Mission, Gītā Jñāna Yajñas, Gītā Chanting Competitions, Bala Vihars, Yuva Kendra, Study Classes, and Vidyalayas — schools with a difference.

You definitely have the Chinmaya brand stamped all over you. Now I see why your aim in life is to make a difference.

The field of management is another area where the Chinmaya impact is seen. Let us meet next week at the Chinmaya Institute of Management, Bengaluru, where I will be addressing a seminar. Hari Om!

Teachers with a difference

Before coming to the Vidyalaya, I thought teaching was just another job. But now I know that what I do is worship.

Smt. V. Lakshmi, English teacher, CV Kolar

Naughtiness got me punished often, but later, ma'am always kissed me and told me that she loved me.

Swastika, Grade V, CV New Delhi

It was tough being a Matron for 84 teenage boys over and above my work as a math teacher. But advised by Guruji I decided to just be there when they needed me. That shift in attitude made all the difference.

Smt. Meera Jackson, former matron, CIRS; Current Principal, CV Coimbatore

Ganesh Sir always gives lifts to elderly and disabled people in his car. He is a person of immense goodness and generosity. Priyadarshini Sivakumar, Grade XII, CIRS

Our Accounts teacher Master Kesavulu was getting married on the day of our Accounts exam and I was a nervous wreck. He jumped the gate of my building at 3 A.M. and sat with me for an hour, clarifying my doubts. Then he came to school, wished all of us well, and went and got married. Amazing!

Jayashree Hemdev, Entrepreneur, CV Chennai alumnus

I believe art is truly for the welfare of the human community; it has worked wonders in my life.

Smt. D. Kamatchi Sundaram, Art Teacher, CV Vadavalli, Coimbatore

I remind myself, 'reach every child before you teach.'

Smt. Sugeetha Rajan, Principal, CV Kannur

One day when I had forgotten to bring my lunch, my teacher gave me her lunch and went hungry that day. That touched me.

R. Shraavan, Grade XI, CV Chennai

Students with a difference

Putting me in the Vidyalaya is the best decision my father ever made.

Manisha Makhecha, ex-student, CV Kannur & CV College Kannur, Yuva Veer, Entrepreneur, CIF Co-ordinator, valued sevak of Mission

The Vidyalaya has taught me not to mock at others' weaknesses, which I often used to do.

B. Nivedita, Grade VII, CV New Delhi

When I asked my daughter Devika to draw something for the 'Silver Jubilee Exhibition,' without prompting she drew a honeybee coming to suck nectar from a flower — both had a smile! My daughter explained that all children go to my school like honeybees to flowers.

Smt. Nitya Paniker, teacher and parent, AAAMCV, Tripunithura

'Hari OM' was the new magic word I learned, and it still remains the first word of greeting to emerge out of my mouth.

Dr. Suchitra Sivadas
2nd batch, 1986 of AAAMCV, Tripunithura

A girl in my class told me that teachers in her previous school made her feel she was stupid, but when she came here, it was as if a rosebud opened on the top of her head.

Annilla Ramadhar, Grade VII, CV Trinidad

Swapnam Kajeria, a star athlete, could have easily won the cross-country race, but he chose to jog to the finish with me so that I could have the satisfaction of having completed the race — a first for me. Winning is important to everyone. To give it up with a smile exhibits nobility.

Anirudh Belle,
passed IB Diploma, CIRS

V

The Age of Management

A great leader leads all toward a noble goal, bringing well-being and prosperity to all in his jurisdiction. He is resourceful, productive, and capable of generating wealth and resources. He is generous and just, and is the very life of all he leads. (agraṇīr grāmaṇī śrīmān nyāyo netā samīraṇāḥ). — Viṣṇusahasranāma 24

Acclaimed as the 'Hindu of the twentieth century,' Gurudev was a leader of the time (yuga puruṣa), a great man (mahā puruṣa), a divine soul (divya puruṣa), and an ideal for millions (uttama puruṣa). He started as a lone crusader and envisaged the very course of spiritual revival and cultural renaissance for India, which is now followed by hundreds of spiritual organizations. To cite an example, many spiritual organizations have developed children's programs modeled on the Bala Vihar system conceived by Gurudev.

He founded, managed, and handed down an ever-expanding international organization — the Chinmaya Mission, which has scores of projects and activities, hundreds of centers, and millions of devotees the world over — and he did all of this without a management degree! Gurudev was both a king and a 'kingmaker.'

The current head of Chinmaya Mission, Swami Tejomayananda, a great man and visionary, was taught, guided, and groomed by him.

Hari Om! Welcome to CIM — Chinmaya Institute of Management.

I believe you too have an MBA from the IIM Ahmedabad. Nowadays, a management degree seems to have become a basic qualification, not just for entrepreneurs, but also for all industries and corporate jobs. Why is that so?

Management is an important aspect of life, especially in professional life, and even more so in the corporate world. Management education gives a holistic perspective as it takes all stakeholders into account. It offers an understanding of various systems at play for the effective completion of a task — be it planning, organizing, communicating, executing, or reviewing. India is rich in talent but poor in management. With limited resources and an ever-growing population, the country requires visionary leaders, good governance, properly functioning systems, and effective managers. In fact, with depleting natural resources globally, this seems to have become the age of management.

There are about 2,000 management colleges in India, and more than 15,000 other colleges offer management courses. Many business schools offer specialized courses, such as Hotel Management, Hospital Management, and Educational Management. Some schools even offer management modules from Grade VII!

So what does CIM offer? Like the Chinmaya Vidyalayas, is it 'management with a difference'?

Yes! It offers an Indian ethos in management. A glimpse of ancient Indian management will give you a better understanding of Gurudev's vision on management.

Ancient Indian Management

Dharma protects those who protect dharma (dharmo rakṣati rakṣitaḥ).

Mahābhārata, Vana Parva

Dharma is that which creates harmony and balance, and following it fosters growth and prosperity of a nation or an organization. It takes care of both — a high standard of living and a high standard of life — material prosperity (abhyudaya) and spiritual growth (niḥśreyasa). Adharma, its opposite, causes an imbalance in society and disintegrates even the best of systems. Rāma Rājya (the dharmic rule of Śrī Rāma) and its opposite, Rāvaṇa Rājya (the adharmic kingship of Rāvaṇa), are classic examples that illustrate this. Ancient Indian life was based on dharma. There was a righteous and healthy give-and-take in society, which ensured a robust economy and the well-being of all. Dharma was the cornerstone of all organizational and management strategies and systems.

Great scriptures like the Rāmāyaṇa, Mahābhārata, and Gītā, and the lives of visionary statesmen and kingmakers like Cāṇakya and his famous treatise — the Arthaśāstra — are legacies of ancient Indian management.

Cāṇakya, the Master Management Guru

Born in fourth century B.C.E, Cāṇakya, also called Kautilya or Viṣṇugupta, was instrumental in laying the foundation of the great Mauryan Empire, and he also served as the Prime Minister of Emperor Candragupta Maurya. He masterminded the defeat of Alexander in India and was the first person to visualize the concept of a 'nation' — Āryavarta, which later became Bhārat, or India. He studied and later taught Political Science in the great ancient University of Takshashila.* He has written many books including *Nīti-Śāstra*. He authored *Arthaśāstra*, while at Takshashila which is India's most influential works in the field of management (with 6,000 sūtras

*Refer to page 14

classified into 150 chapters, covering 180 topics, in 15 volumes). Across the world, it has long served as a reference for rulers and managers in building a nation or an organization on sound management principles and spiritual values.

Cāṇakya gives elaborate instructions on the following seven aspects, for a prosperous kingdom and a successful organization:

> svāmi-amātya-janapada-durga-kośa-daṇḍa-mitrāṇi prakṛtayaḥ.
>
> — Arthaśāstra 6.1.1
>
> The seven pillars of a kingdom (business) are the king (leader/CEO), the minister (manager), the country (market/client/customer/stakeholders), the fortified city (head office), the treasury (capital), the army (team/employees), and the ally (friend/consultant/partner).

Three-way Checklist of Successful Institutions/Organizations

Yantra: The right personnel, resources, infrastructure, machines or instruments, and training in optimizing their use.

Tantra: The right systems, rules, methodology or procedures that govern all aspects of the working of the organization/program/activity. This is to be updated to suit the changing times, and the people concerned must be orientated to the system. Checks and balances are required to strengthen the system.

Mantra: The vision that guides the institution. It should become a source of perennial inspiration; the mantra which empowers, enlivens, and rejuvenates all to give their best. It should motivate all to work in harmony and dedication.

based on Gītā 17.13

So what exactly is the Indian ethos of management, and do Indian management colleges teach Indian tenets of management?

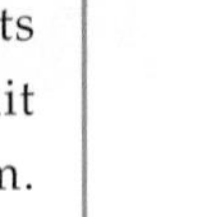

Each country has a unique culture and its management style is based on it. In Japan, the emphasis is on quality, and, in the US, it is on productivity. India has a strong spiritual history and culture. So, Indian management cannot be devoid of spirituality. Unfortunately, our colleges only teach Western management concepts. Indian principles went out of practice during the British Rule, and after India's independence, there were not many who could interpret the

Indian principles in a modern context. But I think Mumbai ḍabbāvālās (lunch carriers) and Amul Dairy are good examples of Indian management principles at work in modern times.

Indian Six Sigma Management: The Mumbai ḍabbāvālās — the Nutan Mumbai Tiffin Box Suppliers Association (NMTBSA) — hold a world record in best time-management. Started in 1880, the association is run by 5,000 self-employed shareholders (ḍabbāvālās) with an average literacy of eighth-grade schooling.

They use local trains, cycles, hand carts, or simply walk to deliver two lakh lunch boxes (ḍabbās) from individual homes to workplaces in a record time of three hours, irrespective of weather or traffic conditions of Mumbai, the most populated metropolis of India. The ḍabbāvālās pray and worship daily, wear the traditional ṭopī (cap) and white clothing, and put kuṁkuṁ (vermilion powder) on the forehead. This uninterrupted service costs each customer ₹350 per month and each shareholder earns ₹8,000 per month; and there are no strikes. It has a Six Sigma performance, which means that 99.999999 percent of the deliveries are made without error!

The Milkman of India — Dr. Verghese Kurien, the founder of the Gujarat Co-operative Milk Marketing Federation, commonly known as Amul Dairy, said to Shailendra Kumar (who worked in his office for 30 years) in 1967, "I am creating an organization that will make India self-sufficient in dairy products. I am looking for young people with integrity

◀ ONE OF THE ICONIC AMUL BUTTER ADVERTISEMENTS

and commitment to the cause for which they work. If they have technical qualifications, well and good; if not, I will teach them." There were no IIT or MBA graduates on his team, but what made his vision come true were simple things like disciplined teaching, daily morning prayers for all, and respect and love for the head of the organization. Once, when on a surprise round, Dr. Kurien saw a worker in the store licking the cream from one of the fresh milk cans. From the next day, every worker was given one litre of milk everyday — free of cost.

Gurudev made an outstanding contribution by interpreting ancient Indian management principles, making them relevant to modern times.

▲ LECTURE AT MELBOURNE UNIVERSITY

Gurudev delivered thousands of public talks on his relentless travels around the world, many of which included addresses to corporate audiences and universities, like MIT and Harvard, on India's holistic approach to management. Subjects he spoke on included Value-based Management, Subjective Management, Dynamism of Togetherness, Manager — Manage Yourself and You Change.

▲ IN DISCUSSION WITH MEMBERS OF THE TAIWANESE PARLIAMENT

He thereby came to be recognized as an inspiring motivational speaker and Management Guru as well as a great Spiritual Master. He then thought of starting a Management Institute at Bengaluru.

Inner Transformation at Chinmaya Institute of Management (CIM), Bengaluru

WE HAVE TO TRANSFORM THIS INDUSTRIAL CULTURE,
DRIVEN BY SCIENCE AND TECHNOLOGY, INTO A CIVILIZATION BASED ON
HARMONY, GROWTH, AND FULFILLMENT OF PEOPLE.

| SWAMI CHINMAYANANDA |

Bengaluru, of Infosys and Wipro fame, was the first IT hub of India. Gurudev's first Yajña in Bengaluru was in May 1956. (The city is also home to two Chinmaya Vidyalayas.) The first-ever management colleges in India were the Indian Institute of Management (IIMs) started in Ahmedabad and Kolkata in 1961, and IIM Bengaluru started in 1973. Understanding well the need of the times, Gurudev inaugurated the Chinmaya Institute of Higher Learning in Bengaluru in 1975, which was renamed the Chinmaya Institute of Management in 1996.

Initially Dr. Thampuram, N. S. Yamuna, Smt. B. Kamala, Śrī K. Ravindran, Śrī H. R. Pandurang, and other senior Mission members contributed their expertise as academicians, entrepreneurs, and senior executives. As the institute grew, Śrī Anil Sachdev, Śrī Mallya, Śrī M. Keshav, Smt. Mytrae Maganti, and Śrī G. N. Seshadri provided quality guidance.

CIM was envisaged as a national and international institute of excellence in leadership studies and research in management, which would inspire new generations of leaders with values anchored in Indian heritage. Gurudev's life-affirming philosophical teachings lie at the heart of all its programs.

The **Motto** (Success through Management) and the **Motive** (Fulfillment through Management)

praśikṣayā yaśo vṛddhiḥ yaśo viśvāsaḥ vardhakam,
viśvāsena parapräptiḥ tataḥ pūrṇatvam ālabhet.

Good Management leads to success. Success enhances confidence. One with confidence aspires for higher goals and perfection — and through perfection one attains fulfillment.

CIM initially also offered seminars on Family Values. Now it offers many diploma and certificate courses in areas such as Skill Management and Supply Chain Management, in addition to Postgraduate Diploma Courses in Hospital Management and Human Resources Management (both affiliated to Bangalore University). Its faculty also conducts various corporate management workshops.

The present Director, Śrī H. V. Vasuki shares his joy of managing the institution realizing that, 'We are actually being managed by a higher force and guided by grace.'

"CIM faculty members were fascinating, inspiring, provocative, and creative in their approach to developing management skills (technical and soft) for our personnel, and we could measure an amazing and visible result both at corporate and site level," says a satisfied client Śrī Sahasranamam, MD, Cimtrix.

Not only does Chennai have maximum number of Chinmaya Vidyalayas, it also has a CIM...

ATM (A Transforming Management) — Chinmaya Institute of Management, Chennai Chapter

The impact of PACT — A Family Quiz on Family Values, with a reach of over three lakh people from Chennai, triggered the establishment of CIM Chennai in September 2010.

"It was quite overwhelming to see people of my parents' and grandparents' age coming to me for advice on relationships," mused Subramanian, a twenty-two-year-old CHYK, one of the young faculty members, who conducted outreach seminars on PACT Family Values as part of the quiz project.

Under the leadership of Swami Mitrananda, the AICHYK President, CIM Chennai focuses on self-unfoldment and self-management programs, offering modules like Anger Management and Svadharma – Identify Your Core Competency. Since coming into existence, CIM's expert faculty, CHYKs and Yuva Veers have trained more than 30,000 students in schools and colleges and hundreds of corporate staff through unique methods, including workshops based on movies, theater, yoga, and outdoor experiential learning.

Geeta Menon, Director, CIM, says, "I love it at CIM. It is thrilling to see the transformation. Those who come with a 'why me' syndrome, walk out with a 'dare me' attitude."

You can clearly see the Indian ethos on management reflected in Gurudev's letter of guidance to the CIMs.

Vedānta and Management

I propose to cover the following topics giving the Vedantic concepts in Management in the Chinmaya Centre that is being opened in Calcutta.

1. Human Enterprise and Organisation: A critical evaluation of the existing concepts and practises (the standard of living and the standard of life/preyas and shreyas), productivity and cosmic harmony, dedicated action (yagna spirit) and ecological balance, sharing and social objectives, human enterprise and individual evolution, dynamics of togetherness, organisation's role in individual's growth, organisation and the social and cultural aspirations of people.

2. Human Nature: Creational aspects (three bodies), functional aspects (five sheaths), dynamic aspects (B-M-I Chart), behavioural aspects (three qualities)

3. Motivation: The roots of motivation - freedom from sorrow (dukha nivrtti) and pursuit of happiness (sukha prapti), concepts of freedom and happiness, motivating factors (three types of inherent tendencies), motivation and human goals (four purusharthas), motivational goals and the social behaviour of man, four stages of life (four asramas), hierarchy of goals and human evolution.

4. Action: Action cycle (avidya-kama-karma/ ignorance-desire-action), knowledge cycle (ichha-kriya-jnana / desire-action-knowledge), types of activity (karma-vikarma-akarma/action-wrong action-inaction), goal of all actions (naiskarmya/ actionless state), work as a means of inner integration and harmony (karma yoga), creative actions and self actualisation, productivity and fulfilment, need-based action and goal-based action.

5. Human Potential Development and Management: Proficiency and efficiency, dynamism and inner integration, regenerative action (buddhi yoga).

6. Human Relationships: The role of ego, love (bhakti), and Self-knowledge (atma-jnana) in human relationships.

7. Self Development: Relaxation and re-vitalisation, japa and meditation.

Chinmayananda.

Letter to Anjali Singh, 30th March, 1977

Gurudev was very versatile. He was equally at ease talking to tiny tots in nursery schools, skeptical youth in professional colleges, faithful seekers in jñāna yajñas, and top executives in management seminars. And his greatness lies in inspiring many such versatile disciples.

Physics Graduate to Metaphysics Master

Swami Tejomayananda, a science graduate, is a Guru who beautifully manages the vast and ever-growing Chinmaya Mission and its global

Chinmaya family. As its Head, he fills devotees' hearts with love as he sings the glories of the Lord, elevates the minds of disciples through his Vedānta talks and addresses MLAs (Members of the Legislative Assembly) on 'Vidhan Sabha, Deśa kī Prabhā' — all in a day's work! His talk on Empowering India at FICCI's (Federation of Indian Chambers of Commerce and Industry) 84th AGM in January 2012 received a standing ovation.

▲ GURUJI WITH KUMAR MANGALAM BIRLA

Designing Spaces to Beautifying Lives — **Swamini Vimalananda**, an honors graduate in Architecture, authors culture series bestsellers, designs spiritual courses, creates visionary educational programs, guides professional educators, and inspires corporate managers toward noble achievements. Her annual talks at the Ahmedabad Management Association are the talk of the town.

Managing Business to Engaging Businessmen — From running a family business in Hong Kong, **Swami Swaroopananda** now globetrots addressing premier universities like Harvard and companies such as Ford. He urges all to 'Make It Happen' through a self-development and management program based on Indian scriptures, now also available online.

PUBLIC ADDRESS, TRAFALGAR SQUARE-LONDON, 2011 ▲

Loyola to Love All — A graduate of the Loyola College, Chennai, **Swami Mitrananda** inspires and manages youth-centred Youth Empowerment

Programmes (YEP), family value-based IMPACT seminars, the nation-oriented 'Awakening Indians to India' quiz, and spiritually-oriented theatrical productions such as 'Surya 108.' He exemplifies the CHYK motto: 'Harnessing youth potential through dynamic spirituality.'

This is just a glimpse of their talent and management skills. There are many other Ācāryas of Chinmaya Mission like Swami Swatmananda, who conducts study classes for business giants like Kumar Mangalam Birla (MD, Aditya Birla Group), and Ajay Piramal (Piramal Industries). Swami Nikhilananda addressed the World Economic Forum in Davos, Switzerland, in 2011, and Swami Ishwarananda, himself an MBA degree holder, also speaks on management at US Universities on the West Coast.

If there are so many management graduates, why are there still so many management gurus? Why do we need to train the trained?

There are several reasons for this. For one, many graduates are poorly trained. Also, in the past, we trained to get a job; now, we train to maintain a job, plus the business scenario is ever-changing. Regular and rigorous training is required, not only in professional and intellectual skills, but also to develop mental abilities like stress management. Having the right attitude is the secret of success, not only for winning an Olympic gold medal, but also for running a small or large-scale business, or country. Many of Gurudev's devotees are now accomplished management gurus.

A SINGLE IDEAL CAN TRANSFORM A LISTLESS SOUL INTO A TOWERING LEADER AMONG MEN.

| SWAMI CHINMAYANANDA |

Son of the SOIL — Anil Sachdev

Love for the motherland and its people and reverence for Gurudev and his teachings led the famous management guru Anil Sachdev on a journey from working at Tata Motors and Eicher to setting up Eicher Consulting Services (ECS), Grow Talent (a top professional service firm), and finally the School of Inspired Leadership (SOIL). The highest standards of ethics and values are the cornerstones of all the institutions founded and led by him.

Value-based Management in Action — We made countless trips to the land authority offices for approval for the construction of SOIL but to no avail. Our entire team makes an annual visit to Gurudev's Mahāsamādhi at Sidhbari, where we pay homage, review what we have done, and plan ahead. Instead of cursing the difficult government authorities for being corrupt and inefficient, inspired by the power of forgiveness and reconciliation, we sent a message of prayer to them. And the magic happened. We obtained the construction approval on the same day!

Narrated by Anil Sachdev.
From 2001 onward, ten percent of the gross profits of his firm are donated to the Chinmaya Organization for Rural Development (CORD)

The Five-level SOIL Solutions — In response to the leadership crisis that the country faces, SOIL has created a five-floor training program in: Mindfulness (through yoga and meditation), Compassion (through sevā), Ethics (through case studies), Sustainability (through green and clean technologies), and Diversity (through the development of multiple intelligences). "India is indeed a land of contradictions where rampant corruption, mismanagement, and poor-quality institutions coexist with successful and honest organizations and institutions," concludes Anil Sachdev.

Sure MANTRA of Success — M. Keshav

Since childhood, Gurudev has been M. Keshav's ideal and altar of worship from where he draws his inspiration and nourishment. He attended schools and colleges in Pune, Ahmedabad, and Mumbai, but he learned the main lessons of life at CHYK.

International Business School — "In the eighties, the term MBA was hardly known. However, I realized later that the CHYK movement was like an international business school where we got practical lessons on leadership and a universal outlook, empowering spiritual thoughts, inspiring visions, and transforming experiences, which molded our entire lives and careers. These intense lesson courses learned in the

abiding unconditional love of a strict, watchful, and thoroughly meticulous Master helped us claim a fair amount of material success as well," says Keshav, who started an Attitude Consultancy firm, MANTRA (Management Training Research Associates), in Chennai. He has conducted over 2,500 workshops on varied modules, including Ego Management, Retirement Planning, and Six Sigma Quality Branding. He is a recipient of many awards and a popular anchor for many radio and TV shows.

He explains: "These are a few of my favorite things adopted from Gurudev. The BMI chart is a well-used tool at MANTRA. I use humor as an effective tool to break the ice, draw attention, and drive home an important point. I also use storytelling and a sense of drama for listening impact. Most importantly, I have cultivated clear goals and the ability to connect with people using my emotions intelligently."

Inspired by Gurudev's clarion call of 'We can! We must!' he fulfills his social responsibility by serving in Chinmaya Mission and promotes knowledge skills for building confidence in underprivileged children, to make them employable through VEMUST (Value Education for Mutual Understanding and Service Trust).

Mentoring Uncle — Kaushik Rindani

'An integrated personality is the key to excellence in performance.' This is what Kaushik Rindani understood by attending many of Gurudev's talks on the Gītā. 'To integrate teachings from the Gītā into management' became his mission in life. Gurudev himself encouraged him to conduct seminars for CHYKs, Mission members, and even students studying in the Sandeepany Sadhanalaya, (later to become Ācāryas).

Uncle Rindani, as he is fondly referred to in the Mission, incorporates the Gītā's teachings into the hundreds of workshops that he conducts for companies, as well as in his ISO 9000 training programs and seminars for management institutions like IIM Ahmedabad.

Gurudev's wish to convert the entire Gītā into a workshop format remains unfulfilled. Uncle Rindani promises to do so, "... if not in this life, then in the next. I know Gurudev's guidance and grace will always be with me."

SHINE in Glory — G. N. Seshadri

SHINE
SHandilya Institute of Nurturing Excellence
Training & Management Consultancy

'The scriptures are the instruction manuals for the right use of the BMI equipment.' This thought of Gurudev, inspired G. N. Seshadri to attend Vijñāna Mandir (intensive study classes conducted by Ācāryas of CM) and lead many study classes in Bengaluru.

After being trained in 1979 by the Dale Carnegie Institute on Leadership and Attitudinal Development at Bengaluru, he efficiently performed both the roles of a senior manager in NGEF Ltd. and a management trainer until 1996. He then started Shandilya Institute of Nurturing Excellence (SHINE) and has trained over 40,000 people from all walks of life, in over 4,000 training programs in English and Kannada.

Through a branch of SHINE at Toppaganhalli in rural Karnataka, Śrī Seshadri, along with his wife, trains teachers and students to sharpen their managerial skills and develop a positive attitude. He shares, "I decided to celebrate my sixtieth birthday in a meaningful way. I gave talks on management in sixty rural colleges." Needless to say, all his training programs, whether in rural or urban areas, use inputs from Indian scriptures.

Corporate Chanakya — Radhakrishnan Pillai

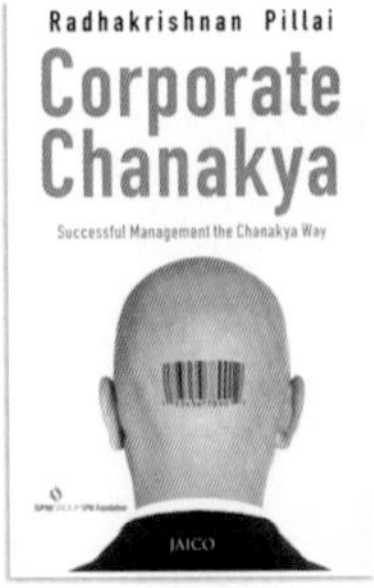

On a fateful day Radhakrishnan Pillai stumbled upon Cāṇakya's Arthaśāstra while browsing in a bookstore. In that same year, he went on a pilgrimage to Kailash Mansarovar, and, as he sat gazing at the divine abode of Lord Śiva, he sensed a divine message: 'Study Arthaśāstra, apply it in your life, and propagate its wisdom to all; make that your goal of life.' He went to Chinmaya International Foundation (CIF) to pursue a deeper study of the text and realized the truth of Gurudev's words — 'If we look back into our rich past, we will find solutions to many of our modern problems.'

As a child, Radhakrishnan met Gurudev and attended Chinmaya Mission's Bala Vihar and Yuva Kendra classes. He ventured into the field of spiritual tourism with his company 'Atma Darshan' but fulfilled his ambition of becoming 'successful in the field of business' by spreading Cāṇakya's management principles.

CIPL
CHANAKYA INSTITUTE OF PUBLIC LEADERSHIP

He has conducted hundreds of talks and seminars on *Arthaśāstra*, authored the best-seller *Corporate Chanakya*, and a film inspired by the book won the 'International Award of Merit' at the 'Indie film Festival,' California, USA, soon after its release. He has hosted over a hundred shows of 'Ask Chanakya' on the Moksha channel, has addressed

▲ RADHAKRISHNAN WITH NARAYAN MURTHY OF INFOSYS

national and international conferences, and is a regular columnist in the Times of India and the Mumbai Mirror. He is also a regular faculty member in institutions like IIT Mumbai, IIM Ahmedabad, and the Defence Service Staff College (DSSC). CIPL, guided by him, provides a professional route to enter public life for future leaders inspired by the ancient Indian wisdom.

"Cāṇakya's principles are now in vogue in the corporate world and Gurudev's grace is very much at work in my personal world!" explains a very satisfied Radhakrishnan.

It is very inspiring to see that not just our home-grown spiritual Gurus but also our management gurus are making a national and international impact.

Gurudev and our Mission Ācāryas have inspired a whole generation of upcoming mentors, motivational speakers, and management gurus.

Touching the Soul — "Don't be a beggar of jobs; provide jobs for others." Gurudev thus inspired **C. K. Suresh** to start ATMA (Attitude Training and Management Association). Trained through managing CHYK events for thousands of youngsters, he now effectively trains youngsters to shoulder responsibility. His 'Tips for Effective Living' has been featured in more than 400 episodes of Udayarasami, a morning talk show on the Asianet TV channel.

Shaping Destinies — Inspired by Gurudev's BMI chart and the Logic of Spirituality talk, **Darren Pereira** set up Success Integrated Inc., a Melbourne-based company, in 2001. His most popular seminar 'Shape Your Destiny' is based on the BMI chart and has been presented to over 150,000 people in Australia, New Zealand, the UK, and India. He pledges to take the BMI chart to every part of the world.

Discovering Your Potential — "It became clear to me that my real purpose in life was in learning and sharing Gurudev's teachings — not as an Ācārya but as a corporate trainer," says London-based CHYK **Milan Samani**, a director of The Real Potential and the founder of Frontier Consulting, UK. He conducts leadership programs for blue chip companies across the world that seek to build visionary leaders. He considers it a true privilege to be Gurudev's instrument in sharing his teachings with some of the largest companies in the world, such as Goldman Sachs, Cognizant, and MTV. "It is both humbling and deeply fulfilling to see business leaders applying Vedāntic teachings in their professional and personal lives."

The influence of Gurudev is truly remarkable. You, too, have changed many destinies, are performing to your full potential, and have touched my soul with this narration. Now tell me your story.

I have learned many management principles from the stories shared by others.

Think Global, Act Rural — Gurudev used to come to my college, BITS Pilani (Birla Institute of Technology), each year for a week-long Gītā Course. Everybody — students and staff — would listen to him, completely spellbound. It was the finest philosophy I have ever heard, so practical and humorous. His teaching about compassion and universal responsibility gave me the courage to give up my corporate job and start working in tribal villages for rural development. It has been deeply fulfilling from the start. I feel one with the world.

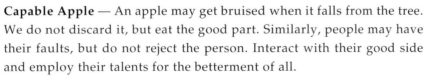

Mathew Cherian, core committee member of the National Human Rights Commission, Chief Executive of Help Age India and Board member of Help Age International. Former Director of Oxfam (UK and India), founded Charities Aid Foundation, Credibility Alliance, and Human Rights Network in India

Capable Apple — An apple may get bruised when it falls from the tree. We do not discard it, but eat the good part. Similarly, people may have their faults, but do not reject the person. Interact with their good side and employ their talents for the betterment of all.

Gurudev to Swami Swaroopananda

Micro to Macro — As CHYKs, we would come up with a small project. Gurudev would make it a national project. We would then have to garner incredible organizational and managerial skills. He would heartily congratulate us on its successful completion. We realized that it was actually his constant guidance, inspiration, and grace that brought success. He thus watched us grow. Swami Mitrananda

Silly to Yours Truly — As CHYKs, we would come up with many silly ideas. Gurudev never rejected them off-hand but asked us to work them out. The ideas changed and transformed into truly inspiring projects. We then owned these projects and worked with them till completion.

Radhakrishnan Pillai

Change Your Destiny — "Sardarji, put your foot down and change your destiny. Tell your father that you want nothing from his business," Gurudev emphatically said to me when I told him about my family problems. I decided to follow his advice, and within a few days, a family friend offered me a job in his finance company. Even though being an employee was a step down from being an employer, Gurudev said, "Take it. One day they will make you a Director." Thereafter, when I was about to set up my own business, he gave my company all the Chinmaya Mission accounts, saying, "When people know I trust you with my accounts, they too will do so." And sure enough my firm prospered. My destiny changed when I heeded his advice.

Rajbir Singh, Founder, Anandini Financial Services which has achieved the 'Top of the Table' status, the highest in the Million Dollar round table for Life Insurance

Kargil Hero — My father was in the army; so are one of my elder brothers and two brothers-in-law. Our hearts beat for India. I own an advertising agency in Delhi, and I felt I had to do something for the families of the deceased Kargil war heroes. We ran an advertising campaign on every TV channel in India over a three-week period and raised over ₹400 crore — an unprecedented achievement. Gurudev always taught us to think big, so we aimed high and reached higher.

Sunil Sachdeva, CEO, Capital Advertising

Union in My Trade — I owned two factories in Delhi — Incowax and Rollatainers. Gurudev taught me never to treat workers as numbers. My wife took personal care of the staff and all felt united as one family. My companies had 1,100 employees and no trade union and so no strikes.

Śrī R. Krishnamoorthy (fondly called tātā, grandfather, in Chinmaya Mission)

Gurudev was indeed a mastermind in management, and this does seem to be the age of management. But, you know, my heart is in art — the art of writing and dancing.

Then, you must come next month to Chinmaya Vibhooti near Pune to write about Chinmaya Naada Bindu, a residential school of Music and Dance. Hari Om!

VI

The Heart of Art

WHAT YOU HAVE IS HIS GIFT TO YOU. WHAT YOU DO WITH WHAT YOU HAVE IS YOUR GIFT TO HIM.

| SWAMI CHINMAYANANDA |

Welcome to Chinmaya Vibhooti — the Vision Center of Chinmaya Mission. How was your bus journey with Gurudev's devotees?

Very interesting. I heard some wonderful stories about Gurudev's informal guidance on education to the young and old all over the world.

His Stories

Mātṛ devo bhava — Gurudev came to our home every year when we were kids. On one occasion, I asked him, "What is religion?" He said, "Serve your parents — that is religion for you."

Śrī Sunil Sachdev, CEO, Capital Advertising, Delhi

Failure and Success — The path to success is often marked by the stumbling blocks of failure. When I informed Gurudev that my daughter had failed in one subject in M.A. Literature exams, he said, "Don't worry. Failures are stepping stones to success."

Smt. Nalini Menon, devotee, Thrissur

Healthy Wealthy and Wise Advice

Continue your daily exercise for a healthy and strong body, plunge yourself in study and score the best you can. Your future career depends upon your healthy mind and continuous efforts. Be regular in your daily prayers and have faith in yourself and the Lord's protection. Fearlessly enter into your chosen field of honest action. You will never know what failure is.

Chinmayananda.

To a teenager, 05.06.1991

Up in the Alps — John C. Corlette was the founder of the prestigious boarding school, Aiglon College in Switzerland. He felt, "I have found my Master," when he met Gurudev in India. Gurudev visited the school for one whole week and conducted meditation classes for all, along with three other sessions each day for teachers and students. From then on, daily morning meditation sessions (contemplation over an uplifting topic) became a part of the school curriculum. Gurudev recommended this school for my sister Nanki and me, as the school's guiding vision was 'to create whole men and women with special emphasis on character development.' Every day was not just about studies. Sometimes the entire morning was spent skiing in the mountains! Study time was often in the afternoon and evenings.

When Nanki once fell from a horse at school, Gurudev wrote to her, 'Even the horse you ride on gets mad, runs wild into the forest to shake you off! Yet you return riding on the animal. Be careful. The ridden will always try to get rid of the rider! Hold on and bring it under your control! That is life.' Once, Nanki

GURUDEV WITH NANKI AND JUJHAR ▲

I conducted a meditation session relating a story she had heard from Gurudev. It was selected as one of the fifty best-ever sessions in the long history of the school. She went on to become the head-girl of the school.

Jujhar Singh, TV Anchor, Delhi

JUJHAR WITH PANDIT SHIVKUMAR SHARMA ▲

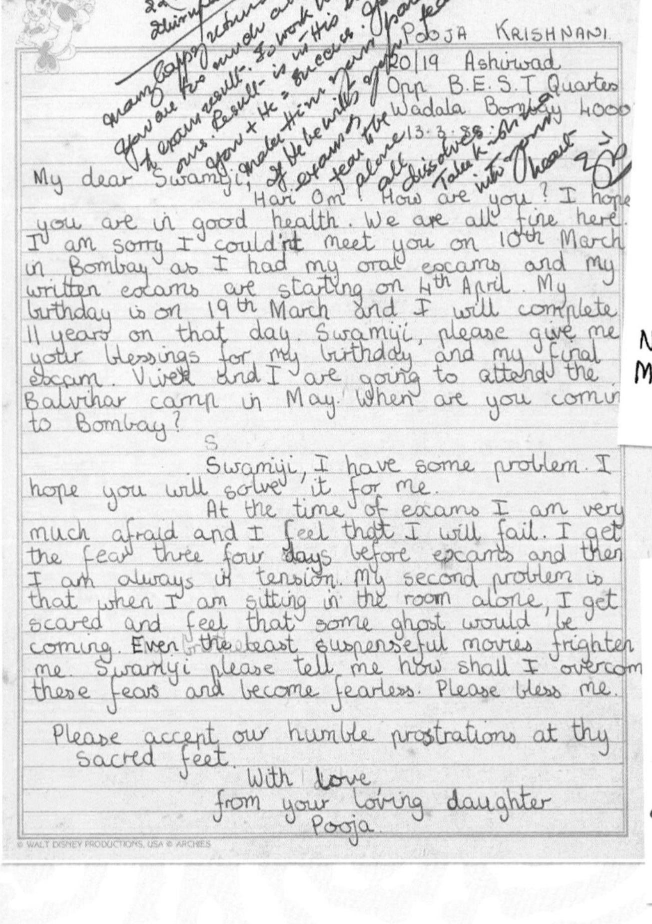

22nd March
Thirupatti
Many happy returns. You are too much attached to exam result. To work hand is ours. Result is in His hands. You + He = Success. You do it, make Him your partner. If He be with you, fear of exams — fear to be alone — all dissolves. Take Him into your heart.

POOJA KRISHNANI.
20/19 Ashirwad
Opp B.E.S.T Quarters
Wadala Bombay 4000
13.3.88

My dear Swamiji,
Hari Om! How are you? I hope you are in good health. We are all fine here. I am sorry I couldn't meet you on 10th March in Bombay as I had my oral exams and my written exams are starting on 4th April. My birthday is on 19th March and I will complete 11 years on that day. Swamiji, please give me your blessings for my birthday and my final exam. Vivek and I are going to attend the Balvihar camp in May. When are you coming to Bombay?

Swamiji, I have some problem. I hope you will solve it for me.
At the time of exams I am very much afraid and I feel that I will fail. I get the fear three four days before exams and then I am always in tension. My second problem is that when I am sitting in the room alone, I get scared and feel that some ghost would be coming. Even the least suspenseful movies frighten me. Swamiji please tell me how shall I overcome these fears and become fearless. Please bless me.

Please accept our humble prostrations at thy sacred feet.
With love
from your loving daughter
Pooja.

© WALT DISNEY PRODUCTIONS, USA © ARCHIES

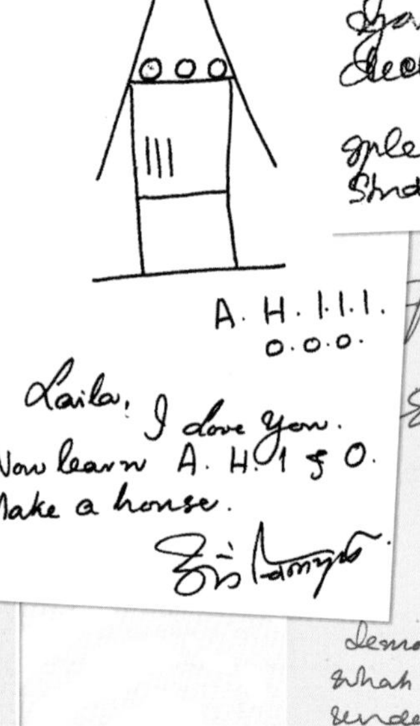

A. H. I. I. I.
O. O. O.

Laila,
I love you.
Now learn A. H. 1 & O.
Make a house.

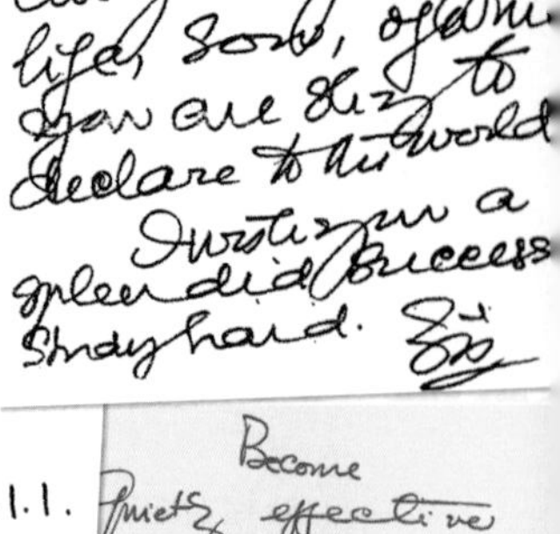

Never ever do anything in your life, Sobi, of which you are shy to declare to the world. Invite you a splendid success. Study hard.

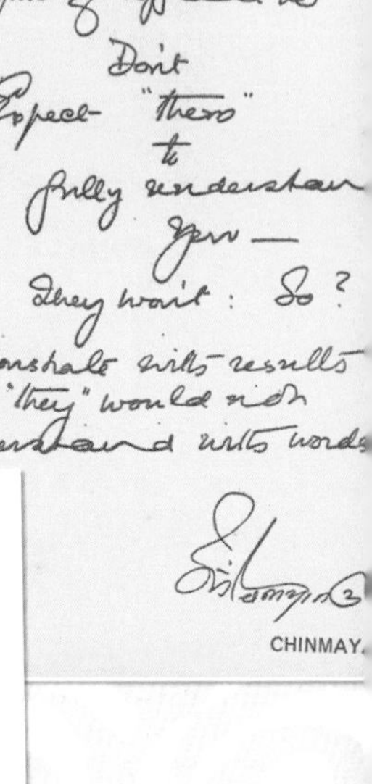

Become quietly effective
Don't expect "them" to fully understand you —
they won't: So?
Demonstrate with results what "they" would not understand with words

CHINMAY

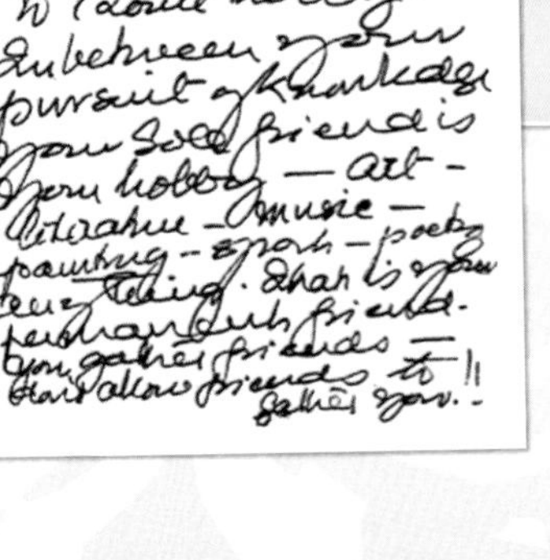

Get wedded to some hobby. In between your pursuit of knowledge your sole friend is your hobby — art — literature — music — sports — poetry painting — etc. What is your ... thing. ... friends — you gather friends — Not allow friends to gather you!!

The First Test — I was tested at my very first meeting with colleagues at university, when I was asked to speak about principles for promoting excellence in learning and teaching. Gurudev's teaching came to my rescue. I offered a simple English translation of the exquisite Vedic invocation 'sahanāvavatu ...,'* adding that it was an ancient contract between the teacher and student, shared with me by the best teacher I had ever had. Needless to say, I passed the test with flying colors.

Christine Grimmer, Sydney, Australia

Master's in Philosophy to Mastery in Photography — Inspired by Gurudev in my very first meeting in 1961, I decided to leave college studies in order to pursue the spiritual path. Gurudev told me, "If you cannot gain mastery in something in the objective world, how will you master the subjective science of the Self, which is far more difficult?" I then completed my Masters in Philosophy. Years later, Gurudev gave me a Nikon camera and said, "Take photographs." From that day onward, I have taken thousands of pictures of Gurudev and other Ācāryas.

Anjali Singh, renowned CM photographer, Delhi

Vedānta Germinating in Germany — Under the guidance of Gurudev, Dr. Annette Wilke undertook a three-year Vedānta Course at Sandeepany West in the U.S.A. She later completed a Ph.D. in philosophy, comparing the teachings of Meister Eckhart with those of Ādi Śaṅkarācārya. Annette has since established a department for the non-theological study of religions at Münster University.

*Refer to page 9

Chinmaya Vibhooti is a beautiful, harmonious blend of man and God's creation.

That is what art is all about. The love for traditional art that Gurudev imbibed as a young boy raised in Kerala stayed with him, giving him a new depth of appreciation as he evolved into the mighty Swami Chinmayananda. He believed that art could transform an individual. His vision of art was in line with the ancient Indian concept of art.

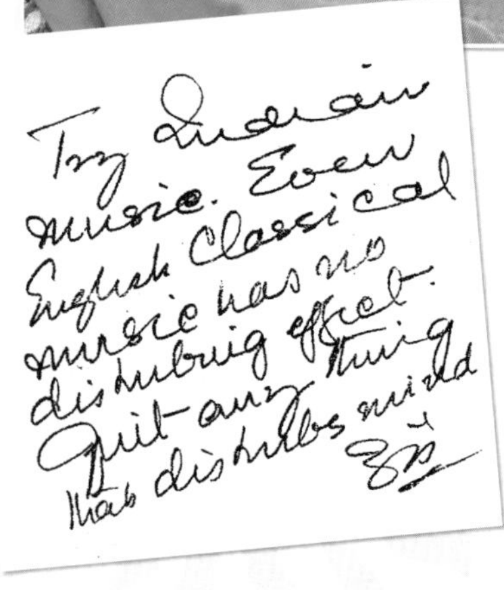
Try Indian music. Even English Classical music has no disturbing effect. Quit any thing that disturbs mind

swami chinmayananda

CHINMAYA TAPOVAN TRUST, SANDEEPANY HIMALAYAS, SIDHBARI-176057, H.P. INDIA. PHONE: 01892-2121/2251.

15 March 1992

Sri A. Chinmaya
s/o V.K.N. Arjun Raja
11, Rajpur Road
Delhi - 110 054

Blessed Self:

Hari Om! Hari Om! Hari Om!
Salutations!

Your kind letter and the enclosed very informative literature. I congratulate you for taking up this sacred work of educating the growing children in the classical arts of ancient India.

In the Western countries, they train their children to appreciate their music by taking them to concerts and many of the parents guide and encourage the children to appreciate the thrill of the classical style. They often take their children to museums and help them to see the rhythm of the colours and the beauty of the strokes in famous and ancient paintings.

As a nation, we have been ignoring these, mainly because of our education is a slavish imitation of what the West left here which train our growing children to have a disrespect to our own Indian art and culture.

I strongly recommend that all our schools in all over the country should encourage this chance provided so easily at their own house. All that the "SPIC-MACAY" wants is only a Hall and the mike. Such a chance our schools can never get. Let them expose all our children from 8th to 12th grades along with their parents.

With Prem and Om,

Thy Own Self,

CHINMAYA

Indian Art

Art is that which manifests joy or divinity. (kaṁ sukham/brahma lāti prakāśayati iti kalā). God is the creator of all arts in creation (kalā-sarga-karaṁ devam). — Śvetāśvatara Upaniṣad 5.14. He is also the first teacher of all arts (akhila-kalā-ādi-guruḥ). — Bhāgavatam. He unites various principles [the artist with his art, the audience with the artist and the audience and the artist with God through the art] (tattvasya tattvena sametya yogam). — Śvetāśvatara Upaniṣad 6.3

NO GREAT ARTIST WILL EVER CLAIM TO HAVE CREATED BEAUTY. HE ONLY DISCOVERS AND UNVEILS THE BEAUTY THAT HAS ALREADY BEEN PLACED BY THE DIVINE ARTIST WHO IS THE CREATOR OF THE UNIVERSE.

| Swami Chinmayananda |

The sculptor chisels away all that is unwanted and brings out the beautiful form from the stone. The sculptor may create many sculptures, but when he makes a statue of God, it is installed in a temple and worshiped. Kings, saints, and the sculptor himself prostrate before the idol. The painting in an art gallery or an idol in the museum is exhibited to appreciate art (pradarśana), whereas the idol in the temple is installed to see divinity (darśana). To manifest divinity is the highest goal of art. When the artist connects his art with God, his heart opens up to grace, as God is the very heart of all art.

Art in every form was essentially spiritual in ancient India. It would fail to be sincere if the artist portrayed Lord Śrī

Rāma without believing in the divine. For example, performing arts were a means to transcend body consciousness; so the artists trained their bodies in order to do so. Art was thus considered a yoga — a means to connect with God.

Also, the artist must be rooted in tradition but not get buried in it. He must have an in-depth knowledge of the art (śāstra jñāna), be well-trained by a Master (tālim), rigorously practice his art (abhyāsa), present himself well (pradarśana), have the right attitude (darśana), and have an altar of dedication (samarpaṇa). The artists were patronized by the royals and the artisans were sustained by the masses. Thus, both the classical and folk arts and crafts thrived in ancient India.

It is said that Sage Nārada was the master of sixty-four arts, which included the sixteen types of cosmetology, embroidery, culinary arts, and performing arts. As in every field of knowledge there were scriptures in ancient India on art, authored by great sages. Nāṭya Śāstra (on performing arts) was revealed to Sage Bharata. Viṣṇudharmottara (which covers a wide variety of subjects, including lexicography, dramaturgy, and painting, and is considered an Upapurāṇa) is compiled as an appendix to Viṣṇu Purāṇa. Vāstu Śāstra (town planning and architecture, also an Upapurāṇa) is believed to have been revealed to Māyā Dānava, or as some believe, revealed to Viśvakarma, the celestial architect. (Interestingly, all the three scriptures mentioned above have a divine origin.)

Dramatic Origin — Lord Brahma revealed the knowledge of **Nāṭya Śāstra** — a treatise on the science and art of stagecraft, considered as the fifth Veda by performing artists. It has the essence of the four Vedas — poetry from *Ṛg Veda*, music from *Sāma Veda*, communicative means from *Yajur Veda*, and aesthetics from *Atharva Veda*. It is extensive and encyclopaedic, with 6,000 verses (currently available), which are classified into thirty-six chapters, covering every aspect of nāṭya. It contains a wholesome combination of what would be the present-day drama, opera, and ballet. The exacting nature of nāṭya — as expounded in the scripture — required the performers to act, sing, and dance to perfection.

The chapters of the *Nāṭya Śāstra* elaborate upon the four methods of communication relevant even today — āngika (movement of the limbs, body language, posture), vācika (dialogue, poetry, lyrics, speech, diction, tone, pronunciation), āhārya (costumes and ornamentation), and sāttvika (moods, expression of emotions and moods).

āṅgikam bhuvanaṁ yasya vācikaṁ sarva vāṅmayam,
āhāryaṁ candratārādi taṁ vande sāttvikaṁ śivam.

Abhinaya Darpaṇa

Prostrations to the divine Lord Śiva. The entire world is His limbs, the entire range of sound is His speech, and the planets and satellites are His ornaments.

India has an undoubtedly rich past. Imagine a sage as a make-up artist and a scripture on body language! As a renowned Swami, Gurudev would have met many artists, wouldn't he?

Gurudev was a patron and a connoisseur of the arts. He encouraged so many devotees who were artists, to excel in their craft. He blessed hundreds of performances of budding artists, as well as accomplished artists by his presence — a trend continued by Guruji. Gurudev wrote and spoke on many occasions on fine arts, the performing arts, and their relation to life and God.

▲ GURUDEV BLESSING YESUDAS

A Master with Maestros: Renowned artists like Pandit Ravi Shankar, Pandit Bhimsen Joshi, M. S. Subbulakshmi, Hari Prasad Chaurasia, Mrinalini Sarabhai, Pandit Jasraj, K. J. Yesudas, Balamuralikrishna, and Purushottam Jalota performed before Gurudev. The budding artists of that time, such as Dr. Padma Subrahmanyam and Anup Jalota, have been blessed by him to become great masters. The artists excelled and performed in ecstasy in his presence.

Blessed One,

Hari Om! Salutations!!

It is not frequent that a nation discovers a Balamurali Krishna in its history. They are very rare. To be born with music in his heart, to hold a recital at his tender age of only eight Deepavalis, to be at once a master in many instruments apart from his unfailing purity of voice, Tal and Rag, clarity of enunciation in more than two-three South Indian languages: these are indeed preciously rare in one single person unless he is a genius.

Music when it rises from the head has a heavy grandeur, but when it gurgles from the heart, soaked in the deep emotions felt by the singer, the fluent music gathers a special pair of wings to dive directly into the hearts of the listeners, cutting across all barriers of language and mood.

Chinmayananda.

Letter to Balamuralikrishna

Mesmerized by MS

On September 10, 1988, the great heart of Smt. M.S. Subbulakshmi shall open up to Him in true deep devotion. The melody that shall burst forth from her lips has the power to spread the fragrance of His vana-mala (garland); perhaps, with a suspicion of a slender smell of a clean cowshed and fresh butter. The audience must arrive on time with a well-prepared mind. Sit completely relaxed–both physically and mentally–surrendering totally to Him, the Lord of your heart (Ishta devata). Listen! Without your total involvement, listening will be impossible. And experience directly the beauty and rhythm of the Lord which is always available in Indian devotional songs. Many of our saints reached truth through singing for Him.

Chinmayananda.

Message for program of M. S. Subbulakshmi

Bhakti Sandhya

Unhook your mind from the outer world. Flow with the rhythm of Padma's movements. Allow her to lift you into realms unknown, where you can be in Bliss Supreme. In this way the evening shall really become Bhakti Sandhya.

Chinmayananda.

Message given for the performance of Dr. Padma Subrahmanyam in 1989 at Delhi

Drop the Glass for a Shattering Silence — My brother invited Gurudev for a classical Indian music performance at his home. By the time Gurudev reached the place, drinks were flowing freely. He told the audience, "To attend a classical Indian music recital with a glass in hand is a contradiction. The music is making the mind quiet and alert; and the alcohol is making it dull. You would be defeating the very purpose for which the music is meant." People put down their glasses, and experienced the beauty of the music!

Narrated by Anjali Singh

Pasyamey — See My Divine Dance

Blessed Child,

See His Dance everywhere ... in the clouds, in the waters, in the wind and the trees, indeed it is all around you, and in you.

Chinmayananda.

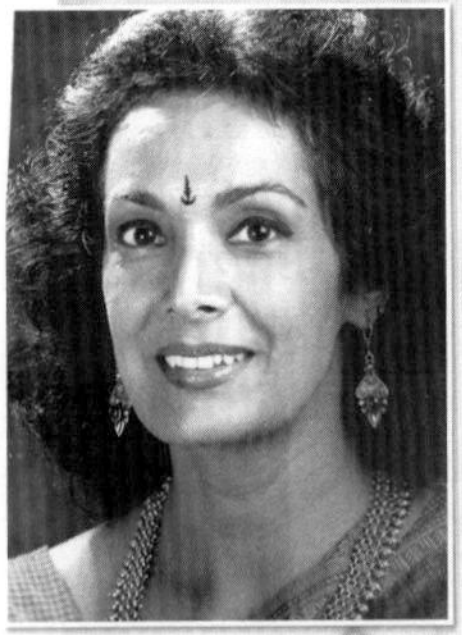

To the famous Bharatanatyam dancer Chitra Sundaram immediately after her Araṅgeṭram. [Inspired by this letter, years later she choreographed and performed 'Pasyamey' — based on the Gītā Chapter 11 at the first International Camp (1983), before an audience of thousands. At the end of the show, Gurudev remarked, "Congratulations!! The audience actually experienced the divine Cosmic Form." She has performed all over the world including the Royal Opera House, London.]

Understanding Abstraction: "When an artist dabbles in abstraction or surrealism, the hope is that the audience will appreciate something that comes close to the artist's intent. Even when the audience loves us, we don't always know if they understand us. But in that moment of meeting Swami Chinmayananda, I can say I felt totally understood," writes Emily Mayne, a U.S.-based dance artist who taught dance at several universities. She has worked as a movement coach for Cirque du Soleil productions, with animators at Walt Disney, Pixar, and Sony Imageworks. Her classical dance works include ballet, Bharatanatyam (under the tutelage of T. Balasaraswati), and Javanese dance.

Noise to Music

SOUND IS A BASIC DISTURBANCE. WHEN IT DOES NOT CONVEY ANY MEANING, IT IS NOISE. WHEN IT HAS MEANING, IT BECOMES A WORD. WORDS ARRANGED IN THEIR RIGHT SYNTAX AND CONVEYING A FULL THOUGHT BECOME A SENTENCE IN PROSE. THE SAME IDEA EXPRESSED IN METRICAL COMPOSITION BECOMES POETRY. POETRY SOAKED IN EMOTION, HAVING ITS OWN HARMONY AND RHYTHM, BECOMES MUSIC.

| SWAMI CHINMAYANANDA |

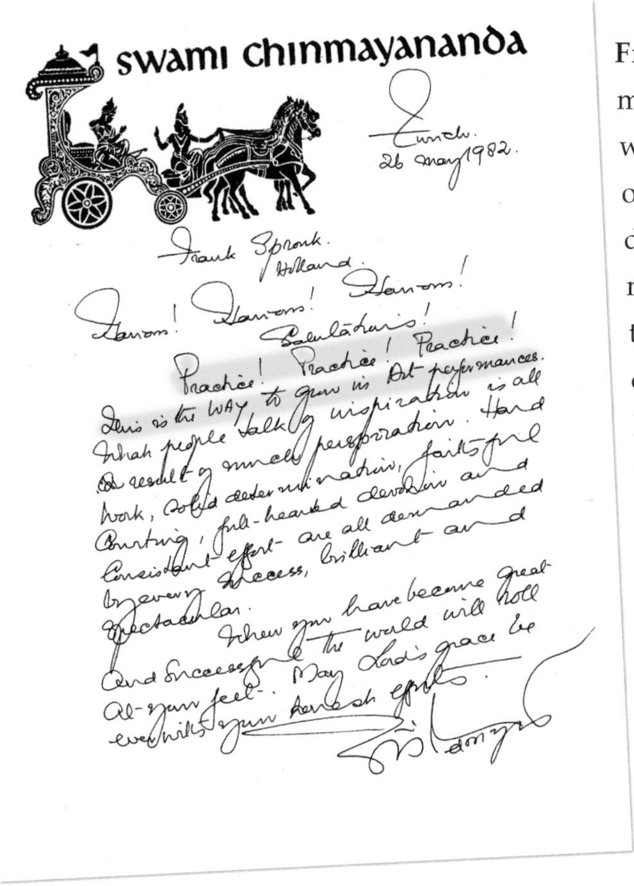

swami chinmayananda

Zurich.
26 May 1982.

Frank Spronk.
Holland.

Hariom! Hariom! Hariom!
Salutations!

Practice! Practice! Practice!
This is the WAY to grow in Art-performances.
What people talk of inspiration is all
a result of much perspiration. Hard
work, solid determination, faithful
Courting, full-hearted devotion and
Consistent effort are all demanded
by every success, brilliant and
spectacular.

When you have become great
and successful the world will roll
at your feet. May Lord's grace be
ever with your honest efforts.

Chinmaya

Frankly Yours: "I had been making and experimenting with music all my life, but only when I met Gurudev did I realize that I was just making a lot of noise," admits the Dutch music teacher, composer and cello player, Frank Spronk. "I met my wife Paula at Gurudev's camp in Switzerland. She did the Vedānta course at Sandeepany, Mumbai, and then we got married. We have two sons who are musically gifted — Gerard plays the cello and Anton plays the violin. Being spiritually inclined, they manage to give even a typical Tchaikovsky romantic melody a divine dimension. Today, the whole family functions in the light of the Guru."

Self-Beautification — "Gurudev, this is my friend Sita Juneja, an interior decorator," Gurudev looked at me and said, "It is good to decorate the interior."

Narrated by Swamini Gurupriyananda,
formerly Sita Juneja

An 'I' for an 'i' — A devotee with a sweet voice kept singing bhajans and chanting ślokas all the time before Gurudev. To the surprise of all, one day he told her, "Spare everyone your singing." We had seen him tolerate bad singing of devotees. Then I realized that Gurudev was annihilating her ego, as she felt she alone was the best singer and would not allow others to sing. He later told her, "Allow Him to sing through you."

Narrated by Swami Swaroopananda

Śaṅkarācārya's Toothless Smile — In 1991, the CM Washington, D.C. Center put up a play on the life of Ādi Śaṅkarācārya. I played the lead role. I was then a six-year-old, with no front teeth. Before the show, Gurudev said to me, "Don't smile! Otherwise people will think Śaṅkarācārya did not have teeth!"

Narrated by Vineet Bhagawat

Yātrā to Cannes: 'I was completely taken in by Gurudev's sense of humor and charismatic presence, right from my teens. He taught me to connect with divinity through my craft.' — Sharanya Rao, CHYK, U.S.A., has written many creative pieces like the theater production, 'Yatra – A Journey Unto the Unknown.' Her first film script, 'Sarathi– The Charioteer,' which focused on the Vedantic concept of being an observer, was screened at the Cannes Film Festival in 2011.

Kalākāra to the Nirākāra — I cannot forget my earliest doodles with paint and the amorphous beings that I generated on paper. Then I decided to draw a birthday card for Gurudev. I drew and redrew. It looked very ordinary (Ammā had put her foot down against drawing Spider-Man or GI Joe on the card at any cost and suggested a vase with flowers). For the first time, I experienced the joy of translating beauty from nature to paper. I finally gave it to him. I remember Gurudev singling out my card from his mail, turning it this way and that, and looking around for the miscreant who could draw so atrociously. I forgot all about the card, except that I had proudly signed and added in brackets 'midukkan kuttī' (smart child) — since Gurudev had called me that. It was an old school trick; somehow, if you reminded the teacher of her last compliment to you, she seemed to go lenient the next time you presented your work to her. And then it happened. I got a letter from Gurudev himself, in reply to a puny, little birthday card from a wisp of a boy he had met just once, a year ago.

Nineteen years and about thirty portraits later, I look back at a hobby that grew on me. No professional aspirations to pursue painting full-time, no frenzy for conducting exhibitions, no lure of the lucre. Art heals for sure, and the mortal pursues art like a plant growing in the direction of light. And Gurudev had been an all-knowing catalyst in the process. His blessings sowed the seed of a vocation that would grow to be my strongest redeeming strength in life. He urged me to perceive art as a passage to divinity — a journey of a kalākāra to the nirākāra.

Nishith Anand attended Bal Vihar and Yuva Kendra classes;
was a student of CV Kannur, and presently teaches Management
at Chinmaya Institute of Technology (Chintech), Kannur

Art of Meditation

NATURE MAKES OUR MIND SILENT. THE ARTIST CREATES BEAUTY, WHICH IN TURN CREATES A BEAUTIFUL, JOYOUS, AND QUIET MOOD IN US. IN INDIA, WE GO ONE STEP FURTHER. GOD IS BEAUTY AND BEAUTY IS GOD. THE FINEST AND SUBTLEST OF ALL ART IS THE ART OF MEDITATION, WHEREIN YOU BECOME ONE WITH GOD, WHO IS OF THE VERY NATURE OF TRUTH, AUSPICIOUSNESS, AND BEAUTY (SATYAM, ŚIVAM, AND SUNDARAM).

OUR MIND IS FASCINATED BY BEAUTY. SEEK IT, AND WHEN YOU FEEL IT, STAY THERE. DON'T INITIATE A NEW THOUGHT. THOUGHTS ONLY REFLECT BEAUTY. GO TO THE SOURCE OF ALL BEAUTY, WHICH IS BEYOND THOUGHTS. STAY THERE IN THE HUSHED SILENCE, EXPERIENCING THE BEAUTY. THE REST WILL HAPPEN. YOU WILL DISSOLVE INTO TOTAL SELF-FORGETFULNESS. YOU ARE NO MORE THE PERSON WHO SOUGHT BEAUTY. YOU BECOME THAT BEAUTY, THE BEAUTY THAT IS REFLECTED IN EVERYTHING THAT IS BEAUTIFUL. THIS IS THE CULMINATION OF ART.

| SWAMI CHINMAYANANDA |

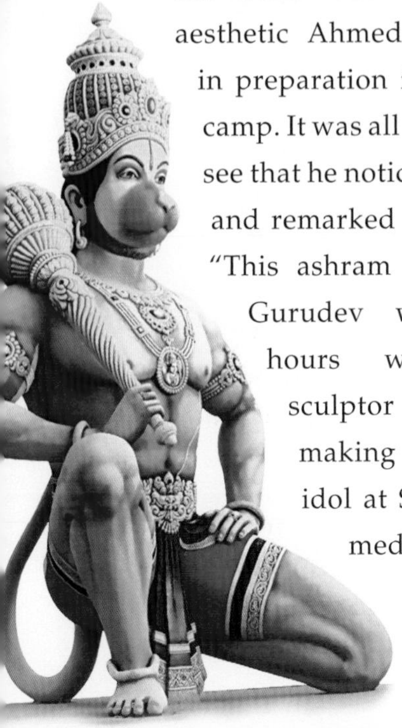

Eye for Beauty — Along with other devotees, I spent days painting the walls with alpanā (designs) and decorating the already aesthetic Ahmedabad ashram, in preparation for Gurudev's camp. It was all worthwhile to see that he noticed everything and remarked several times, "This ashram is beautiful!" Gurudev would spend hours watching the sculptor Kashinath, making the Hanumān idol at Sidhbari. No wonder it is so beautiful! It was a meditation to watch his keen and silent observation.

Narrated by Swamini Vimalananda

Bhajananjali to Swaranjali — The bhajan classes, inspired by Gurudev as a grassroot level activity of the Mission, are weekly meetings for devotional singing. Many music stalwarts like Padma Shankar, Bombay Jayashri, and Shankar Mahadevan emerged from the bhajan group run by Smt. Susheela Acharya in Chembur, Mumbai. She has composed many bhajans on Gurudev that are frequently sung in Chinmaya Mission. Her bhajan group, which ran for thirty years, was called Chinmaya Naada Bindu; it is now the name of the residential school of music and dance at Chinmaya Vibhooti. The bhajan groups evolved into Chinmaya Swaranjali (offering through music), in which members learn the basics of classical music, upon which every bhajan is based. The first Swaranjali group was inaugurated on Guruji's birthday in June 2003. This concept has caught the imagination of many, and now there are many Swaranjali groups functioning in India and overseas.

National Identity

THE ONLY FACTOR THAT CAN BRING US ALL TOGETHER, THAT CAN HOLD THE SOUTH AND THE NORTH IN ONE EMBRACE THAT CAN BRING THE NAGA CHIEFTAINS AND THE KERALA YOUTHS ON THE SAME PLATFORM AS THE KAZHAGAMITES OF MADRAS AND THE NATIONALISTS OF KASHMIR, IS OUR RESPECT FOR AND REVERENCE TO OUR DISTINCT NATIONAL CULTURE, WHICH INCLUDES ALL ITS ARTS.

| SWAMI CHINMAYANANDA |

Unfortunately, art these days seldom reflects these lofty thoughts, especially the Bollywood films, which are trend-setters for many of the arts in India. It would be good to see characters like Gurudev's portrayed more in the movies.

To my surprise, this did happen in one film in the past.

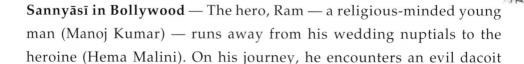

Sannyāsī in Bollywood — The hero, Ram — a religious-minded young man (Manoj Kumar) — runs away from his wedding nuptials to the heroine (Hema Malini). On his journey, he encounters an evil dacoit who poses as Iswara Baba with miraculous powers in order to impress unsuspecting devotees. He then crosses paths with a true sannyāsi, Shanti Baba (Pran), who lays down his life to rescue a helpless woman (Sulochana) from the clutches of the dacoit. Manoj Kumar held Gurudev in great regard. Shanti Baba's role in this 1975 film titled 'Sanyasi' was the characterization of Gurudev, a likeness that can even be seen in the costume and appearance of the character on screen!

PRAN IN SANYASI ▲

This is quite a makeover for Pran, who was the famous Bollywood on-screen villain!

Movies have a tremendous influence, but so does theater. Guided to the last detail and inspired by Gurudev, thousands, especially the young, have been transformed through theater and art shows.

Love-filled Evenings in Delhi: The Bhakti Sandhya (an evening of devotion) cultural programs, organized and executed to artistic perfection by Swamini Gurupriyananda, started as fundraisers for the construction of Chinmaya Vidyalaya in Delhi. Some of the best artists performed before Gurudev. This became an annual feature for Delhites. After Gurudev's Mahāsamādhi, the devotional evening concerts became a monthly Bhakti Pravah (a cascade of devotion). Since the program's inception, hundreds of artists and thousands of audiences have spent love-filled evenings, lost in music and dance.

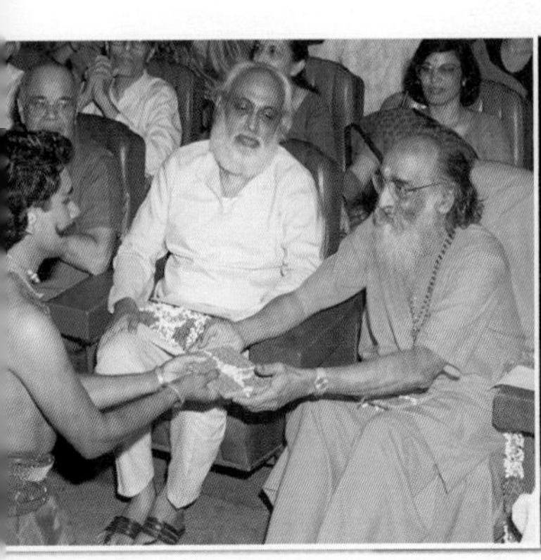

Soul-stirring Nights in Mumbai: Inspired by Gurudev, taught by Smt. Susheela Acharya, and guided by Dr. Madhuriben Sheth, the musically talented and technically gifted CHYKs of Mumbai staged twelve sound and light, music and dance mega-shows called the CHYK Soul Song Nites. These shows also helped the youngsters connect with Indian culture, traditions, and philosophy. Many from this group, such as the Malladi Brothers (Vijayawada) and Padma Shankar (Chennai) have now become leading artists.

▲ GURUDEV WITH MALLADI BROTHERS

Joyful Seasons in Pune: "What the country needs is role models. There was no dearth of them in the past. You must perform a sound and light show on the life of the great Guru of Shivaji Maharaj — Samartha Ramdasa, who is known and revered by all in Maharashtra. It will be a transformation for you and an education for the audience," Gurudev instructed a band of enthusiastic CHYKs in Pune. Thus was born a drama named Anandavan-bhuvani (a joyful dream-kingdom of dharma — Rāma Rājya — conceived of by the saint Ramdasa). It was directed by Rajadutta, with a musical score by Datta Rawjekar and a script by Sudhir Moghe, all famous in the field of Indian theater. This multi-stage, open-air mega-event included a cast of over a hundred youngsters who performed sixty-six shows between 1982 and 2009. Milind Tilak, who played the lead role for all the shows, says that he "received lots of prizes and surprises, pleasures and treasures that I will carry even beyond my grave." One devotee

MILIND TILAK AS SAMARTHA RAMDASA ▶

was apprehensive about the disco lights being used in the show. He felt that the young audience would think about the disco during the show. Gurudev retorted, "Remember! They will also think of Samartha Ramdasa each time they go to the disco."

ON THE STAGE, 'BE REAL.' IN REAL LIFE 'ACT WELL.'
| Swami Chinmayananda |

Dramatic Years in Chennai: Gurudev was recounting his experience of witnessing a grand Rāmalīlā show when he suddenly said, "Why don't you all stage a Tamil version of Rāmāyaṇa based on Kamba Rāmāyaṇa." He then asked Smt. Padma Narasimhan of the TTK Group to take charge of the project. Gurudev sent detailed letters of loving instructions along the way as a group of CHYKs practiced day and night. "In your life, you have to play many roles. Play them to meet the expectations of the world around you! Also remember that Lord Rāma lives in each one of us and we only need to invoke Him with our beautiful thoughts and words, like Kamban did." This multistage, open-air show started in 1981 with a cast of over one hundred, with the script written by Śrī Srinivasan, music composed by K. V. Mahadevan, and songs rendered by Vani Jayaram and S. P. Balasubramaniam. There was no stopping the CHYKs thereafter. The dramatic years continued with fifty shows of Kamba Rāmāyaṇa, followed by wonderful productions like 'Sambhavami Yuge Yuge,' 'Gnana Ganga,' 'LOC–Line of Control,' 'Surya 108,' 'Death,' '1947 to 2047,' and other titles, under the guidance of Swami Mitrananda,

STILL FROM 1947 TO 2047 ▲

who was a part of the original Kamba Rāmāyaṇa cast. "My life changed for the better even though I played the role of Rāvaṇa," jokes the then CHYK Secretary, M. Keshav. "We were struggling young professionals during the day and magical stars of Tamil theater by night. We discovered our own potential, learned to appreciate the cultural nuances of language, music, dance, and drama that make Tamil culture so special. I also discovered a world of artistic excellence, commercial profitability, prudent planning, and professional responsibility that has helped me succeed professionally."

Till the Last Breath — Devotees were worried about Gurudev's deteriorating health at the final camp at Sidhbari in May 1993. A group of CHYKs were very keen to perform a play. With oxygen clamped to his wheelchair, he came and watched them perform. He said, "600 youngsters have come to perform for me. How can I disappoint them and dampen their enthusiasm? They are the future. They will be the ones who will carry the message forward."

Narrated by Smt. Prarthana Saran, Delhi

◀ INTERNATIONAL CHYK PERFORMANCES

Here, There, and Everywhere: In North America, there have been cultural shows of dance, music, and drama, right from the time of Gurudev as fund-raisers and cultural fests. Recently, the UK CHYKs staged shows like, 'Colours of Krishna' and 'Swami Tapovanam: A God without Temple.' The Melbourne CHYKs created spectacular productions like 'Ramayana in the Park (RAP),' which was witnessed by over 5,000 people. The performers transformed the park into the magical world

of Rāmāyaṇa, with its splendid palaces, mystical forests, and awe-inspiring battlefields, while the magnificent cast brought the timeless characters to life, depicting righteousness, sacrifice, devotion, and valor.

I wish I were a part of such mega-shows. What bonding and camaraderie they create; what a boost to one's confidence and a sense of fulfillment, that, too, in a safe and spiritual environment. This is so different from the cheap, competitive, and commercial scenario of present-day stage shows, television serials, and film productions.

Do join our next production in Chennai. Speaking of TV, Gurudev inspired a TV serial named 'Upanishad Ganga.' Remember his vision of bringing the knowledge of the Upaniṣads to the masses as he sat on the banks of Gangaji at Uttarkashi?

The Perennial Sacred Flow of Self-Knowledge — Upanishad Ganga

'If the mountain will not come to Mohammed, then Mohammed must go to the mountain.' This fifty-two episode TV serial on the fundamental concepts of Vedānta came alive on screens across the world on March 11, 2012. This is the first-ever comprehensive TV production on the Upaniṣads and is produced by Chinmaya Mission. Presented in a unique style, each episode has a sūtradhāra (a traditional story-teller) who takes viewers through one concept of Vedānta, using the medium of story-telling from India's rich heritage, enacted on stage through

◀ SCENE FROM UPANISHAD GANGA

drama and offstage as in a film. Conceived by Guruji, researched by the Mission ācāryas, directed and scripted by Dr. Chandraprakash Dwivedi (of Chanakya serial fame), with music by Aalap Desai and Amod Bhatt, art direction by Nitin Desai and Muneesh Sappel, and enacted by professional artists, it excels in content, presentation, and esthetics. Farid Khan, the co-writer with Dr. Dwivedi, considers that the knowledge of the Upaniṣads has the power to unite humanity in the real sense.

"Until now, I had only got roles of a villain! It is only after 'Upanishad Ganga' that people see me as an actor who can take a main and positive role," relates Abhimanyu Singh, the actor who plays thirty-three different roles in 'Upanishad Ganga.' Sargam, his wife, named their son Nachiketa after she learned about Kaṭhopaniṣad.

Sounds fascinating. I will watch it every Sunday on Doordarshan. Many great saints like Gosvāmī Tulasidāsa and Tyāgarāja were excellent composers and musicians and created immortal works of literature, art, and music. Gurudev, too, had his artistic side. I've read some of his poems, and his prose, too, was poetic and profound.

A life of spiritual practice does bring out our latent talents. I will introduce you to just a few artistic ācāryas of Chinmaya Mission.

Stilling me softly with his song ... Guruji, with his saintly heart filled with devotion, is a great vāk gāyaka — one who not only sings well, but also composes wonderful lyrics and the music for his compositions. His songs and his singing pull at the heartstrings of devotees and still the minds of the listeners in divine love.

He entered my life as a lifeless stone.

But now, this Black Beauty rocks ...

on my heart's throne ...

Ārādhanā of Rādhā ... Love for her beloved Kṛṣṇa and love for His beloved Rādhā keep Swamini Aradhanananda engaged in penning exquisite poems of love and sweet stories for her bāla-gopālas, the children who read the Bala Vihar magazine.

An artistic offering ... Brni. Nivedita Chaitanya is a sensitive and gentle soul whose artistic talents create endearing and cuddly characters, like Siddha the leopard, Bhalu the bear, and Appu the elephant.

Samvit ekarūpā na bhidyate ... A playwright and an actor, a dancer and a director, a chef and a Sanskrit master, Br. Samvid Chaitanya is an ardent worshiper of the divine Mother, from whom he draws his inspiration and succor.

With such a plethora of talent in Chinmaya Mission, it is little wonder that a music and dance school came into being. Tell me the story of Chinmaya Naada Bindu.

Chinmaya Naada Bindu — the Sura and Tāla of Chinmaya Vibhooti

The Visionaries That Guide

God is beyond names, forms, and attributes (bindu-nāda-kalā-atīta). Gurudev's love for Indian art and culture and his vision of a cultural renaissance inspired Guruji to manifest His divinity through Chinmaya Naada Bindu (CNB) — a modern gurukula (residential school) of Indian Classical Music and Dance, inaugurated on September 13, 2009.

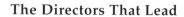

The Goals That Fulfill

The aim of CNB is reflected in its vision statement — To develop the arts of music and dance, as a means of inner purification and Self-realization, and to create artists and art-lovers as the finest ambassadors of universal love, peace, and harmony. The motto of CNB is 'Swara to Ishwara' (to reach the Almighty through music) and 'Nartan to Paramatman' (to attain the Divine through dance).

The Directors That Lead

Pramodini Rao, Resident Director, CNB, adept in Hindustani classical music, began her initial training under her talented mother, Smt. Susheela Acharya, and is lovingly called the nightingale of Chinmaya Mission.

Himanshu Nanda, Music Director of CNB, is a flutist, and student of the world-renowned Pandit Hariprasad Chaurasia. He chose to lead

at CNB even though offered the opportunity to head his music guru's gurukula in Odisha.

Ramaa Bharadvaj, Dance Director, CNB, is a renowned dancer and choreographer, trained by Vazhuvoor Ramaiah Pillai and Padma Bhushan Kamala in Bharatanatyam, and by Dr. Vempatti Chinna Satyam in Kuchipudi. She returned to India after thirty years of living in the United States, to fulfill Gurudev's wish to promote dance in India.

The Seekers That Sight: CNB has conducted many workshops such as 'Monsoon Masti,' 'Dancing Voices Singing Bells,' and 'Singing with

Love.' CNB also conducts art festivals like 'Naada Bindu Festival of Arts,' 'Nrtya-Sura-Bharati,' and 'Kalaateet.' It provides the perfect atmosphere for sincere students and established artists to further their art. Many students, among them Kshitij Saxena (Odisha), Taka Kanozawa (Japan), Tessa Ramburn (Mauritius), and Asha Sukumar (San Diego, US), have stayed for long intense periods of music and dance training.

The Luminaries That Alight: Some of the greatest names in the orchestra of Indian classical music, such as Pandit Hariprasad Chaurasia, Pandit Ulhas Kashalkar, Pandit Shivkumar Sharma, and Kala Ramnath, have strum and sung and Geeta Chandran has danced at CNB.

▲ KALA RAMNATH ON VIOLIN

This place is amazing. I feel so fortunate to be among such inspired and inspiring people. I feel so much at home with all.

Now that you are a part of the Chinmaya Family, I'm sure we will meet again soon.

These have proved to be unforgettable and transformational journeys. I feel humbled to know, what it is to be truly educated and cultured. What started as an interview for an article will now become my maiden attempt at writing a book on education. Thank you for being with me on this journey of evolution. Hari Om!

Dear Reader, the life transforming vision of Gurudev — of manifesting divinity through holistic education — is now a reality. I hope your journey through Gurudev's thoughts, words, and deeds on education has been fruitful. I came as a skeptical journalist and became a learner. So can you!

With the lovely prayer song that I heard in Chinmaya Vidyalaya, written by Pūjya Guruji, I pay obeisance and pray to Param Guru Swami Tapovan Maharaj, the great visionary Master Pūjya Gurudev Swami Chinmayanandaji, Pūjya Guruji Swami Tejomayanandaji, and bid you all Hari Om!

त्वं हि नो नेता त्वं हि नो दाता। यत्र त्वं नयसि तत्र गच्छामः ॥ १ ॥
कापि नो चिन्ता क्वापि नो भयम्। यदाश्रये तव वर्तामहे सदा ॥ २ ॥
रक्षकस्त्वं हि संकटे क्वापि। शिक्षकस्त्वं हि शोभने पथि ॥ ३ ॥
देहि नः शक्तिं बुद्धिं तथा भक्तिम्। दर्शिते मार्गे चलनाय नित्यं हि ॥ ४ ॥
यदि विस्मरामस्त्वां त्वं न विस्मर नः। बालकास्तव हे करुणाकर प्रभो ॥ ५ ॥
हे प्रभो! हे विभो! हे गुरो!

You are our leader and our provider; and we shall follow you wherever you lead us.
We have no worries or fears, for we are always under your protection.
You are indeed our guardian in difficulties and Master on the path of goodness.
Grant us strength, wisdom, and devotion to always walk on the path you have shown us.
O compassionate Master! Please forget us not, even if we do so, as we are your children.
O Omniscient Master! O Omnipresent Master! O Guru!

Activities in Chinmaya Vidyalayas

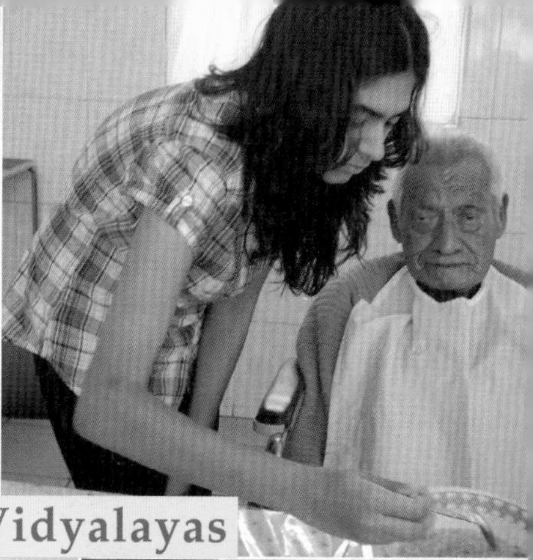

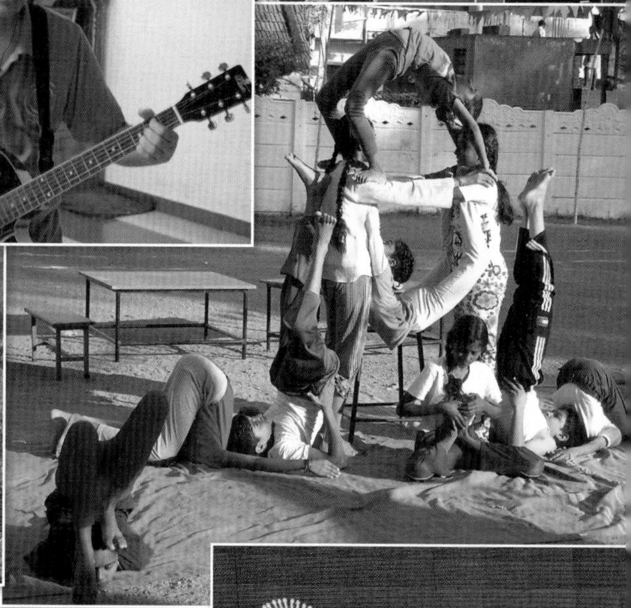

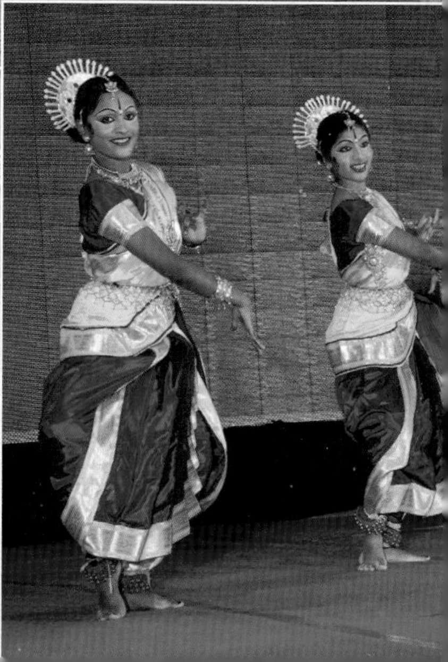

Sports in Chinmaya Vidyalayas

Pūjās in Chinmaya Vidyalayas

I washed my mother's feet and applied kuṁkum and candana. After the ritual, I saw tears rolling down my mother's cheeks. I strongly recommend that Matru Pūjā be made compulsory in all schools, homes, and wherever possible.

Parag Makhecha, Businessman and TV presenter.
13 years in CV Kannur

Honestly, I have never touched my parents' feet before I came to CIRS.

Pragathee, Grade XII, CIRS

It is always divine and heavenly to hear the chanting of the 108 names of Gurudev.

B. Nivedita, Grade VIII, CV New Delhi

Festivals in Chinmaya Vidyalayas

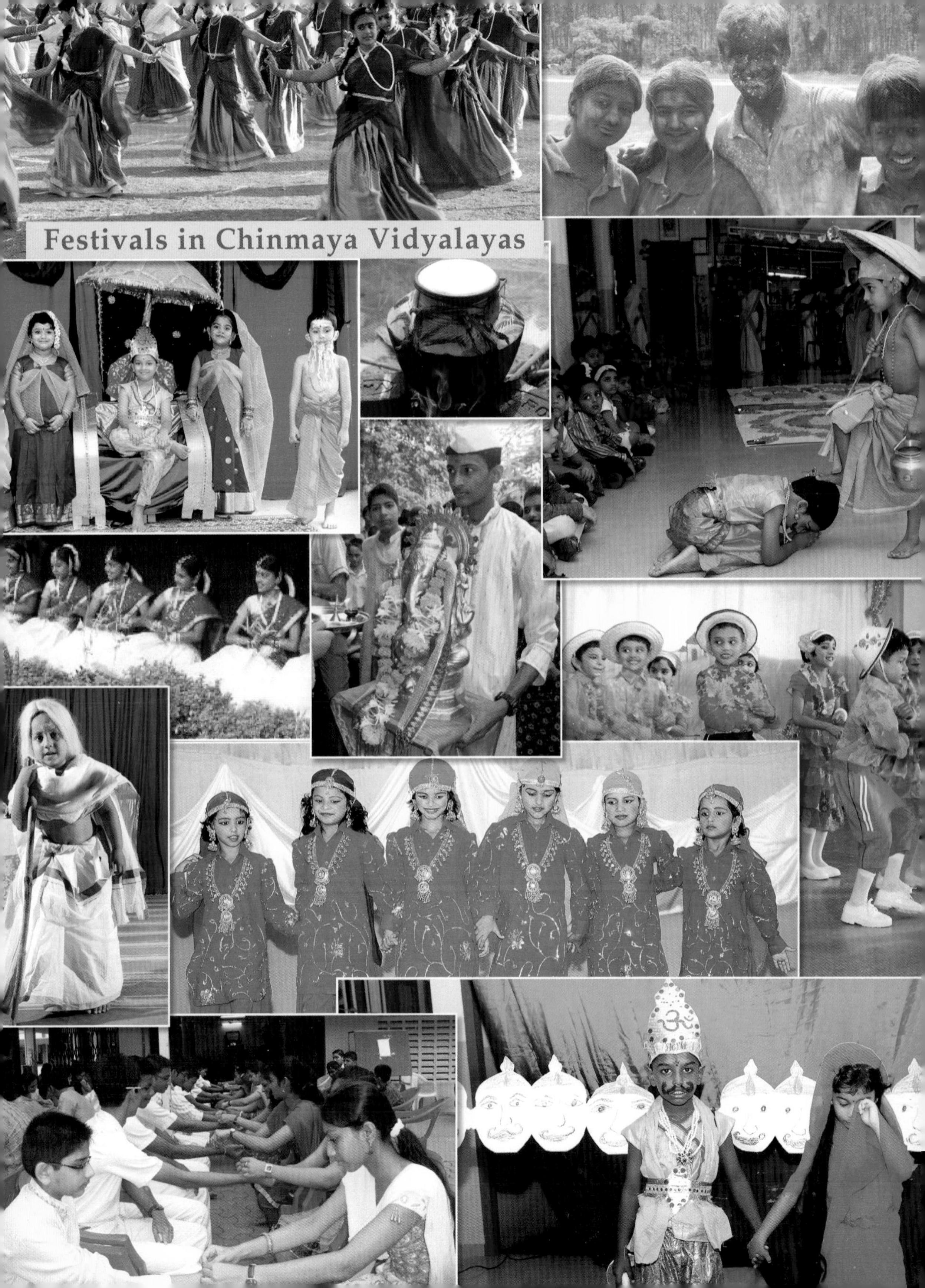

Thus Spoke Gurudev...

"Be like a flower. Give fragrance to all," has inspired me to share goodness.

B. Nivedita Grade VIII, CV New Delhi

I have learned to "give my best and leave the rest to God." When things don't work my way, then I believe something better is in store for me.

S. Anand Sankar, ex-student CIRS

"Only sheep follow, lions walk by themselves" has inspired me to walk bravely ahead in life.

Annilla Ramadhar, Grade VIII, CV Trinidad

"Let us be Hindus" said Gurudev. Now I will be a true Hindu.

K. Tharun Grade VIII, CV Bengaluru

"Plan out your worl and work out your plan motivates me to be regula and systematic in life.

Aishwarya G. Unnithaı
Grade X, CV Tarapu

"The glory of life is in risin each time we fall" inspire me to accept failures an begin afresh.

Nisarg Save, Grade X, CV Tarapu

I've learned to "Keep Smiling" — not a sarcastic mockin smile, but one of hope and determination, which I hav when I face difficulties.

Adithya S., Grade XII, CV Kannu

What is the special SWAD of this school?

It feels more like a temple than a school. There is a visible purity and simplicity among the teachers as well as students.

How do you guide the parents?

Many parents want to fulfil their dreams through their children. I explain to them about svadharma and karma, and they do seem to understand.

How do you view your work as a school Ācaryā?

I see this work as worship to Pūjya Gurudev and service to my motherland.

Brni. Sucheta Chaitanya, Acharya, CV Bokaro

What impact will a Chinmaya Vidyalaya child have on society?

Externally they may excel in their professions, but internally they will be spiritual. The spiritual touch will bring peace and harmony in society.

Ācaryā devo bhava

They have such passion that they instill confidence in us to take up all sorts of challenges.

Shan Abdul Rahman, BBM Chinmaya Arts and Science College, Kannur

The best thing about Swami Prakashananda is the positive atmosphere he creates whenever he's around us. Plus he's so funny!

Alisa Pandey, Grade VIII, CV Trinidad

Ācaryās are like lighthouses, guiding not only the students, but also teachers.

Rajeshwari Satish, Economics teacher, CIRS

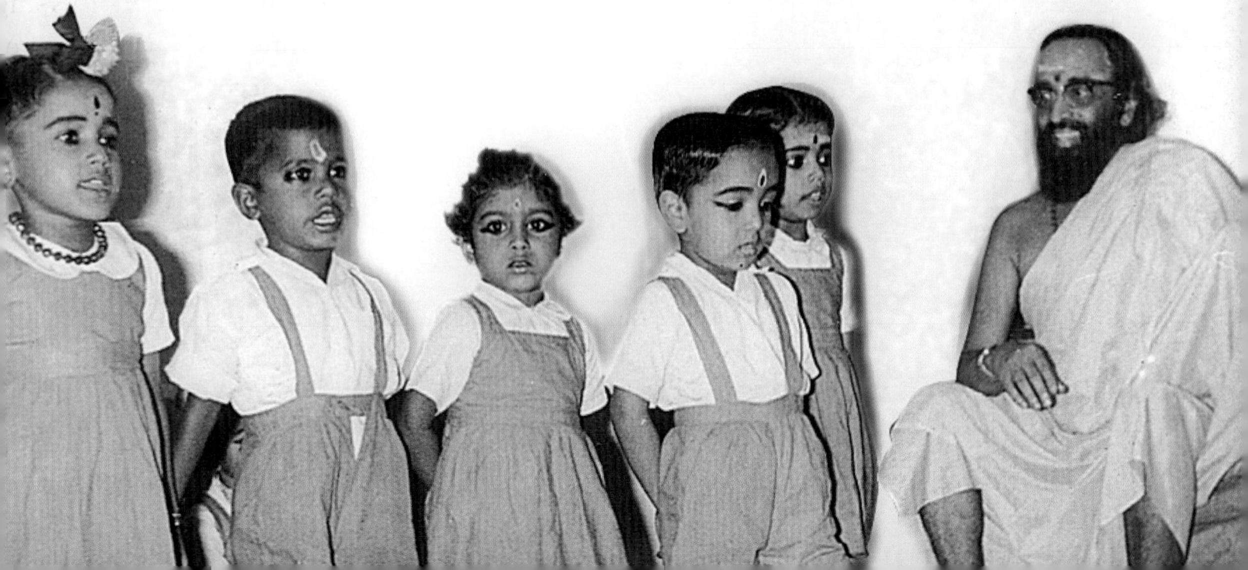

Acharyas with Vidyalayas and Colleges

Glossary

A	*Ācārya*	Teacher; also in this book, initiated disciples — Brahmachari or Swami of Chinmaya Mission
	adhārmic	pertaining to adharma — unrighteousness
	Ādi Varāha	the third incarnation of the Hindu God Viṣṇu
	ahaṁ brahmāsmi	Vedic declaration which means 'I am (in essence) the infinite Truth.'
	āndolan	gentle oscillation of a musical note in Indian classical music
	annā	elder brother (Tamil); in the book, referred to as male helper
	anuvādi svara	accompanying notes of a rāga (melody) in Indian classical music
	araṅgeṭram	debut performance of a Bharatanatyam dancer
	Aryan Invasion Theory	It posits that India was invaded by Indo-European tribes (Aryans) from Central Asia (1500-1000 B.C.E.) who conquered its native Dravidians. The British employed this theory to divide India along north-south, Aryan-Dravidian lines. Based on new evidence in archeology, geography, mathematics, astronomy, and linguistics, numerous scholars from both India and the West now reject this theory
	āśrama	residence or center of a spiritual teacher, which often includes lodgings for students

	āyās	female helpers who do menial work
	āyurvedic	pertaining to Āyurveda — the oldest form of traditional Indian Medicine, in practice even today
	bāla-gopālas	young cow-herders, childhood friends of Lord Kṛṣṇa; in the book, referred to as children
B	*bhaiyā*	elder brother (Hindi)
	bhajans	rendering of hymns
C	*candana*	sandalwood (paste)
	Chitragupta	Hindu deity who keeps a complete record of actions of human beings on earth
	crore	ten million
	cūlā	traditional Indian cooking stove, usually made of mud, that uses biomass, wood, or charcoal as fuel
D	*deśa kī prabhā*	glory of the Nation
	desis	slang term referring to the people of the Indian subcontinent
	dharma	essential nature of a thing; duty; righteousness
	dhārmic	pertaining to dharma — righteousness
	dīdī	elder sister (Hindi)
	Divālī	a major Hindu festival, the festival of lights, celebrating the victory of good over evil
G	*gamaka*	ornamented note in Indian classical music
	Gaṇeśa	Lord revered as the remover of obstacles
	garbhādhāna	Vedic ceremony of purification performed by parents before conceiving a child
	Gāyatrī mantra	a sacred Vedic mantra invoking Lord Sun, who also symbolizes God, Truth, the Self
	ghuṇgrūs	tiny bells strung together to form a musical anklet worn by Indian dancers
	gurubhāī	spiritual brother by virtue of having the same Guru
	gurukula	ancient Indian residential school
H	*havan*	ritualistic fire worship which involves offerings into the fire with sacred chants into a receptacle

	Hitopadesa	Book of Counsels — a popular collection of Sanskrit tales and fables imparting knowledge and wisdom, written in the 12th century C.E.
J	*Janmāṣṭamī*	Hindu festival celebrating the incarnation of Lord Kṛṣṇa
	japa	repetition of a sacred mantra, chanting of the Lord's name
	jāta karma	purification ceremony performed immediately after the birth of a child
	Jataka Stories	folklore with morals featuring the previous lives of the Buddha
	jñāna mudrā	'knowledge gesture,' signifying the oneness of the individual with the Supreme
K	*kabaddi*	traditional Indian game
	kalākāra	artist
	Kali Yuga	last of the four ages according to Hindu Scriptures
	Kazhagamites	people belonging to a Kazhagam, a forum or association or political party (Tamil)
	kheṅca	stretching of the musical note in Indian classical music
	kuṁkuṁ	red dot applied on the forehead for religious and social purposes
L	*lakh (or lac)*	in the Indian numbering system, a lakh is equal to 100,000
M	*Mahābhārata*	the longest historic epic in the world (100,000 verses) composed by Sage Veda Vyāsa
	Mahāsamādhi	end of physical being of a spiritual Master
	mahāvākya	great Upaniṣadic statement indicating the essential oneness between the individual and the infinite Truth
	Manu Smṛti	book giving the tenets of dharma (code of conduct) by Manu
	marma	certain vital points in the body; also, a juncture where two or more types of tissue meet, such as muscles, veins, ligaments, bones, or joints. They are important in Āyurvedic treatment

	Medhā Sūktam	powerful Vedic hymn in praise of Sarasvati, the goddess of knowledge and learning, known to improve memory and kindle intelligence
	mīṇḍa	glide from one note to another in Indian classical music
N	*Naga*	referring to a tribe living in parts of Northeast India
	nagara saṅkīrtanam	processional singing of hymns in the town
	namaskāra	Indian way of greeting with folded hands
	neem	Azadirachta indica, a common Indian tree whose bark, fruit, and bitter leaves have numerous medicinal properties
	nirākāra	formless
O	*Om*	universal name of God or Truth
P	*pādukā pūjā*	worship of the Master's sandals
	pān masālā	chewing mixture of catechu, areca nuts, seeds, and spices. It often contains tobacco and has carcinogenic properties.
	pañcakarma	five-fold Āyurvedic detoxification therapy for purification of the body
	Panchatantra	collection of animal fables providing instruction on human values
	pāṭhaśālā	traditional Indian school
	pradakṣiṇā	circumambulation of the deity in a temple
	prāṇāyāma	breath-control exercises advocated in Yoga
	puṁsavana	ritualistic ceremony performed for the birth of a noble child
	purāṇic	pertaining to the Purāṇas. The eighteen Purāṇas are scriptures that impart spiritual and social guidance through stories of the Lord and His devotees
	pūrvāśrama	referring to the life of a renunciate before renunciation
R	*Rādhā*	beloved of Lord Kṛṣṇa, symbolizing bliss, devotion, and surrender
	rāja vidyā	royal knowledge

	Rāja yoga	in the book referred to as the particular position of the constellations which predicts greatness and fame, arrived at through the reading of the horoscope
	rākhī	thread representing love and protection that the sister ceremoniously ties to the brother on a special day
	Rāmāyaṇa	great epic depicting the life of Lord Rāma, originally composed by Sage Vālmiki
	raṅgolī	traditional decorative designs made with colors in front of the house as an auspicious welcome
S	*ṣaḍaja – sā*	first musical note in Indian classical music
	sādhanā	spiritual practices
	saṁvādi svara	accompanying notes of a melody in Indian classical music
	samvit ekarūpā na bhidyate	Consciousness is one (unique), without any differences. Pañcadaśi 1.4. In this book, referring to the uniqueness of Samvid Chaitanya
	saṅkalpa	thought, will, or resolve
	sannyāsa	initiation into the last stage of life — a life of renunciation
	sannyāsi	renunciate
	śānta	peaceful
	Śāradā pīṭha	first of the four Hindu monastic orders established by Ādi Śaṅkarācārya at Sringeri in the state of Karnataka
	Sarasvati pūjā	Hindu ritual worshiping Sarasvati, the deity of knowledge
	sardār	leader
	Sardarji	respectful term for a Sikh gentleman
	satsaṅga	company of the noble souls
	satyāgrahis	freedom fighters who followed Mahatma Gandhi's principle of peaceful protest against unrighteousness, and for a righteous cause
	Satyameva jayate	India's National motto, which means 'Truth Alone Triumphs'

	sevā	service done in a spirit of selflessness
	shanti yatra	procession for peace
	sīmanta unnayana	symbolic ceremony during the seventh month of pregnancy
	Śiva	Lord expressing as Destroyer
	Śivarātri	Hindu festival celebrating the sacred midnight when Lord Śiva manifests as a column of light
	subhāṣita	literally meaning, 'well-spoken'; Sanskrit verses of wise sayings and instructions
	svara saṁvāda	music conference
U	*upanayana*	the sacred thread ceremony that initiates a young man into scriptural study
	Upaniṣad	portion of the Vedas that pertains to knowledge of the Self
	Upaniṣadic	relating to portions of Vedas that pertain to knowledge of the Self
V	*vādi svara*	main note of a rāga (melody) in Indian classical music
	vaidya	āyurvedic physician
	vāsanās	tendencies dictated by past actions
	Vedānta	section of the Vedas that deal with the knowledge of the supreme Reality
	Vedas	basic scriptures of the Hindus, a compilation of knowledge revealed to the sages
	Visharad	degree signifying proficiency in a subject
	Vijaya Daśamī	Hindu festival celebrating the victory of Lord Rāma over the demon king Ravaṇa
	vīṇā	Indian stringed instrument
Y	*yogāsana*	postures of yoga
	Yuva Veer	youth who has undergone the Youth Empowerment Programme (YEP) run by Chinmaya Yuva Kendra

Patrons and Contributors

Grateful acknowledgement and special thanks to our

MAJOR CONTRIBUTORS

CIRS COIMBATORE, CVs CHENNAI, CIM CHENNAI, CV RAJAPALAYAM (TAMIL NADU)

CV THRISSUR, CMC THRISSUR, CHINTECH KANNUR, CV VADUTHALA KOCHI,

AAAM EDUCATIONAL AND CHARITABLE TRUST, TRIPUNITHURA (KERALA)

CV TARAPUR (MAHARASHTRA), CV DELHI, CV BOKARO (JHARKHAND),

CVs ROURKELA (ODISHA)

ARYA GURUKULA (MAHARASHTRA), M. KESHAV, CHENNAI,

MARGARET & DAVID DUKES, TORONTO, CANADA,

SCHOOL OF INSPIRED LEADERSHIP (SOIL), GURGAON

OTHER CONTRIBUTORS

CV KOLLENGODE, CVs TRIVANDRUM (KERALA), CV TRINIDAD, (CARIBBEAN), CV BISTUPUR,

VBCV JAMSHEDPUR (JHARKHAND), CV HUBLI (KARNATAKA),

HARI HAR CV ELLAYAPALLE (ANDHRA PRADESH), CV NAGAPATTINAM (TAMIL NADU),

MILAN SAMANI (LONDON), RADHAKRISHNAN PILLAI MUMBAI,

CHINMAYA NAADA BINDU, G. N. SESHADRI BENGALURU (KARNATAKA),

CIM BENGALURU (KARNATAKA)

TRANSLITERATION AND PRONUNCIATION GUIDE

In the book, Devanāgarī characters are transliterated according to the scheme adopted by the International Congress of Orientalists at Athens in 1912. In it one fixed pronunciation value is given to each letter; f, q, w, x and z are not called to use. An audio recording of this guide is available at www. chinmayamission com/scriptures.php. According to this scheme:

	sounds like		*sounds like*
a	o in s*o*n	ḍh	dh in a*dh*esive
ā	a in f*a*ther	ṇ	n in u*n*der*
i	i in d*i*fferent	t	t in *t*abla
ī	ee in f*ee*l	th	th in *th*umb
u	u in f*u*ll	d	th in *th*is
ū	oo in b*oo*t	dh	dh in Gan*dh*i
ṛ	rh in *rh*ythm*	n	n in *n*ose
ṝ	**	p	p in *p*en
ḷ	**	ph	ph in *ph*antom*
e	a in ev*a*de	b	b in *b*oil
ai	i in del*i*ght	bh	bh in a*bh*or
o	o in c*o*re	m	m in *m*ind
au	o in n*o*w	y	y in *y*es
k	c in *c*alm	r	r in *r*ight
kh	kh in *kh*an	l	l in *l*ove
g	g in *g*ate	v	v in *v*ery
gh	gh in *gh*ost	ś	sh in *sh*ut
ṅ	an in *an*kle*	ṣ	s in *s*ugar
c	ch in *ch*uckle	s	s in *s*imple
ch	ch in wit*ch**	h	h in *h*appy
j	j in *j*ustice	ṁ	m in i*m*provise
jh	jh in *Jh*ansi	ḥ	**
ñ	ny in ba*ny*an	kṣ	tio in ac*tio*n
ṭ	t in *t*ank	tr	th in *th*ree*
ṭh	**	jñ	gn in *gn*osis
ḍ	d in *d*og	'	a silent 'a'

* These letters don't have an exact English equivalent. An approximation is given here.

** These sounds cannot be approximated in English words.

'Keep Smiling' for Me.

Love,

Louis Armstrong